Contents

Introduction

Bike Rides

Appendix

THE BEST BIKE RIDES IN THE MID-ATLANTIC STATES

Best Bike Rides Series

THE BEST BIKE RIDES IN THE MID-ATLANTIC STATES

**Delaware · Maryland · New Jersey
New York · Pennsylvania · Virginia
Washington, D.C. · West Virginia**

Second Edition

by

Trudy E. Bell

A Voyager Book

The Globe Pequot Press

Old Saybrook, Connecticut

Cover photograph ©Tony Demin/International Stock Photo

Text photo credits: Pg. 13: Barbara Lloyd; pg. 45: Carroll County Tourism Office; pg. 141: Mark Scholefield; pg. 221: courtesy of the Washington, D.C., Convention & Visitors Association; pg. 235: courtesy of Nancy Taylor; pg. 259: Pamela "Sam" Withrow, Camera One. All others by the author.

Library of Congress Cataloging-in-Publication Data
Bell, Trudy E.
 The best bike rides in the Mid-Atlantic states: Delaware, Maryland, New Jersey, New York, Pennsylvania, Virginia, Washington, D.C., West Virginia/by Trudy E. Bell—2nd ed.
  p. cm.—(Best bike ride series)
 "A Voyager book."
 ISBN 0-7627-0049-1
 1. Bicycle touring—Middle Atlantic States—Guidebooks. 2. Bicycle trails—Middle Atglantic States—Guidebooks. 3. Middle Atlantic States—Guidebooks. I. Title. II. Series.
 GV1045.5.M53B45 1997
 796.6'4'0974—dc21   97-12107
                                                              CIP

♻ This book is printed on recycled paper.
Manufactured in the United States of America
Second Edition/First Printing

To my mother,
Arabella J. Bell,
and to the memory of my father,
Rev. R. Kenneth Bell,
for their lifetime of love and friendship

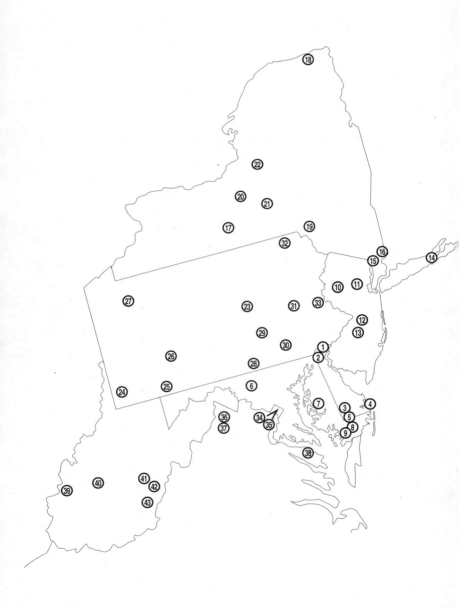

Introduction

A Variety Tour of the Mid-Atlantic States

The Mid-Atlantic region of the United States is one of the most beautiful areas of the country in which to bicycle, whether you're a novice wishing to venture beyond your home neighborhood for the first time or a strong rider trying for a century (100 miles in a day) every weekend.

Because the Mid-Atlantic states were settled centuries ago, when many byways were still footpaths and dirt wagon tracks joining local communities, the region offers a vast network of wandering secondary and tertiary roads bypassed by the more direct interstate and toll highways. Even in today's automobile-oriented society, these small roads are almost undisturbed by cars—and they pass through some of the loveliest countryside a cyclist could hope for.

For scenery you can choose fragrant pine forests, cultivated farm fields, or meandering river valleys. For terrain you have the choice of virtually flat (on New York's Long Island, in southern New Jersey, and in parts of Delaware and Maryland), rolling (in Washington, D.C., Virginia, and southeastern Pennsylvania), or mountainous (West Virginia). Stop to pet the horses standing next to the rails of a horse farm; pick your own apples in the fall at wayside orchards; open your picnic lunch next to a waterfall; pedal through great Civil War battlefields. And after the day's exercise, camp under the stars in the bracing forest air or luxuriate in a soaking bath at a bed-and-breakfast inn. These and other choices are offered on this book's lovely routes, which were contributed by local bicycle clubs, state tourism organizations, commercial bicycle touring groups, and dedicated individual cyclists.

Some of the rides take you through areas that are the acknowledged favorite of many cyclists—such as the Pennsylvania Dutch farm land, the Finger Lakes region of New York, and the Delmarva Peninsula. On a summer weekend in those areas, you are very likely to exchange a wave and a smile with dozens of other riders you pass on the road. Other routes guide you through places as yet largely undiscovered by road-touring cyclists, such as the hills of West Virginia (see "A Special Word about West Virginia" below), where you can pedal for days before meeting another cyclist. Thus, you can even choose a ride based on the society or solitude you seek!

Something for Everyone

To aid in your selection, the rides in this book are categorized by their difficulty.

Rambles are the easiest, designed to be completed by almost anyone; they are under 35 miles long, and their terrain is flat or gently rolling.

Cruises are intermediate in difficulty, ranging from 25 to 50 miles, with the terrain being rolling or moderately hilly.

Challenges require adequate training and preparation; they range from 40 to 70 miles in total distance and may include long climbs.

Classics, the equivalent of the "black diamond" slopes in skiing, are longer than 60 miles, and their terrain may be hilly or mountainous; they will satisfy the strong, expert rider.

Having noted this, less experienced riders should *not* be discouraged at seeing so many challenges and classics in the list of rides at the beginning of each state chapter. The rides are named after their longest incarnation, and most of the long rides have cutoffs to turn them into shorter cruises or rambles. Alternatively, some of the longer rides can be broken up into shorter rides by staying overnight along the way. In fact, because of variations on rides, this book actually contains 63 rides well-distributed over the four levels. Specifically, there are 16 rambles (rides 3, 4, 7, 8, 10, 11, 12, 15 (two variations), 19, 25, 27, 28, 32, 33, and 34), 24 cruises (rides 1 (two variations), 2, 5, 6, 11, 13, 14, 16, 18, 19, 20, 22, 24, 26, 28, 29, 30, 31, 32, 35, 38, 39, 41, and 43), 17 challenges (rides 4, 7, 9, 16, 17, 19, 21, 23, 24, 26, 32 (two variations), 36, 37, 39, 40, and

42), and 6 classics (28, 31 (two variations), 36, 38, 40, and 42).

As terrain is as much a factor as distance in determining a ride's difficulty, some long rides that are very flat (such as the 51-mile-long "Strawberries and Wine Cruise" on Long Island) may be easier than some short rides that are very hilly (such as the 25-mile-long challenging "Hillsboro Farm Land Cruise" in West Virginia).

How to Use This Book

Each ride is preceded by a short description to give you a feel for the specific area and what you are likely to see. The description usually mentions roadside attractions, as well as inns or camp-grounds for spending the night; where possible, telephone num-bers are also provided.

The most crucial section of the description is "The Basics." There you will find information about the ride's mileage, including mileage options for shortened routes; terrain; automobile traffic; and availability of food. Where possible, the routes start near pub-lic rest rooms, water, and sources of food, but for a few of the more isolated rides, you will have to bring all your provisions with you.

Last is "Miles & Directions"—a cue sheet, in bicycle-touring par-lance. As much as possible this book observes several conventions. A "T intersection" is one where the road you are on dead-ends into a perpendicular road where you must turn either left or right. A "Y intersection" is one where the road you are on appears to split into a fork.

A word about maps: Take several. The best is a county map showing all the local streets. (*Note:* Some rides pass through several counties. The names of the counties are given for every ride.) Ide-ally, if you can find more than one map put out by different pub-lishers, take along two or more. Why weigh yourself down that way? First, maps can help you spontaneously shortcut or add to your ride midway through it, beyond what's shown in this book. Second, road construction begun after this book's publication may block off part of the directed route, in which case a supplemental map can help you find a detour and guide you back to the main route. (If this happens to you, please write to the author so that the rides can be correctly updated in subsequent editions; see "A Modest Request" and "Disclaimer" on page 11). Third, as maps do contain errors in the way roads are drawn and labeled, having two maps by different publishers allows you to compare the versions to ascertain which one better matches your current situation. For more information see "State Bicycling Maps and Guides" in the Appendix.

A Word about This Second Edition

No bicycle route is good forever. In the march of Progress, developers bulldoze fields and forests, build houses and malls, and reroute or widen roads—destroying with amazing speed what not long ago had been a lovely ride. Such was the fate of Maryland's "Sykesville Hill-Climbing Cruise," the old Ride 7 in this book's first edition. Increased automobile traffic also forced the rerouting of the first leg of Delaware's "Inn-to-Inn Triangle Three-Day Ramble," which is still Ride 3, and the elimination of the Amawalk Reservoir from New York's old Ride 16, the "Two Reservoir Cruise," creating the smaller new Ride 15, the "New Croton Reservoir Ramble." If a cyclist must battle cars instead of being soothed by babbling creeks, a bike route is no longer *the best*, and no longer qualifies for inclusion in this book.

Touring cyclists are ever exploring farther afield for better routes. Luckily, many are also generous in sharing their discoveries. Thanks to their generosity, this second edition features several new tucked-away gems in the Mid-Atlantic: in New York, the "St. Lawrence River Church Cruise" (Ride 18) and the "Cannonsville Reservoir All-Class Challenge" (Ride 19); in Pennsylvania, the "Montour Preserve Challenge" (Ride 23) and the "Endless Mountains Challenge" (Ride 32).

New also to this second edition is part of a whole new state: the northern section of Virginia. In the eyes of many, Virginia is part of the Mid-Atlantic (and it was originally to have been part of this book's first edition); in the eyes of others, however, Virginia is viewed properly as a southern state (and so it was claimed by Globe Pequot's first edition of *The Best Bike Rides in the South*). A Solomon-like division does work with states, however, allowing Virginia to be part of both books. So for the first time, this Mid-Atlantic book describes three lovely bicycle tours in the northern part of Virginia.

A few rides, however, have been pruned away, because they were too close to another representative ride, and because making room for new material always entails tough decisions (*sigh*). Thus, possessors of the first edition of this book might want to hang onto it if they still wish to try the "Wonders of Glass Cruise" (old Ride 19), the "Cazenovia-Erieville Cruise" (old Ride 22), the "Blue Bell All-Class Challenge," (old Ride 33), and the "Springs to Springs Cruise" (old Ride 42). Despite such trimming, the net number of rides in this second edition has increased, from 42 to 43.

Lastly, every ride from the first edition that reappears in the second edition has been completely updated and corrected. This checking required a veritable army of volunteer experienced cyclists, who—for the modest incentive of a copy of the second edition and a hot lunch—carefully verified each mile, direction, and map. For some rides, the changes were minimal; for others, the corrections were unexpectedly demanding. To each of the cheerful and dedicated souls who lent their skill and time, we all—the readers who will enjoy these rides as well as I the author—raise our water bottles in a toast of gratitude. May you always have the wind at your back!

A Special Word about West Virginia

West Virginia's roads are so different from those elsewhere in the Mid-Atlantic that they require a few notes. The gist is this: The state is gorgeous, but the cycling is only for riders both experienced and strong.

West Virginia is the state of diehard mountain-bikers. Virtually all the bike shops are geared toward mountain-biking, as are the tour companies and cycling campgrounds. Trails abound for mountain-bikers, as do packaged tours, books, and informal notes.

Because of the mountain-bike orientation of West Virginia, one of the West Virginia rides—the "Williams River Trail Cruise"—is an introductory mountain-bike ride that requires a true all-terrain bike with 2-inch knobby tires. For this ride a cross or hybrid bike—one designed for riding on both paved roads and some dirt—is *not* advisable. By comparison, road cyclists are rare: In the five days I spent there one May—prime weather for cycling—I saw only two cyclists on road bikes on principal roads and *no* road cyclists of any description on the best backroads. In fact, the first edition of this book may well have been the first to publish *road* rides in West Virginia.

Part of the reason so few road tours may exist is that West Virginia has not, until recently, recognized its potential for tourism of any form, according to Greg Cook, West Virginia's bicycle coordinator for tourism and parks. Attracting road cyclists is part of that change in focus. Now the state helps sponsor several annual professional road races and amateur day-long tours. You may want to time your own cycling visit to coincide with one of these events.

But West Virginia's roads themselves make the state forbidding to all but experienced road cyclists in peak physical condition. There's a reason West Virginia is called "hill country" or the "Mountain State." Both main and secondary roads commonly grind up miles-long, unremitting climbs and plunge down miles of switchbacks at grades of up to 8 and 9 percent. Believe me, 9 percent is *steep*, as you will see for yourself on the brief 9 percent descent that is unavoidably included in "The Hillsboro Farm Land Cruise." Although grades that steep certainly exist in western Pennsylvania, northern New York, and elsewhere in the Mid-Atlantic, most are mercifully short—under a mile. West Virginia arguably has the *longest* steep grades you're likely to find outside the Rocky Mountains, minus about 10,000 feet in altitude. The hilly terrain is the reason that none of even the shortest West Virginia rides classifies as a ramble.

Many of the main roads are only two lanes and are traveled at 55 miles per hour by cars and logging trucks alike. Scarcely any have paved shoulders. What shoulders do exist are narrow, below pavement level, and inevitably of gravel. There is a *lot* of gravel in West Virginia, and all too much of it ends up on the pavement— so, especially on downhills, ride with *extreme caution*.

That being said, please note that the pavement itself is generally good to excellent, even on the one-lane backroads; you will encounter noticeably fewer potholes than you might find, say, in New York State (undoubtedly due to West Virginia's milder winters producing less frost heave). Moreover, West Virginia's secondary roads have so little traffic that four cars in an hour would be a lot. In fact, it is not an exaggeration to characterize cycling the narrow, paved backroads of West Virginia as almost like riding along your own private paved bike path.

Probably the best road ride in West Virginia is not included as a separate ride in this book: the two-lane Highland Scenic Highway 150 near Marlinton, which curves in a 23-mile-long letter *C* through the western part of the Monongahela National Forest, with its northern tip on busy Route 219 and its southern tip on busy Route 39/55. Reminiscent of the gorgeous Blue Ridge Parkway in Virginia, the Highland Scenic Highway commands spectacular views of line after line of the forested ridges that are so beautifully characteristic of West Virginia. Moreover, its pavement is so superb and the summer automobile traffic so light that "we Rollerblade all over it," remarks Gil Willis of the Elk River Touring Center in Slatyfork. But be forewarned: The scenic highway has no services outside of primitive campgrounds, and there are very long climbs—probably 7,000 to 8,000 feet of altitude gained and lost over the 23 miles, Willis estimates. A short section of this gorgeous road is included in Willis's contributed mountain-bike ride, the "Williams River Trail Cruise" (Ride 41).

One appealing aspect of West Virginia is that even on the eve of the twenty-first century, traveling in the state is almost like it used to be driving cross-country in the 1950s: Outside of towns the size of Elkins, Bartow, and Marlinton, major chain hotels, motels, and fast-food restaurants have not yet blighted the countryside with commercialism. Overnight accommodations are often mom-and-pop enterprises that are few and far between and may be open only during the summer.

The flip side is that on some of these routes you may pedal 20 to 40 miles between places to refill your water bottles and stomach—and then your only culinary choices may be what many cyclists consider high-fat "junk": hamburgers, hot dogs, and pizza. Advice: Carry three water bottles, take advantage of *any* opportunity to provision up, and pack more Fig Newtons, sports bars, fruit, and other carbos than you think you could possibly want. Also, as bicycle shops are even fewer and farther between than are food and accommodations, carry a more complete set of tools than you might be inclined to take on less isolated rides, and know how to use them.

Safety and Comfort on the Road

Like skiing, boating, and many other sports, bicycling has distinct hazards, some of which have claimed lives. But the chance of injury can be minimized by proper equipment and technique. Moreover, there are ways to increase your comfort, allowing you to enjoy hours in the saddle day after day.

Most important of all: Always wear a helmet. If you bicycle regularly, it is not a matter of *if* you will fall but of *when*. A helmet can make the difference between a serious injury that ends your journey or just some road rash and a story to tell. For maximum protection buy one that has the sticker inside indicating that it has passed the rigorous safety standards of the Snell Memorial Foundation. A white or yellow helmet will reflect the sun's heat the best and offer maximum visibility at night. Adjust the inside fit of the helmet with the different sized pads provided. You want the helmet to hold on to your head firmly enough to stay on when you bend over upside down even without the chin strap fastened. Then adjust the chin strap so it's loose enough to be comfortable when your neck is extended forward but taut enough so the helmet cannot be pushed backward off your forehead.

Wear fingerless, padded cycling gloves for two reasons: to buffer road shock to your hands as you ride and to minimize abrasion should you fall. Even roads that look smooth are bumpy enough to make unprotected palms and heels of your hands feel weary at the end of a day's ride. Plus, the open oval on the back above the glove's closure will give the backs of your hands the characteristic "bicyclist's suntan," which can be a nice conversation-starter in social situations!

Use a rear-view mirror to monitor automobile traffic approaching from behind. With a mirror you will not be startled if a car suddenly materializes to your left and honks. Also, you will not have to take your eyes off the road ahead to know what is going on behind. The most effective rear-view mirrors mount to your helmet or eyeglasses; the ones that mount to your bicycle handlebars may vibrate too much to stay aligned or to produce a clear image.

Wear light, bright colors so you are visible to motorists, particularly on overcast days or toward sunset. Yellow is the best of both worlds. Some neon colors, such as neon yellow and lime, are even better. For maximum visibility apply reflective tape to your bicycle frame and helmet, especially if there's a chance you'll be riding after dark. Headlights and taillights for the bicycle, required by many states, also alert motorists to your presence.

Last, **ride defensively.** The traffic laws in most states recognize the bicycle as a vehicle, with all the rights and responsibilities thereof. That means stopping at all stop signs and red lights, using left-turn lanes, and using arm signals to indicate your intentions. On roads where you must share the right-hand lane with vehicular traffic, rely on your ears and your rear-view mirror to monitor cars and trucks approaching you from behind. Do not block your ears with earphones; not only are they illegal, but they will deprive you of auditory warnings. Most state laws call for cyclists to ride as far to the right as practicable—but "as far right as practicable" does not necessarily mean blindly clinging to the far right-hand edge in all circumstances. On fast downhills where you feel insecure at the far right because the road's edge is broken or littered with gravel, you are legally permitted to take the lane—that is, to ride far enough to the left (about where the passenger in a car would sit) so that cars approaching from behind must slow down to pass you—and then immediately move back again to the right when the hazard is passed or you're traveling slower again. When passing parked cars, look carefully inside each for the silhouettes of heads of people who might suddenly open a door in your path. Buy a cyclist's bell, the loudest one you can find, and use it to warn cars and pedestrians of your presence; do *not* use a police whistle—not only is it illegal in some places, but it often offends people, and many times they do not think the whistle blast applies to them. For more information on safe techniques for riding in traffic, read John Forester's classic *Effective Cycling*, 6th edition (MIT Press, 1992).

Now that you're equipped for safety, here are a few additional words about simple comfort.

Padded cycling shorts will minimize saddle-soreness. Saddle-soreness is produced by the transmission of road shock from your saddle through soft flesh to your "sit bones" (ischial tuberosity). The most effective padding is made of genuine or artificial chamois; polypropylene is more effective for wicking away moisture than protecting against saddle-soreness. For additional protection you can buy a seat cover of either sheepskin or gel; both are equally effective, although the gel has a longer lifetime. A bonus: Cycling shorts, which usually extend down to the knee, also protect the skin of your inner thighs against chafing and blisters that otherwise can be caused by rubbing against either the saddle itself or the seam of ordinary short or long pants.

Bicycling jerseys also serve several practical purposes. Their light colors increase your visibility; their polypropylene or wool fabric increases the wicking of perspiration to keep you dry; their longer cut in the rear shields your lower back from the sun and wind; and their rear pockets allow you to carry a wallet and keys without your legs hitting them at the top of every pedal stroke.

Take at least one water bottle, and always pack a minimum "emergency snack" of raisins or Fig Newtons, even for the shortest rides. On hot days pack a salty snack as well; ideal are pretzels, which are also low in fat and high in complex carbohydrates.

A word about tools: As many of these routes deliberately take you away from human habitation, you may not find a bike shop nearby. Take bicycle tools—at the very least, tire levers, a patch kit, and a pump for repairing a flat tire—and either know how to use them or travel with a friend who does. In fact, if you anticipate bicycling a lot, one of the best favors you can do yourself is to sign up for a simple "roadside bicycle repair" class, offered by many continuing education schools, bicycle clubs, and youth hostels. If you lack knowledge and tools, a simple flat tire can immobilize you for hours, requiring you to flag down a van or truck to take you back to civilization, whereas if you're equipped, you can fix the problem and be back on the road again in less than twenty minutes.

A Modest Request

If readers pedaling these routes have suggested corrections, updates, or additions, I would be grateful to receive them for a subsequent edition. Moreover, I would welcome the contribution of altogether different rides to round out the geographic representation of the best bike rides in the Mid-Atlantic. Also, if you would enjoy being a volunteer to verify rides for a later edition, I'd love to hear from you. Please send changes for the existing rides, cue sheets and maps for new rides, or any other comments to Trudy E. Bell, c/o The Globe Pequot Press, P.O. Box 833, Old Saybrook, CT 06475; e-mail: tebell@mcimail.com, or visit our website at http://www.globe-pequot.com.

Disclaimer

Neither the author nor The Globe Pequot Press assumes any liability for accidents happening to, or injuries sustained by, readers who engage in the activities described in this book.

Delaware

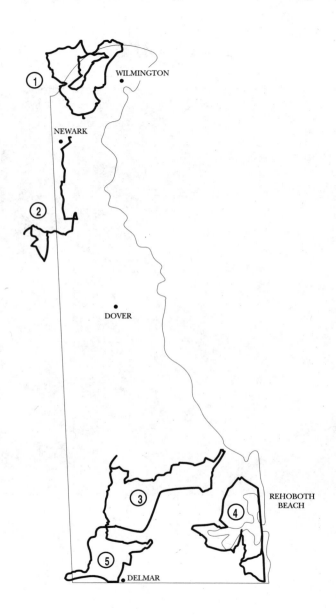

WILMINGTON

NEWARK

DOVER

REHOBOTH
BEACH

DELMAR

1

2

3

4

5

Delaware

Note: It is an eccentricity of some counties in Delaware that most roads—even small farm lanes—are not named but are instead known by their route number (state or federal) or road number (county). With the advent of 911 emergency service, this custom is now being changed, and you may find that more and more roads are starting to acquire names.

As a general rule, road numbers of intersecting roads are listed on small, black and white signs placed on each side of the sign post just below the intersection's stop sign. Road numbers may also appear on black and yellow signs just below intersection warning signs that appear about 75 yards before an upcoming intersection. In the text and on the maps, numbers for Rds. are County road numbers and for Rtes. are State route numbers.

1

Delaware-Pennsylvania Hill-Climbing Cruise

Delcastle Recreation Area—Kennett Square— Cossart—Delcastle Recreation Area

This hilly, challenging ride along less traveled roads offers lovely forest and wooded area scenery, with many old homes of lots of historical character. You'll wander on backroads that the developers have not yet discovered, as you ride from the outskirts of Wilmington, Delaware (New Castle County), into Pennsylvania toward Philadelphia (Chester County). For the least traffic pedal early on a Saturday or Sunday morning, as some of the main two-lane roads do see heavier automobile traffic during the week, suggests David Shackelford, bicycle-commuter expert of Wilmington's White Clay Bicycle Club, who contributed the ride. (The directions have been updated by Shackelford and by Bruce and Alfreda Clinton of Wilmington.)

The route is shaped as if you were tracing the outline of the letter *V*. The longer 37.5-mile version dips down into the center of the V to include a stop at the Ashland Nature Center (302–239–2334), where you can stretch your legs on some nature trails. Then the ride continues by taking you through one of Delaware's few remaining covered bridges. The shorter 26.7-mile version eliminates the 10-mile dip down the center of the V-shaped route, turning the route into a simple triangle. Both rides take you near a second covered bridge.

About 9 miles into both the longer and the shorter versions of the ride, you'll pedal along the southern edge of Kennett Square, a small town whose downtown shopping district is quaint but whose outskirts have the typical convenience stores.

Because the ride takes less traveled roads, there are no services on the route itself; neither does the route pass any bike shops or bed-and-breakfast inns, although there are a number in the general area, Shackelford notes. The two covered bridges and the Ashland Nature Center offer scenic places to stop for a packed snack or lunch. Another good lunch stop is a rustic restaurant and bar called Buckley's Tavern in Centerville (5812 Kennett Pike, 302–656–9776), about 30 miles into the longer ride (about 20 miles into the shorter ride); if you plan to stop there, call ahead for the tavern's hours, which are somewhat limited. Another nice lunch stop is the Hoopes Reservoir, where you can sit and enjoy the view of the lake. Near the end of the route, you'll pedal by the Mount Cuba Astronomical Observatory (call 302–654–6407 for information on activities and public observing hours).

The Basics

Start: Millcreek, Delaware, at the public parking lot of the Delcastle Tennis Center at the north entrance to the Delcastle Recreation Area. There is a portable toilet next to the parking lot near the tennis courts; water fountains are scattered throughout the recreation area. To get to the start, take Rte. 41 (Newport Gap Pike) to Millcreek Rd. Head west on Millcreek Rd. for 0.3 mile and turn left on McKennans Church Rd. into the Delcastle Recreation Area.

Length: 26.7 or 37.5 miles.

Terrain: Moderately hilly. Traffic is generally light on weekends, although during the week it can be moderate to moderately heavy on some main roads.

Food: Across from the Delcastle Tennis Center is the Delcastle Inn Restaurant, 801 McKennans Church Rd. (302–994–4600), at the Delcastle Golf Course. Open daily to the public for casual breakfast, lunch, and dinner from 7:00 A.M. to 9:30 P.M. Typical clientele are golfers so dress is casual. Other that that and Buckley's Tavern there are no convenience stores, restaurants, or water stops directly on the route, although detours of 1–2 miles will bring you plenty in Kennett Square and Chadds Ford. Pack your own snacks and water.

Miles & Directions

- 0.0 From Delcastle Recreation Area, turn right onto McKennans Church Rd.
- 0.3 Turn left at the second traffic light onto the unmarked Millcreek Rd.
- 1.1 Bear right to continue on unsigned Millcreek Rd. You are now on Delaware's Bicycle Route 1, a north-south bicycle route.
- 2.3 Turn right at the stop sign to stay on Millcreek Rd.
- 4.3 Turn left at the T intersection onto unsigned Old Lancaster Pike, followed by an *immediate right* onto Yorklyn Rd. Follow the green Bicycle Route 1 arrows. Cross Lancaster Pike to continue straight on Yorklyn Rd.
- 4.9 Turn left onto Old Wilmington Rd., leaving Delaware Bicycle Route 1.
- 5.4 At the bottom of the hill, bear right at the stop sign to continue on Old Wilmington Rd.
- 6.3 Turn right onto Chandlers Mill Rd. You have now entered Pennsylvania. Look for road signs on brown wooden posts with the road name engraved vertically on the post.
- 6.7 At the bottom of the hill, bear right as Chandler Mill Rd. merges with Kaolin Rd., then immediately turn left to stay on Chandler Mill Rd.
- 7.1 Turn right to stay on Chandler Mill Rd. and immediately cross a one-lane stone and metal bridge built in 1910.
- 8.7 Turn right at the stop sign onto Hillendale Rd., which truly takes you over hill and dale.
- 9.4 At the five-corner intersection with the stop sign and flashing red light, continue straight across Kaolin Rd. to stay on Hillendale Rd. To visit the stores, shops, and restaurants of Kennett Square, Penna. (which is promoted as the Mushroom Capital of the World), turn left here and proceed about 1 mile.
- 12.2 At the seven-corner intersection with a stop sign, turn right onto Rosedale Rd., followed by an immediate right onto Norway Rd.

- 13.0 Bear right at the stop sign to stay on Norway Rd.
- 13.7 Turn right at the T intersection onto Burnt Mill Rd.

Note: For the 26.7-mile ride, at this T intersection turn left instead onto Burnt Mill Rd. At mile 14.1 turn left onto Center Mill Rd., and then resume following the directions at mile 25.0 below.

- 14.4 Bear right at the stop sign onto Old Kennett Pike.
- 14.5 Turn left onto Nine Gates Rd. You have now reentered Delaware.
- 15.6 As you come to a stop sign at Lower Snuff Mill Row, bear left to stay on Nine Gates Rd.
- 15.7 Turn right at the T intersection onto Snuff Mill Rd.
- 15.8 Turn left at the T intersection onto unmarked Rte. 82 (Creek Rd.). You are now riding alongside Red Clay Creek on a winding, two-lane road with no shoulder and many sharp, diagonal railroad crossings. Be very careful.
- 16.8 Turn right onto Sharpless Rd.
- 17.9 Turn left at the T intersection onto Old Wilmington Rd.
- 18.6 Turn left at the stop sign onto unmarked Brackenville Rd.
- 19.8 Bear left at the stop sign onto unmarked Barley Mill Rd. Now you will be able to see the single-lane covered bridge you will cross. Just before you cross it, on your left is the entrance to the Ashland Nature Center.
- 20.1 Immediately after you cross the railroad tracks, turn left at the T intersection onto Rte. 82 (Creek Rd.).
- 20.2 Make the first right onto Ashland Clinton School Rd.
- 21.7 Turn left at the T intersection onto Old Kennett Pike.
- 21.8 Make the first right onto Snuff Mill Rd. (Rd. 244).
- 23.4 Turn left at the T intersection onto Rte. 52 (Kennett Pike). To visit Buckley's Tavern and other stores and shops in Greenville, turn right and proceed along Kennett Pike. Buckley's will be on your right within half a mile.
- 23.9 Turn left onto Burnt Mill Rd. You are now back in Pennsylvania.
- 25.0 Turn right onto Center Mill Rd. *It is at this intersection that the 26.7-mile ride rejoins the longer route. Those doing the shorter ride should turn left onto Center Mill Rd.*
- 25.9 Bear right at the stop sign onto Fairville Rd. While riding

on Fairville Rd., you will cross Rte. 52 (Kennett Pike). There are several antiques stores (but no food or drink) immediately to your left in the village of Fairville on Rte. 52 (Kennett Pike).

- 26.6 Turn right onto unmarked Cossart Rd. Enjoy the long downhills here on this rough road; you'll pay for them later.
- 28.3 Turn right at the T intersection onto unmarked Rte. 100 (Chadds Ford Rd.). Where the road crosses back into Delaware, it changes its name to Montchanin Rd.
- 29.0 Turn right onto unmarked Twaddell Mill Rd. (Rd. 234), where you will begin climbing some steep hills.
- 30.4 Watch for the hidden stop sign at the top of the hill before crossing Rte. 52 (Kennett Pike), and then continue straight on Owl's Nest Rd. At that intersection you're at the center of the historic town of Centerville, containing several offices, boutique and antiques shops, and Buckley's Tavern.
- 32.4 Continue straight where Owl's Nest Rd. becomes New London Rd. and also joins Rte. 82 North.
- 32.7 Make the first left onto Hillside Mill Rd. (Rd. 269). On this road you'll pass by Hoopes Reservoir and Deer Valley Ln. on your left, which will take you to the Mount Cuba Astronomical Observatory. It has a planetarium and telescopes open at certain times to the public (for information, call 302–654–6407).
- 33.6 Immediately after crossing over the railroad tracks, turn left onto Mt. Cuba Rd.
- 34.0 Turn left at the T intersection onto unmarked Barley Mill Rd. (Rd. 258).
- 35.0 Turn right onto Rolling Mill Rd. While on Rolling Mill Rd., as you pass Foxhill Ln., look to the right at another covered bridge.
- 35.6 Turn right at the T intersection onto Rte. 48 (Lancaster Pike). Watch for heavy traffic.
- 35.8 Turn left at the first traffic light onto Hercules Rd., which becomes Millcreek Rd. after crossing Rte. 41.
- 37.2 Turn left onto McKennans Church Rd.
- 37.5 Turn left into the Delcastle Tennis Center parking lot of Delcastle Recreation Area.

Two-State Breakfast Cruise

Newark—Chesapeake City—Newark

This 48-mile route from Newark, Delaware, to Chesapeake City, Maryland, has long been a popular "breakfast" ride with the White Clay Bicycle Club (WCBC), headquartered in Wilmington, Delaware. The destination: Jack and Helen's Restaurant (410–885–5477), a down-home diner that "serves really good, inexpensive breakfasts, sandwiches, and platters. Very 'bicycle friendly,'" notes Nancy Estilow, the editor of WCBC's newsletter *Tailwind*, who contributed and updated the cue sheet on which this ride is based.

The ride starts at Casho Mill Barksdale Park near the Newark campus of the University of Delaware in New Castle County. At first you will pedal along some fairly busy roads, but they generally have wide shoulders. Soon you will cross Summit Bridge over the Chesapeake and Delaware Canal and pass through the Canal National Wildlife Area. The canal, which first opened to traffic in 1829, is now one of the busiest canals in the world, averaging more than 22,000 vessels a year; you may be lucky enough to see large international oceangoing freighters plying their way between Baltimore and Philadelphia. You can also hike or mountain-bike along the unpaved service roads paralleling the canal and hunt for fossils in the canal's banks.

As the canal separates the upper and lower Delmarva Peninsula, you'll feel as though the pace of life has slo-o-owed down. You cycle through open corn fields and past farmhouses and barns. Once you head west into Maryland, you'll take a scenic loop through some of Cecil County's thoroughbred horse farms.

At this point, 27 miles into the ride, you'll undoubtedly have worked up quite an appetite. Chow down at Jack and Helen's, where the waitresses know everyone, as most of the patrons are locals. "Their pancakes are #1 on our list and are typically what we order," notes Estilow. Crowded on weekends, especially very early in the morning, Jack and Helen's is open before dawn seven days a week.

After remounting your bike, you can pause to let some of the feast digest by stopping less than a mile into the return to gaze at the exhibits in the Chesapeake & Delaware Canal Museum. The 21-mile return leads you back essentially along the outward route minus the scenic loop.

The Basics

Start: Newark, Delaware, at Casho Mill Barksdale Park, at the corner of Barksdale Rd. and Casho Mill Rd. Park cars in one of the three lots. In the summer there are portable toilets set up, but no water. From I–95 take Rte. 896 north along College Ave. South, Christina Pkwy., and Elkton Rd.; turn left onto Casho Mill Rd., right onto Barksdale Rd., and left into Casho Mill Barksdale Park.
Length: 48 miles.
Terrain: Flat to gently rolling. Traffic is generally moderately light to light, except on main roads, where it is much heavier—but the main roads compensate by having wide paved shoulders.
Food: Available near 1 mile and 6 miles into the ride and at Jack and Helen's at mile 27. But carry water and snacks, as there are some long stretches without services.

Miles & Directions

- 0.0 Turn right out of the parking lot of Barksdale Park.
- 0.2 Turn left at the traffic light onto Casho Mill Rd.
- 0.8 Turn right at the T intersection onto Rte. 2/896 (Elkton Rd.). Use caution; this road is busy but has wide paved shoulders. Be very careful in passing the shopping center on your

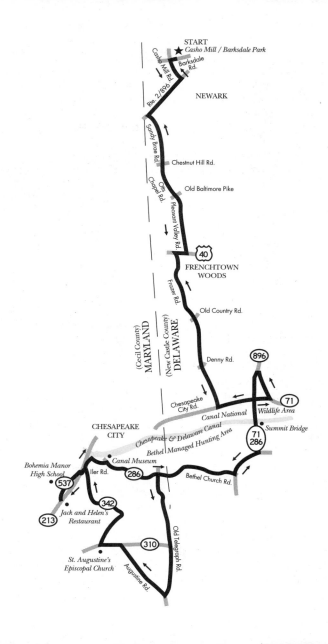

right, watching for cars turning right. (This shopping center includes a grocery store and deli.)

- 2.0 Turn left at the traffic light onto Sandy Brae Rd. This road changes its name several times. After crossing Chestnut Hill Rd., it becomes Otts Chapel Rd. (Rd. 397). At mile 4.3, after crossing the Old Baltimore Pike, keep heading straight on Pleasant Valley Rd. (Rd. 8).
- 5.9 Turn right at the T intersection onto Rte. 40 (Pulaski Hwy.), watching carefully for cars. This road is busy but has a wide paved shoulder. (*Note:* If you were to turn left instead of right onto Rte. 40, you would reach a shopping center with a grocery store, deli, fast-food restaurants, and gas stations.
- 6.1 Take the first left onto Frazer Rd. (Rd. 391), a nice rural change of pace after busy Rte. 40. At mile 8.0, cross unmarked Old County Rd. At mile 9.4 cross Denny Rd. (Rd. 396).
- 10.5 Turn left at the T intersection onto Chesapeake City Rd.
- 11.8 Turn left at the T intersection onto Rte. 71 (Red Lion Rd.).
- 12.6 Turn left at the T intersection onto Rte. 71/896 (Summit Bridge Rd.), which is moderately busy but has wide paved shoulders that narrow when you reach Summit Bridge. Cross Summit Bridge over the Chesapeake and Delaware Canal.
- 14.7 Turn right onto Bethel Church Rd. (Rd. 433).
- 15.6 Turn right to stay on Bethel Church Rd. (Rd. 433) where Choptank Rd. continues straight. At the Maryland border Bethel Church Rd. changes its designation to Rte. 286.
- 17.6 Turn left onto Old Telegraph Rd. At mile 19.5 keep heading straight at the stop sign at the unmarked intersection with Rte. 310 (Cayots Corner Rd.).
- 20.8 Make a sharp right onto Augustine Rd. (the sign says St. Augustine, although the maps say Augustine).
- 22.5 Turn left at the T intersection onto Rte. 310 (Cayots Corner Rd.).
- 23.1 Turn right at St. Augustine's Episcopal Church onto Rte. 342 (St. Augustine Rd. N.).
- 25.9 Turn left onto unmarked Iler Rd.; watch carefully, for this turn is easy to miss. Immediately cross Rte. 286 and pass under the very high bridge of Rte. 213. At mile 26.7 head straight onto unmarked Rte. 537 (Basil Ave.).

- 27.0 Bear left at the Bohemia Manor High School to stay on Rte. 537 (Basil Ave.). Cross Rte. 213 to Jack and Helen's Restaurant for a well-deserved breakfast. Leave the restaurant parking lot by turning right to head north on Rte. 213.
- 27.9 Bear right onto Rte. 286.
- 28.4 Turn right at the deli to stay on Rte. 286 (here called 2nd St.) On parallel 1st Street, 1 block away, is the "main drag" of South Chesapeake City, with quaint shops, a bed-and-breakfast inn, a fancy restaurant on the water, and other amenities.
- 28.9 Turn right at the T intersection to stay on Rte. 286. The Chesapeake & Delaware Canal Museum is across the road to your left. At mile 30.3 you'll pass Old Telegraph Rd., and then you'll leave Maryland and reenter Delaware. At the border Rte. 286 becomes Bethel Church Rd. (Rd. 433).
- 32.3 Turn left at the stop sign to stay on Bethel Church Rd. (Rd. 433).
- 33.1 Turn left at the blinking light onto Rte. 71/896 (Summit Bridge Rd.), watching carefully for traffic.
- 35.2 Turn right onto Rte. 71 (Red Lion Rd.).
- 36.0 Bear right onto Chesapeake City Rd.
- 37.3 Make the first right onto unmarked Frazer Rd. (Rd. 391).
- 41.7 Turn right at the T intersection onto Rte. 40, watching carefully for traffic.
- 42.0 Take the first left at the traffic light onto Pleasant Valley Rd. (Rd. 8), which changes its name first to Otts Chapel Rd. (Rd. 387) and then to Sandy Brae Rd.
- 45.9 Turn right at the T intersection onto Rte. 2/896 (Elkton Rd.), watching carefully for traffic.
- 47.1 Turn left onto Casho Mill Rd. Caution! This intersection is busy. If you happen to miss the turn, you'll know it because the paved shoulder disappears.
- 47.7 Turn right at the traffic light onto Barksdale Rd.
- 47.9 Turn left into the parking lot of Casho Mill Barksdale Park.

3

Inn-to-Inn Triangle Three-Day Ramble

Laurel—Lewes—Greenwood—Laurel

Nestled between Chesapeake Bay tributaries and the Atlantic Ocean lies the gentle, scenic coastal plain of lower Delaware—terrain ideal for cycling at any level of experience. Although strong riders may want to make this flat ride through Delaware's rural Sussex County a one-day near-century challenge, it is best savored as it was designed: three days meandering leisurely from one luxurious bed-and-breakfast inn to the next.

Designed by cycling-enthusiast innkeepers Gwen North of Spring Garden Bed & Breakfast in Laurel and Betty Sharp and Cora Tennefoss of Eli's Country Inn in Greenwood, this ride takes the route offered as a self-guided package by their outfit, Biking Inn to Inn Delaware. (That hassle-free package—which is quite moderate in price—includes three nights in the inns for double occupancy, the transportation of your luggage from one inn to the next, three breakfasts and three dinners, snacks at each inn on arrival, detailed maps and cue sheets of side trips, parking for your car, and secure bicycle storage. For reservations or more information, call Ambassador Travel at 800–845–9939. Tell 'em you read it here.)

This trip, verified and updated by Bruce and Alfreda Clinton of Wilmington, Delaware, begins in Laurel (although beach-lovers may choose to start and end in Lewes). Once a thriving shipping center and port town, Laurel boasts more than 800 structures on the National Register of Historic Places. One of these is your starting point, Spring Garden Bed & Breakfast (302–875–7015), a restored eighteenth-century country manor furnished with eighteenth- and nineteenth-century antiques and fine art.

After a hearty breakfast you'll head for the beach town of Lewes (pronounced "Lewis")—the "First Town in the First State." The cycling is virtually flat, along agricultural backroads with little traffic. At Lewes, there are a growing number of bed-and-breakfast inns within half a mile of the Second Street business district (where, among other places for treats, you can visit the Lewes Bake Shoppe and King's Ice Cream—homemade!).

After a filling breakfast full of the complex carbohydrates that fuel a cyclist's legs, you'll head cross-country past farm lands and ponds and through historic Milton. One treat will be passing Colvine's Bison Farm—yes, buffalo in Delaware: On Route 16 just before your arrival at Greenwood, you are likely to see the out-of-place-looking creatures pasturing right on the side of the road. Just north of Greenwood is Eli's Country Inn (302–349–4265), a renovated family farm where you can sit and rock forever in the porch swing on the ample front and side porches, listening to the birds trill.

The return ride to Laurel includes passage on Delaware's last free cable ferry across a Chesapeake Bay tributary, the Nanticoke River, and a visit to the quaint shipbuilding village of Bethel, the only village in Delaware listed in its entirety on the National Register of Historic Places. Once again at Spring Garden B&B, you can retrieve your car and wave farewell to Gwen North as you head home.

The best times of year to take this ride are spring and fall, as it can "get bleeding hot" in the summer, with high humidity, remarks a local. You may want to pack some insect repellent as well.

The Basics

Start: Spring Garden Bed & Breakfast in Laurel, 0.2 mile west of Rte. 13 on Delaware Ave. Extended.

Length: 98.2 miles, divided into day-long segments of 34.5, 35.2, and 28.5 miles.

Terrain: Mostly flat. Traffic mostly light, except around the three towns.

Food: Occasional convenience stores en route, but carry some snacks and water. If you do this ride as part of the Biking Inn to Inn Delaware package, your breakfasts and dinners are included, and picnic lunches are available at an extra charge.

Miles & Directions

Note: Follow directions carefully, as not every small street is shown on the map.

First Day (Laurel to Lewes)

- 0.0 From the Spring Garden B&B parking lot, turn left onto Rd. 466 (Delaware Ave.).
- 0.3 Cross Rte. 13 and make an immediate right onto Rd. 465.
- 1.6 Bear left after passing Chipman's Pond and Old Christ Church on your left to stay on Rd. 465.
- 2.2 Turn left at the T intersection onto Rd. 74.
- 3.0 Turn left onto Rd. 446. There is no road sign for Rd. 446 except on the stop sign at the intersection. At about mile 8, cross Rte. 9 to continue on Rd. 446.
- 14.3 Turn left at the T intersection onto Rte. 9 (which is also County Rd. 28). In 0.4 mile, you'll pass a shopping center on the right. At mile 14.8, cross Rte. 113 and enter Georgetown.
- 15.4 Enter the traffic circle and turn right onto Rd. 431 (South Bedford St.). In 0.2 mile, Bodie's Dairy Market is on the left for drinks and snacks.
- 16.3 Turn left onto Rd. 318 at sign pointing to State Fire Marshall.
- 18.3 Turn right onto Rte. 47. At mile 20.5, Wilson's General Store is on your left at the stop sign at Rte. 30 (which is also County Rd. 248).
- 24.3 Turn right at the T intersection onto Rte. 5.
- 24.9 Turn left at Rte. 48 at sign to Christ Church. Indian Mission Church is on far left at this intersection and Wise Buys auto business is on the near right.
- 25.6 Turn left onto Rte. 23 (which is also County Rd. 285).

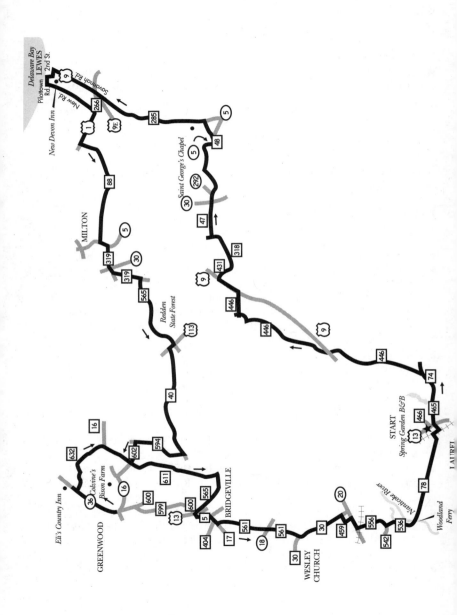

Christ Church is on the far left at this intersection.
- 31.5 At end of Rte. 23, turn left and immediately right at traffic light onto Rte. 9E.
- 31.7 Cross Rte. 1 at the traffic light. Stay in the middle lane of this very busy intersection and proceed straight on Rte. 9. Continue to follow signs for Rte. 9E.
- 32.3 Bear left at the sign to Lewes.
- 34.4 Turn left onto 2nd Street 1 block before the traffic light. In 0.1 mile, Lewes Bake Shoppe is on the left and King's Ice Cream is 1 block farther on right. Bike around and enjoy this peaceful coastal community before arriving at your chosen bed-and-breakfast inn.

Second Day (Lewes to Greenwood)
- 0.0 From your chosen inn, proceed down 2nd St. Turn right at the T intersection onto Shipcarpenter St. and then turn left at the T intersection onto Pilottown Rd.
- 0.8 Turn left onto New Rd. (Rd. 266).
- 3.6 Turn right at the T intersection onto Rd. 266B.
- 3.9 At the yield sign merge onto the wide shoulder of the very busy Rte. 1N.
- 5.5 Turn left onto Rd. 88 at the sign to Milton.
- 11.4 At the stop sign turn left onto Rte. 5 (Federal St.). (A large dish-type TV antenna with the name TONY'S TV is on the ground just before this intersection and the Goshen Methodist Church is on the far side.) (*Note for a detour:* If you turn right or go straight at this intersection, you can visit the town of Milton, which has a number of lunch spots the [Town Cafe or Norma's], 198 homes on the National Register of Historic Places, a lovely pond, and the mouth of the Broadkill River. King's Ice Cream is on Union St. on the left. Pick up snacks at Bodie's Dairy Market or the IGA. After your excursion return to this intersection to continue the main ride.)
- 11.9 Turn right onto Rd. 319 at the produce stand on your left.
- 15.0 Turn right onto Rd. 565 at the sign for Ockels Farm Airport. At mile 16.4, Redden State Forest is a wonderful area for bird-watching. At mile 18.7 you'll pass a picnic area on your left.

- 19.2 Turn right onto the wide shoulder of busy Rte. 113. Watch carefully for traffic! (Relax, you'll be on this road only 0.2 mile.)
- 19.4 Turn left onto Rd. 40 at the signs for Bay Bridge and Bridgeville. At mile 21.5 you'll pass another picnic area on your left.
- 25.5 Turn right onto Rd. 594.
- 28.2 Turn left onto Rd. 602 soon after the sign reading DEAF CHILD.
- 30.3 Turn left at the T intersection onto Rte. 16. At mile 30.8, Elmer's Market is on the right for fresh fruit and veggies. At mile 31.5, you should see the buffalo from Colvine's Bison Farm on your right.
- 32.4 Turn right onto the busy Rte. 36 at the traffic light. Be careful, as there is only a narrow road shoulder on Rte. 36.
- 35.2 Turn left into Eli's Country Inn.

Third Day (Greenwood to Laurel)
- 0.0 Turn right out of Eli's Country Inn onto Rte. 36. Watch for traffic!
- 0.9 Turn left onto Rd. 632
- 3.3 Bear right onto Rd. 611. In 0.2 mile, keep heading straight across Rte. 16 at the stop sign.
- 7.7 Turn right at the T intersection onto Rd. 565.
- 9.4 Turn left at the T intersection onto Rd. 600. At the stop sign at mile 10.1, be especially careful when crossing the four-lane Rte. 13.
- 10.3 Bear left at the stop sign onto Rd. 5. In 0.2 mile, Smith & Sons Fruit Market is on your left; in the fall, the market features fresh-pressed apple cider.
- 10.9 Turn right at the traffic light onto Rte. 404W. (*Note for a detour:* If you go straight at this intersection, you may tour Bridgeville and visit the Rappa Brand Scrapple House.)
- 11.3 Continue straight at the traffic light onto Rte. 17. Do not follow Rte. 404, which heads right at this traffic light.
- 11.4 Turn left onto Rd. 561. Immediately, Delagra Corp. will be on your left.
- 15.7 Turn left at the T intersection onto Rd. 30. Wesley

Church is on the near right of this intersection.

- 18.5 Turn right at the traffic light onto Rte. 20 (Stein Highway). (*Note for a detour:* If you turn left or go straight at this intersection instead, you may tour Seaford and visit the John Ross Mansion and its Plantation.) In 0.1 mile, the Nylon Capitol Shopping Center is on the right, including a pizza parlor and Chinese restaurant. The pizza parlor has very clean rest rooms and the Chinese restaurant has the better facility for bicycle security (bikes can be viewed while eating at inside tables while the windows at the pizza parlor shield visibility).
- 19.2 Turn left onto Rd. 556.
- 20.2 Bear right at Craigs Pond onto Rd. 542A.
- 20.4 Turn left at the T intersection onto Rd. 542.
- 21.1 Bear right at the stop sign onto Rd. 536.
- 22.4 Turn left at the T intersection onto Rd. 78. In 0.2 mile, follow Rd. 78 as it turns left, and proceed to the Woodland Ferry. Take the ferry, which operates seven days a week from 6:00 A.M. to 8:00 P.M. (7:30 A.M. to 6:00 P.M. in the winter) at no charge, whenever its staff see people waiting to cross. Enjoy the two-minute ride across the Nanticoke River.
- 22.7 From the ferry dock, continue straight on Rd. 78. (*Note for a detour:* At mile 25.3, you may elect to turn right at the traffic light and tour the town of Bethel.)
- 28.0 Cross Rte. 13A at the traffic light and bear left onto Rte. 9.
- 28.2 Turn right onto Short Ave. at the end of the school field.
- 28.4 Turn left at the T intersection onto Delaware Ave.
- 28.5 Turn left into Spring Garden Bed & Breakfast. Welcome back!

4

CRABS Challenge

Delaware Seashore State Park—Fenwick Island—
Dagsboro—Millsboro—Rehoboth Beach—
Delaware Seashore State Park

This tour of the scenic inland estuaries of Delaware is the route featured by the annual Come Ride Around the Bays of Sussex (CRABS) organization in its fund-raising tour early each May, the entrance fee for which benefits the Delaware Inland Bays Estuary education program. The scenery varies from farmland to seashore. Although the land is largely flat, differing from the normal challenge ride by not having long hills, "we regularly have medium to strong prevailing winds that local riders refer to as Delmarva mountains," says CRABS route designer Larry Wonderlin of Rehoboth, Delaware. A steady headwind has often been likened to a hill that never quits.

"I have twice cycled from Portland, Maine, to Orlando, Florida, with Pedal For Power, and I believe Delaware has the best cycling roads on the East Coast," declares Wonderlin. "Although we have been 'found,' traffic is still lower than in most places." Even the shoulders of Delaware's busy roads are wide enough to be adequate for a single cyclist, if not two abreast. Moreover, motorists are still friendly toward cyclists: "We're over 30 miles into this ride and no one has honked a horn," marveled a cyclist from Sherbourne, New York, who rode in the 1993 CRABS.

Also, wildlife abounds. Delaware is the northernmost point to which pelicans migrate in middle to late June, and you'll also see a profusion of wading birds, such as the egret and the great blue heron. Sussex County is in the north-south flyway for all species of song birds, many of which have flown all the way from South America to arrive at the same time that the horseshoe crabs are mating on Delaware's beaches. By feeding on the crab eggs, the birds double their body weight before crossing the Delaware Bay and continuing north.

The CRABS benefit ride, as verified and updated by Alfreda and Bruce Clinton of Wilmington, Delaware, features a metric century (100 kilometers, or in this case 64 miles—close enough for government work) and a short ramble of 27 miles. The shorter version can be ridden by almost anyone. Come hungry for an early lunch, because there are several good opportunities to chow down on the local delicacy of (appropriately enough) crab cakes: Harpoon Hannah's and the Sharks' Cove (at opposite ends of the bridge at mile 11.4) and Tom and Terry's on Route 54 (passed at mile 16.2). Later on in the ride, you can try more crab cakes at The Rusty Rudder (mile 58.0).

There are also nonculinary highlights of the ride. One is Holts Landing State Park on the Indian River (mile 24.5), which has picnic tables, a pavilion, a playground, a boat ramp, and a wading beach. The water is potable, but it sometimes has color, odor, and an obnoxious taste—so do not refill your water bottles unless you are dying of thirst. Another highlight is the museum of the Native American Nanticokes, who live in the Oak Orchard area (miles 39–45); by timing your visit for the weekend after Labor Day, you'll arrive while they are hosting their large annual powwow. And bring your bathing suit, for there are many opportunities for swimming in either the ocean or the bays.

If you would like to take this tour in the company of other cyclists at the next CRABS benefit, write to Larry Wonderlin, 28 Marshall Road, Rehoboth, DE 19971, or call him at (302) 227–3697.

For those wishing to stay a night or two in the area, there are many bed-and-breakfast inns and motels in the towns through which you will pass—including Rehoboth Beach, Dewey Beach, Bethany Beach, South Bethany, Fenwick Island, and Millsboro. For specific information call the Delaware Tourism Office at (800) 282–8667 from within Delaware or (800) 441–8846 from out of state.

The Basics

Start: Delaware Seashore State Park Bath House parking lot just south of the Indian River Inlet Bridge on Rte. 1, on the ocean side of the road. The parking lot and beach are accessible year-round, although the bathhouse is open only from May 1 through September 30.

Length: 27 or 64 miles.

Terrain: Flat, although there can be strong winds requiring low gears in some sections. Traffic is generally moderately light to nonexistent, but in the few populated sections where it is heavy, the roads have wide paved shoulders.

Food: An assortment of fast-food places and restaurants are available from mile 4.0 to 16.0; the next available food is in the towns of Millville (mile 21.4), Dagsboro (mile 30.5), and Millsboro (mile 35) and at occasional convenience stores thereafter. Wonderlin's favorite lunch stop is Casapullas at mile 52.7, where the steak sandwiches "rival South Phillie steaks," and Ashby's Oyster House is "better than average" for seafood. Once on Route 1 again, Wonderlin notes, "you're in hog heaven."

Miles & Directions

Note: Follow directions carefully, as not every small street is shown on the map.

- 0.0 Turn right out of the parking lot and make a U-turn under the bridge.
- 0.3 Turn right onto Rte. 1S. At mile 4.8 continue straight at the intersection of Rte. 26. (*Note for a detour:* Turn left here for an enjoyable visit to the shops and restaurants of Bethany Beach.) At mile 6.0 do you brake for doughnuts? Here's a Dunkin' Donuts—also a McDonald's for those who want a quick McMuffin.
- 10.8 Turn right at the traffic light onto Rtes. 20 and 54. The next 3 to 4 miles are busy with motor vehicles and a narrow road shoulder. Use caution.

- 14.6 Turn right onto unmarked Rd. 381, just before a Texaco service station.
- 16.7 Bear right onto Rd. 384. In 0.5 mile you'll pass Lil Red School House—a nursery school that is indeed painted red. Decision time is approaching.
- 17.6 Bear left onto Rd. 84. Do not follow the sign to Camp Barnes unless you have decided to take the shorter route.

For the shorter route, turn right instead onto Rte. 363 (sign reads TO CAMP BARNES. *At mile 18.9 bear right to stay on Rd. 363. At mile 21.0 turn right at the T intersection onto Rd. 361 and ride over Little Assawoman Canal Bridge. At mile 22.4 turn right at the T intersection onto Rte. 26. At mile 22.5 turn left at the traffic light onto Rte. 1N. At mile 27.0 turn right into the parking lot alongside the bridge and re-enter Delaware Seashore State Park and return to the start.*

- 17.9 Bear right to stay on Rd. 84.
- 19.9 Turn left onto unmarked Rd. 352.
- 21.0 Turn left at the stop sign onto Rte. 26 in the village of Millville.
- 21.4 Turn right onto Rd. 347 (White Neck Rd.).
- 23.4 Bear left at the stop sign onto Rd. 346. (If you were to turn right instead, you would pass the entrance to Holts Landing State Park in about a mile.)
- 25.4 Turn right at the stop sign onto Rte. 26.
- 30.5 In Dagsboro, turn right at the T intersection to stay on Rte. 26.
- 30.8 Go straight through the traffic light.
- 31.7 Turn right onto Rd. 331 (where the sign unfortunately reads for 336A, which intersects with Rd. 331 just after this turn), just across from the S&J Restaurant.
- 34.1 Bear left at the Y intersection to stay on Rd. 331.
- 35.1 You've now entered the town of Millsboro. To avoid waiting at the two traffic lights, turn right onto Morris St. and then turn left onto Dodd St.
- 35.3 Turn right onto Rte. 24.
- 39.4 Turn right onto unmarked Rd. 310A.

REHOBOTH
BEACH

DEWEY
BEACH

Rehoboth Bay

MILLSBORO

Indian River Bay

Holts Landing State Park

Indian River
Yacht Club

START
Delaware Seashore
State Park
bathhouse
parking lot

MILLVILLE

DAGSBORO

BETHANY
BEACH

SOUTH
BETHAN

Turn left here for 64-mile ride;
turn right for 27-mile ride

Little
Assawoman
Bay

Fenwick
Island

- 40.2 Turn left onto Rd. 313A as Rd. 310 dead ends at the waterfront.
- 40.6 Turn right at the stop sign onto Rd. 312. In 0.5 mile you'll pass the Indian River Yacht Club.
- 43.0 Turn left at the T intersection onto Rd. 297.
- 45.0 Turn right at the traffic light onto Rte. 24E. At mile 48.0 continue straight through the traffic light. At mile 50.6 Casapullas in Peddler's Village on your left offers good steak sandwiches. At mile 53.2 cross over Love Creek Bridge.
- 53.6 Turn right at the traffic light onto Rd. 275.
- 54.3 Turn left at the stop sign onto Rd. 274.
- 54.6 Turn right onto Seaside Dr. into the small residential area of Rehoboth Shores.
- 54.8 Turn right at the stop sign onto Airport Rd.
- 55.1 Turn right onto Rte. 1S to Rehoboth Beach. The next 9 miles have heavy motor vehicle traffic, but the road has a wide, well-paved shoulder.
- 64.0 At the bottom of the bridge, immediately turn right. Re-enter Delaware Seashore State Park. In 0.4 mile you'll reach the parking lot.

5

Sussex Ponds Cruise

Delmar—Portsville—Bethel—Trap Pond—Delmar

Aside from being ideal for cycling with its almost traffic-free and wooded backroads, Delaware's Sussex County has a fascinating ecology. Two of the ponds this ride passes—Trap Pond and Trussum Pond—represent the northernmost extent of the bald cypress trees growing out of the water in swamps for which the Deep South is famous. At Trussum Pond you may feel as though you're pedaling through a Louisiana bayou instead of in a corner of the Mid-Atlantic. Trap Pond is in a state park, which—in addition to views of the pond—offers picnic tables, rest rooms, drinking water, a camp store, and overnight camping during the summer (for more information call the Delaware Division of Parks in Dover: 302–736–4702).

This ride, devised and verified by Gilbert M. Turner of Salisbury, Maryland, has long been a favorite of the Salisbury Bicycle Club. The outbound route through flat, agricultural land will take you right through the place where the corner of Delaware juts into Maryland—the cornerstone there was the first laid by the surveyors Mason and Dixon in 1768. As the route passes through Portsville, unpack your binoculars for a bird-watching detour into the Nanticoke Wildlife Area.

The Basics

Start: Delmar, a town that straddles the border of Delaware and Maryland (and whose name obviously borrows from both states), in the parking lot for the strip mall in the Delaware half of the town; it is just north of Rte. 54 and just west of the southbound lane of Rte. 13. Park near Bonanza Restaurant at the south end of the parking lot.

Length: 42 miles.

Terrain: Flat. Traffic is light except on Rte. 54 and crossing Rte. 13.

Food: Many options at the start in Delmar; a country store just off the route in Bethel about 20 miles into the ride; and seasonal camp stores at Chipman Pond (mile 26) and at Trap Pond (mile 34). No other services in between, so carry snacks, water, and tools.

Miles & Directions

Note: Follow directions carefully, as not every small street is shown on the map.

- 0.0 Leaving the south end of the parking lot, turn right (west) onto Rte. 54 at the Delaware state line. At mile 6.5 continue straight to stay on Rte. 54 (don't follow curve to the right). At mile 7.8 you'll pass the cornerstone monument marking the Mason-Dixon Line and will now be riding briefly in Maryland.
- 8.7 Turn right onto Norris Twilley Rd.
- 9.3 Bear right onto May Twilley Rd. In about 0.75 mile you'll re-enter Delaware, where the road you're on becomes Rd. 507.
- 11.2 Immediately after crossing Rd. 76, turn right onto Rd. 508.
- 12.7 Where Rd. 508 jogs right to continue straight, turn left onto Rd. 509.
- 14.8 Turn left onto Rd. 514.
- 15.8 Cross Rte. 24 and continue straight on Rd. 493 into Portsville. (To detour into the Nanticoke Wildlife Area, at Portsville turn left onto Rd. 496 and ride to the end; return the way you came in.) At Portsville continue on Rd. 493, which bends east past the pond and takes you into Bethel at mile 19.8. Cross the bridge and pass a country store on Main St. to your left. Continue on Rd. 493.
- 22.4 Cross Rte. 13A and continue straight on Rd. 470.

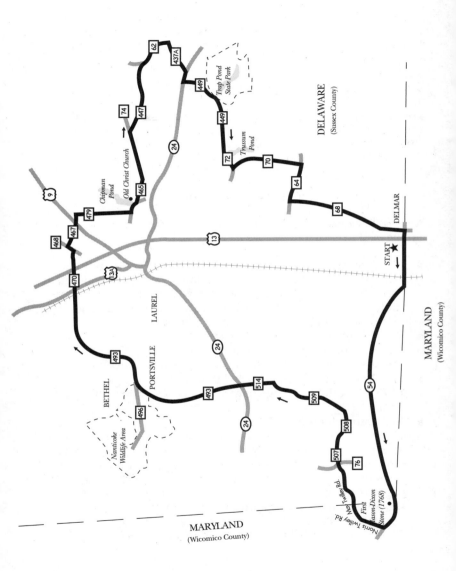

- 23.0 Cross Rd. 13 and continue straight on Rd. 470 until the end.
- 23.7 Turn left at the T intersection onto Rd. 468.
- 23.8 Turn right onto Rd. 467. In 0.7 mile you'll cross US Rte. 9/Rte. 28.
- 24.7 Turn right onto Rd. 479.
- 26.2 Turn left onto Rd. 465. Just after this corner is a camp store, where you can provision up if you're hungry or thirsty. In 500 feet cross over Chipman Pond Dam. Less than 0.25 mile later is Old Christ Church on your left, an early-eighteenth-century "chapel of ease," where the interior—including the pews—is still original, unpainted wood. By the way, for the next 5 miles you'll be riding on the first 5 miles of Ride 3.
- 27.2 Bear left to join Rd. 74.
- 28.5 Turn right onto Rd. 447.
- 30.7 Bear right to join Rd. 62.
- 31.5 Turn right onto Rd. 437A.
- 32.5 Turn right at the T intersection onto Rte. 24.
- 32.7 Turn left onto Rd. 449 at the sign to Trap Pond State Park. At mile 33.9 is the entrance to the park itself. South of the park Rd. 449 bends right (west). At mile 35.5 cross over the dam for Trussum Pond, which lies to your left and is very pretty with its stand of bald cypress trees.
- 35.7 Continue straight on Rd. 72.
- 36.0 Turn sharply left at the stop sign onto Rd. 70 where Rd. 72 curves right. Go slowly here, for this intersection is easy to miss.
- 37.9 Turn right at the T intersection onto Rd. 64.
- 38.9 Turn left onto Rd. 68.
- 42.1 Turn right onto Rte. 54/Rd. 419.
- 42.2 Cross Rte. 13 at the traffic light. Turn right into the mall parking area.

Maryland

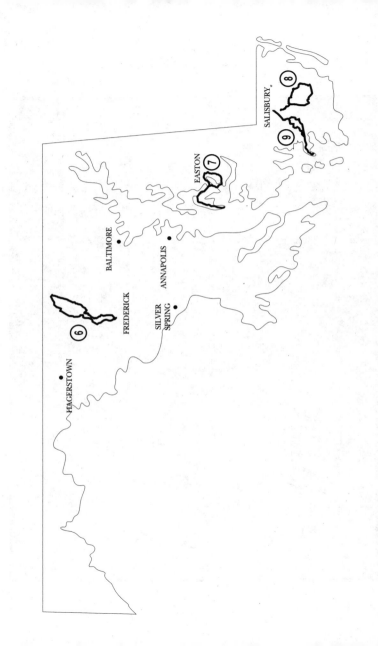

Maryland

6

Three Covered Bridges Cruise

Frederick—Motters—Thurmont—Catoctin—Frederick

Be sure to pack your camera for this 44-mile jaunt into the northern part of Frederick County. Rolling, lightly traveled roads take you through a valley from which you can gaze at the distant Blue Ridge Mountains. At the northernmost section look for the imposing shrine of Mount Saint Mary's College in the mountains.

Besides the three nineteenth-century covered bridges through which you will ride, you might want to spend some time at the Catoctin Mountain Zoological Park (301–271–7488), one of two privately owned zoos in Maryland. And don't miss the chance to poke around the ruins of an old lime kiln in the historic Catoctin Furnace area; the kiln dates back to the late 1700s. South of Thurmont you'll ride past various fish hatchery ponds.

This ride, one of a series produced by the Tourism Council of Frederick County, Inc., along with the Frederick-based bicycle shop Wheel Base, Inc., and verified by Jeffrey H. Marks of Baltimore, is especially nice on a spring day when the orchards are fragrant with flowers, or in the autumn when their boughs are heavy with apples. Leave some space in your panniers to stash a few of each!

For those wishing to break up the 44-mile cruise into an easier two-day jaunt, there are several overnight options in Thurmont, 26 miles into the ride. Campers may set up a tent at Catoctin Mountain Park (301–663–9330) or at Crow's Nest Campground (301–271–7632). Those preferring luxury can rent a secluded cabin at Ole Mink Farm (301–271–7012) or relax with a free continental breakfast at the quaint Cozy Country Inn (301–271–4301). Staying at Thurmont then makes the second day's return to Frederick a mere 17 miles.

Frederick also has several bed-and-breakfast inns. Particularly notable is the Tyler-Spite House (301–831–4455), an elegantly restored three-story 1814 Federal-style mansion, where your stay includes afternoon tea and an evening carriage ride through the historic district. For information on other choices, contact the Tourism Council of Frederick County at (800) 999–3613.

The Basics

Start: Frederick at Culler Lake, at the corner of W. 2nd St. and College Ter. Free parking is available on the street. Rest rooms are open near the tennis courts from May through October. To get to the start from I–70 or I–270, take Rte. 15 north to the Rosemont Ave. exit. Go straight at the light onto 2nd St. Culler Lake will be on your right. Park along 2nd St.
Length: 44 miles.
Terrain: Moderately rolling hills. Traffic generally light but heavier around Frederick. *Note:* Verifier Marks led the successful campaign to get Maryland traffic law changed to allow bicyclists to use the shoulders of most non-freeway controlled-access highways, such as Rte. 15.
Food: Readily available in Frederick and Thurmont, with convenience stores scattered along the rest of the route. To be on the safe side, carry snacks and water.

Miles & Directions

- 0.0 Make a U-turn and head west on W. 2nd St. The lake should now be on your left.
- 0.2 Turn right onto Fairview Ave.
- 1.3 Turn left onto Motter Ave.; after crossing Rte. 15 a mile or 2 later, the name changes to Opossumtown Pike. At about

mile 4, at McClellan Rd. and the Willowbrook Housing Development, bear left to stay on Oppossumtown Pike.

- 5.5 Turn right (at Ford Rd.) to stay on Opossumtown Pike.
- 6.1 Bear left at the bottom of the hill to stay on Opossumtown Pike.
- 6.2 Turn right onto Masser Rd.
- 8.0 Turn right onto Mountaindale Rd.
- 8.2 Turn left onto Hansonville Rd.
- 8.4 Cross Rte. 15 and turn left onto unmarked Rte. 806, here called Hessong Bridge Rd.
- 9.5 Turn right onto Utica Rd. Here you'll pass through the first of the three covered bridges, Utica Mills Covered Bridge, built about 1850.
- 10.7 Turn left at the T intersection onto Old Frederick Rd.
- 14.7 Bear left at the stop sign onto Rte. 550 (Creagerstown Rd.).
- 15.0 Turn right onto the continuation of Old Frederick Rd. At mile 17.1 you'll pass through the Loys Station Covered Bridge, also built around 1850. If you're so inclined, stop to have a snack at the picnic tables at Loys Station Park or to use the rest rooms there.
- 21.0 Turn left at the stop sign onto unmarked Rte. 76 (Motters Station Rd.)   50   50

at Holly View Farm.

- 21.6 Turn left onto Old Kiln Rd. Soon you'll pass the old lime kiln on your right. Watch for gravel on the road.
- 24.1 Turn left at the T intersection onto unmarked Roddy Rd. At mile 25.7 you'll pass through the third of the covered bridges, Roddy Covered Bridge, built about 1856. Keep going straight where the road becomes Apples Church Rd., in the village of Thurmont.
- 26.8 Turn right at the T intersection onto Rte. 77 (E. Main St.).
- 27.5 Turn left onto Rte. 806 (Water St.). (*Note for a detour:* Continue west on Rte. 77 a bit more than 3 miles, past Catoctin Visitor's Center, to Conningham Falls Trail on the left. It's only a quarter of a mile to the falls on this level, wheelchair-accessible trail. Return to the main ride by retracing your route downhill on Rte. 77, which is narrow and winding, with weekend traffic.)

- 27.6 Turn right to stay on Rte. 806, which is now called Frederick Rd. Several miles ahead the Catoctin Mountain Zoological Park will be on your left. Stay on Rte. 806 as it crosses Rte. 15, changing its name to Auburn Rd. (no sign). Be careful at that crossing, as traffic is fast and heavy.
- 33.4 Turn right onto the wide, smooth shoulder of busy Rte. 15.
- 34.1 Turn left onto Fish Hatchery Rd. Now you will pass fish ponds.
- 34.7 Turn left onto Bethel Rd.
- 39.4 Turn left onto Yellow Springs Rd. at the stop sign. In Frederick this road becomes Rosemont Ave. Watch for dangerous grates and traffic.
- 44.0 Turn right onto W. 2nd St.

7

Delmarva Challenge

Easton—Oxford—Saint Michaels—
Tilghman—Easton

Delmarva—a long peninsula encompassing *DEL*aware, the eastern shore of *MAR*yland, and a part of *Virgini*A—lies between the Chesapeake Bay and the Atlantic Ocean. Much of it is still commercial farmland for raising chickens, grain, and corn. Most of the land is flat coastal plain and gently rolling farm fields with little-traveled backroads, making for ideal cycling—although at times variable winds, generally from the south, can present stiff opposition on parts of a ride.

Both the shorter and the longer versions of this Talbot County ride have everything for a perfect weekend getaway: lovely views of the water, antiques shops, superb seafood restaurants famous for their Maryland crabs, a nautical museum, and a short ride on the oldest continuously operating ferry in the United States. The 27-mile ramble through the Chesapeake Bay towns of Easton, Oxford, and Saint Michaels in Maryland is an easy, scenic meander that is a favorite of many clubs and commercial bicycle touring companies.

By adding 32 more miles out to Tilghman Island—which most likely will include bucking headwinds on the way out—stronger cyclists can find their match. The full 59-mile challenge to Tilghman Island also includes a view of one of the last remaining fleets of skipjacks: nineteenth-century sailing vessels still used to dredge for oysters. (Another such fleet can be seen on the bicycle ride to Deal Island; see Ride 9). For those antsy to push the pedals even farther, there are also any number of beautiful side jaunts along quiet necks into the water.

There is so much to see and do that, rather than trying to cram all the miles into one day, you would do better to plan your stay to include at least one night. And you can really pamper yourself if you take the whole weekend. This entire area offers a wide assortment of luxurious bed-and-breakfast inns. Among them are the rambling Pasadena Inn in Royal Oak (410–745–5053), the Tidewater Inn in Easton (410–822–1300), the Robert Morris Inn in Oxford (410–226–5111), and Harrison's Chesapeake House on Tilghman Island itself (410–886–2123).

Because this is such a popular resort area, traffic and population density on summer weekends can be higher than someone seeking peace and solitude might desire, particularly in the towns themselves. Try your visit instead in September or October, when the autumn colors can be spectacular. Or play hooky from work to slip away for some midweek R & R and time for yourself and maybe your love. Although a fair amount of the cycling is along main highways (because they are the only access on the narrow necks), the state of Maryland is so civilized that the wide, smoothly paved shoulders are marked as bicycle lanes! Enjoy!

The basic loop ride, contributed by Frank J. Pondolfina of the Freestate Derailleurs Bicycle Club of Baltimore and verified by Robert Moore, Sr., of Baltimore, starts at the Tred Avon Square Shopping Center in Easton, where you can park your car. There is also a municipal lot several blocks away. If you plan to stay overnight, park at the inn of your choice and pick up the ride near there instead.

The Basics

Start: Easton, Maryland, at the Tred Avon Square Shopping Center on Rte. 322 and Marlboro Rd. To get to the start from Rte. 50, exit onto Route 322 into Easton and turn left onto Marlboro Rd. and right into the Tred Avon Square Shopping Center.
Length: 27 or 59 miles.
Terrain: Mostly flat, although there can be stiff headwinds out to Tilghman Island. Traffic ranges from light to moderate, heavier in

the towns and on summer weekends.

Food: Excellent seafood restaurants in the towns, plus convenience stores. You might want to pack a snack, though, for the stretch from Saint Michaels to Tilghman Island.

Miles & Directions

Note: Follow directions carefully, as not every small street is shown on the map.

- 0.0 Turn left out of the Tred Avon Square Shopping Center onto Marlboro Rd. and left onto Rte. 322E.
- 1.7 Turn right at the second light onto Rte. 333S (Peach Blossom Rd.) toward Oxford, riding in the bicycle lane along the right shoulder. Stay on this road for the next 10 miles until it ends at the ferry dock in Oxford. At mile 4.2 you'll pass Bailey's Neck Rd. on your right—a delightful 8-mile round-trip detour out toward the Tred Avon River if you're feeling energetic. If you're hungry for an early lunch when you reach Oxford, make a sharp left at the tennis courts onto unmarked S. Morris St. and turn right at the second block onto W. Pier St. for a cyclists' popular lunch stop at the Pier Street Restaurant and Marina. You can also picnic and swim at the beach of the Oxford town park across from the Oxford Mews. Just before the ferry dock, you'll pass the Robert Morris Inn.
- 11.2 Where the road ends at the ferry dock, pay the nominal fare to take the Tred Avon Ferry for a breezy, beautiful, and all-too-short five-minute ride across the Tred Avon River to Bellevue. From the dock continue riding straight.
- 11.5 Turn right at the T intersection onto Bellevue Road, following the signs for Saint Michaels.
- 14.1 Turn left at the stop sign at the T intersection onto Rte. 329 (Royal Oak Rd.), following the signs for Saint Michaels. Royal Oak is a thriving center of antiques stores. In less than 0.25 mile, you'll pass the Pasadena Inn on your right.
- 15.0 Turn left at the stop sign onto Rte. 33W, riding in the bi-

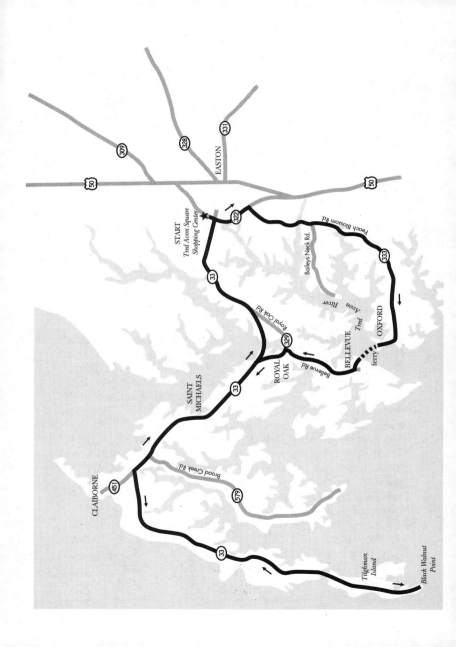

cycle lane on the right shoulder. At mile 18.1 you'll reach Saint Michaels. Here you may, if you wish, splurge for some calories at Justine's Ice Cream Parlor, on the right at Railroad Ave., or turn right onto Mill St. to explore the Chesapeake Bay Maritime Museum.

If you wish to make this ride only a 27-mile ramble, leave Saint Michaels the way you came in, heading east on the bike lane on the shoulder of Rte. 33E. At mile 27.3 turn left at the first traffic light onto Rte. 322. One block later turn right into the Tred Avon Square Shopping Center.

- 18.1 If you wish to visit Tilghman Island, continue heading west out of Saint Michaels on Rte. 33W. At mile 20.6 you'll pass the intersection with Rte. 579 (Broad Creek Rd.) on your left; if you're up for some extra exploring, that spur will lead you down 8 miles along some of the least-traveled roads you are likely ever to pedal, for some views of the sparkling water. At mile 21.2 you'll pass Rte. 451 heading off to your right; that 2-mile optional spur will take you into the charming village of Claiborne and to Rich Neck Manor, the plantation home of Michael Tilghman, a member of the Continental Congress during the American Revolution. At mile 30.5 stop at the Tilghman Island drawbridge for a lovely vista of the sailboats. Half a mile beyond that, turn left onto a small wharf where there is one of the last remaining fleets of skipjacks. At mile 31.2 is Harrison's Chesapeake House, an inn popular with duck hunters and sports fishermen. In another 2.5 miles you've reached the end of the line: the Coast Guard station at Black Walnut Point.
- 33.7 Turn around and retrace your entire route out Rte. 33W, on which you will remain for the next 25 miles, through Saint Michaels and past the turnoff on Rte. 329 to the Pasadena Inn.
- 58.6 Turn left onto Rte. 322. In 1 block turn right into the Tred Avon Square Shopping Center.

8

Iron Furnace Ramble

Salisbury—Furnace—Colbourne—Salisbury

Bicycling doesn't get much better than it does on this ride, one of the favorites of the Salisbury State University Cycling Club. On this ride—an easy 33-mile meander through woodlands preserved by the Nature Conservancy in Wicomico County in southeast Maryland—the scenery is idyllic, the trees shelter you from prevailing winds, the pavement is smooth, the road is flat, and automobile traffic is light. Ah-h-h!

Just to make life even easier, the cycling club has marked the entire route with white arrows numbered 33 (the length of the ride and the number given it when the club first marked it for the 1989 National Rally of the League of American Wheelmen)—markings that have been kept up to date, notes club representative Joseph K. Gilbert, who contributed this ride. (It was verified by Robert Moore, Sr., of Baltimore.) All in all, it's a perfect choice for warming up early in the season or for introducing a novice to the joys of two-wheeled touring.

The nominal destination, Furnace Towne, is a restored iron-smelting village. During summer weekends you might see a blacksmith pounding hot iron on an anvil, a candle-maker dipping wicks into tallow, or a broom-maker assembling straw on a wood handle. Stop long enough in Furnace also to stroll along the 0.25-mile-long nature trail, which leads you into a marsh where discreet signs identify exotic cypress trees and other plants.

Although the starting place of this ride is the university campus, you might prefer instead to begin and end from Snow Hill, a couple of miles southeast of the route on Route 12. There you can make a weekend of it at the Snow Hill Inn (410–632–2102), the Chanceford Hall Bed & Breakfast (410–632–2231), or the River House Inn (410–632–2722); for further information contact Somerset Community Information in Princess Anne, Maryland, at (410) 651–0852. Outside the town is Pocomoke River State Park (410–632–2566), where those preferring to camp can pitch a tent.

In addition to restaurants, canoe rentals, and other services, Snow Hill has *Tillie the Tug* (phone: 410–632–0680); a tugboat that, for a few dollars, will take you chugging down the Pocomoke River. Keep alert—you might even spot a bald eagle wheeling overhead.

The Basics

Start: Salisbury, at the front of the Maggs Physical Activity Center at Salisbury State University. Parking there is free to the public, although it may be crowded during the school year. To get to the university from Rte. 13, turn west onto Bateman St. and proceed .75 mile.

Length: 33.7 miles.

Terrain: Virtually flat. Mostly on well-paved country roads with very little traffic.

Food: Stock up in Salisbury, because this ride is so rural that there are no places to stop for food or drink unless you make a detour of 4 miles each way to the town of Snow Hill halfway through the ride (adding the detour to Snow Hill lengthens the route to 42 miles).

Miles & Directions

Note: At the start of the ride, follow the big white arrows painted on the pavement until the ride is marked with smaller white arrows numbered *33*. When approaching the university on your return route, follow the green arrows marked with an *H* (for *Home*).

■   0.0 Depart from the exit in front of the gym across from the parking lot.

- 0.1 Head straight onto Bateman St. Cross the very busy Rte. 13 (S. Salisbury Blvd.) by using the tunnel underneath it.
- 0.3 Turn right at the T intersection onto S. Division St., which eventually becomes Coulbourne Mill Rd.
- 2.6 Turn right onto Union Church Rd.
- 4.2 Turn right onto Pocomoke Rd., which, after crossing St. Lukes Rd., becomes Stevens Rd.
- 10.4 Turn left onto Old Furnace Rd. (the road is unmarked, but follow the sign pointing to Snow Hill). At mile 16.3 you will pass the Nassawango Iron Furnace on your right; the sign to it faces oncoming traffic. You might like to stop here and wander around the village restoration and the nature trail. There are also public rest rooms and water.
- 17.5 Turn left onto Rte. 12 (Snow Hill Rd.). *If you wish to visit the town of Snow Hill for lunch or other sightseeing, turn right instead and ride 4 miles; although traffic is moderate, there is a lane-wide paved shoulder.*
- 18.1 Turn right onto Mt. Olive Church Rd.
- 24.3 Turn left onto Spearin Rd.
- 27.3 Turn right onto Rte. 12 (Snow Hill Rd.).
- 28.0 Turn left onto Old Fruitland Rd.
- 29.4 Bear right at the yield sign onto the unmarked Coulbourne Mill Rd. After crossing over a bridge, follow the main road as it bears right and joins S. Division St.
- 33.4 Turn left onto Bateman St. Cross Rte. 13 (S. Salisbury Blvd.). Enter the Salisbury State University campus.
- 33.7 Head straight into the Maggs Physical Activities Center parking area.

9

Deal Island Skipjack Challenge

Salisbury—Jason—Deal Island
Princess Anne—Salisbury

Nautical history buffs particularly ought to enjoy this ride, as its destination—Deal Island in the Tangier Sound—is the home of one of the last remaining skipjack fleets. Skipjacks are sailing vessels that by law may not be motorized. In the nineteenth century they were the primary way fishermen tongued for oysters. Today, at the threshold of the twenty-first century, the dozen or so skipjacks at the small Deal Island harbor are one of the last fleets of the waterman's work boats. If you're lucky enough to time your visit for the proper weekend in the spring, you may be able to cheer on the annual skipjack races; for details call Somerset Community Information in Princess Anne at (410) 651–0852.

On the way out, in addition to cycling through miles of pastoral farmland of Wicomico and Somerset counties, you'll pedal through the tidal marshland of the Deal Island Wildlife Management Area. Birders might enjoy packing a small pair of binoculars and looking for great blue heron and other shore birds.

On the return the route takes you through the historic town of Princess Anne. There you will ride by the two-century-old Washington Hotel (410–651–2525), where George Washington's mother once spent the night; if you wish, you can do so today. In the winter the hotel is worth a stop for a steaming bowl of oyster stew; in the spring try the soft-shell crab sandwich. (The weather in this southeastern peninsula of Maryland is so moderated by the surrounding bodies of water that you can comfortably bicycle year-round.)

For the most part the terrain is flat, but don't let that fool you. The land is exposed and there is a significant prevailing wind from the west, and so on the way out "you work," remarks Joseph K. Gilbert, representative of the Salisbury State University Cycling Club who contributed to this ride. (It was verified by Robert Moore, Sr., of Baltimore.) But the payoff is that "you have a wonderful tailwind coming home," he adds.

The club designed this ride for the 1989 National Rally of the League of American Wheelmen held at the university, marking the pavement with orange arrows and the number *62* (for its approximate mileage). Where roads have not been repaved since, many of those arrows will still guide you.

Because this route is so rural, services are limited. There are two mom-and-pop stores for buying snacks and drinks in Monie and Deal Island, as well as public rest rooms at the gas station on Deal Island. For those wishing to make the ride into a more leisurely weekend trip, Princess Anne has a number of beautiful bed-and-breakfast inns (again, call Somerset Community Information for suggestions). And Salisbury itself has all the major chain hotels, motels, and restaurants.

The Basics

Start: Salisbury, at the front of the University Center at Salisbury State University. Parking there is free to the public, although it may be crowded during the school year. To get to the University Center from Rte. 13, turn west onto Dogwood Dr. and proceed for 0.2 mile.

Length: 63 miles.

Terrain: Virtually flat, although there can be persistent headwinds on the way out (remember, headwinds have been likened to hills that never quit). Very low traffic, and Rte. 363 has a lane-wide shoulder almost its entire length.

Food: A couple of convenience stores along the way, plus all services in Princess Anne and Salisbury.

Miles & Directions

Note: Follow directions carefully as not every small street is shown on the map. Follow the big orange arrows at the start until the ride is marked with an orange *62* and smaller arrows. When you approach the university on your return, look instead for green arrows marked with an *H* (for *Home*).

- 0.0 Head straight out the exit of the University Center parking lot. Turn left onto Dogwood Dr.; turn right onto Wesley Dr.
- 0.3 Turn right onto unmarked Pine Bluff Rd.
- 0.5 Turn left onto Camden Ave.
- 2.3 Bear right at the Y intersection onto Allen Rd. After you pass through the village of Allen (which has a small convenience store), the road changes its name to Loretto Allen Rd.
- 8.3 Turn right onto Polks Rd. Stop in at Foggy Bottom, a discount store, for delftware and other items; it has "good prices" and "will ship," notes Joe Gilbert.
- 10.3 Turn left onto New Rd.
- 11.5 Turn right at the T intersection onto Ridge Rd.
- 13.7 Turn left at the T intersection onto Mt. Vernon Rd.
- 14.5 Make the first right onto Black Rd.
- 16.6 Turn left at the T intersection onto Drawbridge Rd.
- 17.3 Make the first right onto Fitzgerald Rd.
- 19.8 Turn right at the T intersection onto Rte. 363 (Deal Island Rd.), and stay on it to Wenona Harbor at the very end. At mile 32.1 you'll reach Deal Island. Stop to explore. To return, turn around and retrace your route, pedaling 18 more miles straight into Princess Anne. At mile 50.3 you'll cross busy Rte. 13.
- 50.4 Turn right onto Mansion St.
- 50.5 Turn left onto Prince William St.
- 50.7 Turn left onto Rte. 675 (Somerset Ave.) and look for the Washington Hotel on your left.

- 52.1 Turn right onto Rte. 529 (Old Loretto Rd.). At mile 54.7 cross Rte. 13. Watch carefully, as the traffic is heavy and there is no traffic light. After this intersection Old Loretto Rd. becomes Loretto Allen Rd.
- 56.9 Bear left onto Allen Rd., which eventually becomes Camden Ave.
- 62.8 Turn right onto Pine Bluff Rd.
- 62.9 Turn left onto Wesley Dr.
- 63.0 Turn left onto Dogwood Dr.
- 63.1 Turn right into the Salisbury State University Center parking lot.

New Jersey

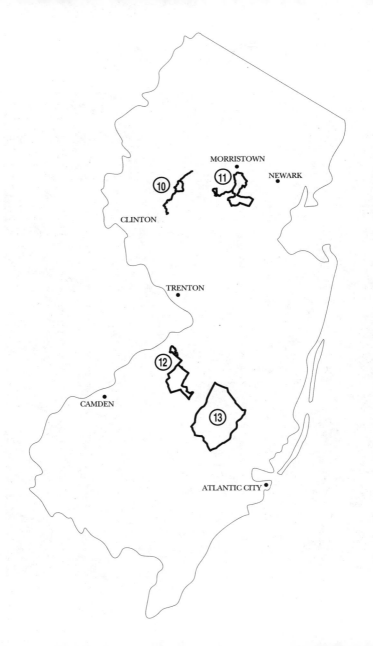

New Jersey

10

Raritan River Gorge Ramble

Clinton—Califon—Clinton

This peaceful meander in western New Jersey is one of the nicest you're likely to encounter. In late June, the route is festooned with wild rose, fragrant honeysuckle, and edible mulberries. It is so shaded that it would be cooling even on a hot day; it has little automobile traffic; its gently rolling terrain is accessible to nearly everyone; and its scenery—especially the gorge cut out by the Raritan River—is unparalleled. So slow down; bring your fishing rod, binoculars, and picnic lunch; and introduce a friend to the joys of bicycle touring.

This charming ride, based on a route contributed by Leonard C. Friedman and Gail Waimon of Short Hills, New Jersey, and verified by myself and my family, starts in the town of Clinton in Hunterdon County. There you can park either along the street or in the public lot in back of the Clinton Bakery, where you can pick up breakfast, snacks, or lunch on any day but Monday. Clinton's small historic downtown district is worth a walking tour, especially the Hunterdon Historical Museum (908–735–4101) and the Hunterdon Art Center (908–735–8415)—two former gristmills on either side of the cast-iron bridge. The Clinton Falls Country Store and Eatery overlooking the waterfall is a nice place to relax for a drink or bowl of soup after the ride. Clinton is also the home of the Amber House bed-and-breakfast inn at 66 Leigh Street; call (908) 735–7881.

First you'll leave Clinton by Center Street, which is lined by mature gingko and maple trees and gracious old homes. The ride from

Clinton to Califon, which follows the Raritan River upriver, is a net uphill, although generally very gentle; the few notable inclines are short enough only to make you glow.

The highlight is the 1.8-mile unpaved section of Raritan River Road (uniformly abbreviated RIVER RD. on the street signs) paralleling the fast-flowing, boulder-strewn south fork of the Raritan River deep in the rocky wooded gorge of Ken Lockwood Gorge Park. Although the rutted dirt road can be navigated even by thin-tire bikes, you'd be happier on a hybrid or true mountain bike, especially if the road is muddy after a rain. In any event take your time—maybe even pause for an hour or two to watch the birders gazing through their spotting scopes or the fly fishermen in waders casting for rainbow, brown, and brook trout.

Your destination, Califon, feels like a town that time forgot. The roads are so sleepy that geese sit right in the middle of them, hammocks swing from front porches, and the nineteenth-century buildings of the bank and general store still have false fronts (170 of these structures are included on the National Register of Historic Places). Sit by the river to enjoy your picnic lunch.

You can return by the path out, if you want to revisit the river gorge and have a generally easy return. Or you can follow the directions in the cue sheet for a bit of variety, climbing over a ridge just for the challenge and some green vistas (also a good detour for both directions if River Road in the gorge is too muddy). In either case the return to Clinton is a net downhill, and the distance is identical. There are some tricky intersections in both directions, but if you remember not to cross any of the bridges over the Raritan River, you'll do fine.

The Basics

Start: Clinton, in the public parking lot on Lower Center St. behind the Clinton Bakery. Take I–78 to exit 15, following Rte. 173 (Hunterdon County Rte. 513) to Clinton; at the brown sign for the Historical Museum and Art Center, turn left onto West Main St.,

cross the painted iron bridge, and make the first left onto Lower Center St.; the public parking lot is around the bend on your right.
Length: 19 miles.
Terrain: Flat to gently rolling, with one steeper hill on the return. After some initial traffic around Clinton, there are few automobiles the rest of the ride.
Food: Available in Clinton and Califon but not in between. (Califon's shops have limited hours, so pack a snack just in case.)

Miles & Directions

- 0.0 Turn right out of the public parking lot onto Lower Center St. As soon as you cross the first intersection (Halstead St. heading left over the bridge, Leigh St. heading right), the name changes to Center St.
- 0.8 Turn left at the light, following the signs for Rte. 31N over the overpass.
- 1.0 Turn left at the T intersection, following the signs for Rte. 31N. Now you're pedaling on an onramp.
- 1.1 Turn right onto Grayrock Rd., just before the onramp joins Rte. 31N. Grayrock Rd. immediately becomes a country lane through cornfields.
- 2.1 Turn right onto Jericho Rd. (not crossing the bridge over the Raritan River 0.2 mile ahead). *Watch for the bicycle-tire–eating grates on the curve.* Soon the river will parallel your path on your left.
- 2.9 Turn right at the T intersection onto Arch St. and ride through the right arch of the double-arched stone bridge, paralleling the river flowing through the left.
- 3.3 Turn right at the T intersection onto Washington Ave., which bends left and passes silent factory buildings.
- 3.9 Keep heading straight; as soon as you cross over a babbling creek, you're on River Rd. (Rte. 639).
- 5.0 Turn left at the T intersection onto the unmarked Cokesbury Rd., just past the dark green clapboard house on your left. *Immediately* bear right just before the bridge to stay on Rte. 639

Raritan River South Fork

Main St.

CALIFON

Raritan River South Fork

Raritan River Rd.

Hoffman Crossing Rd.

Ken Lockwood Gorge Park

Mt. Grove Rd.

Cokesbury Rd.

River Rd.

Raritan River South Fork

Washington Ave.

Arch St.

Jericho Rd.

Graysock Rd.

78

22

31

Center St.

CLINTON

31

START
(Parking lot in back of Clinton bakery)

(River Rd.). For the next 4 miles the south fork of the Raritan River will be rushing among the boulders on your left. At mile 5.5 the deteriorating pavement ends as you enter the Ken Lockwood Gorge, and you'll be riding on a flat, rutted gravel road. From time to time wild rabbits may hop alongside your tires. At mile 7.2 the road becomes paved again as you leave the park. At mile 7.5, keep heading straight through the stop sign at Hoffman Crossing Rd. At mile 9.2 River Rd. ends at a T intersection with Main St. in Califon.

- 9.5 To return, retrace your route back along River Rd. (Rte. 639).
- 10.9 Turn left at the stop sign onto Hoffman Crossing Rd. and begin climbing. Near the top stop and look back at the green valley and the distant wooded ridges—now, isn't this solitary beauty worth the effort?
- 11.8 Turn right at the T intersection onto Mt. Grove Rd.
- 12.8 Turn right at the T intersection onto unmarked Cokesbury Rd. After a short initial climb, enjoy the downhill coast.
- 13.8 Follow the main road (double yellow line) left just before the dark green clapboard house onto River Rd. Now you're re-tracing the route out.
- 15.0 After crossing over a small creek, continue straight onto Washington Ave. Follow the main road as it bears right past the factory.
- 15.4 Turn left at the gas station onto Arch St., again just before a bridge over the river. Ride back through the arches.
- 15.8 Make the first left onto Jerricho Rd. (here spelled with two r's) just before a bridge.
- 16.6 Turn left at the T intersection onto unmarked Grayrock Rd.
- 17.7 Turn left at the T intersection, following the signs to Rte. 31S and to Clinton and Flamingo, and make an *immediate right* onto the overpass over Rte. 31.
- 18.0 Turn right at the traffic light onto Center St. Head straight across Leigh (or Halstead) St. onto Lower Center St., and at mile 18.8 turn left into the public parking lot.

11

The Great Swamp and Jockey Hollow Cruise

*Convent Station—Green Village—Meyersville—
Jockey Hollow—Convent Station*

Tours in and around the 6,800-acre Great Swamp National Wildlife Refuge and the Jockey Hollow Encampment Area of the Morristown National Historic Park are ever-popular among nature-loving bicyclists. Even in winter you'll get a wave and a smile from one or two lone riders—and on summer weekends you're likely to be overtaken by a whole group from the Bicycle Touring Club of North Jersey or even from the commercial company Brooks Country Cycling and Hiking from New York City. This Morris County ride, which I devised and ride several times a year, is one of my personal favorites; for years a variant of the shorter version also delighted students in my course "Bicycle Touring: An Introduction" offered by the South Orange–Maplewood Adult School.

The Loantaka Brook Reservation–Great Swamp portion of this ride ranges from flat to gently rolling, with about 1.5 miles of gravel. But the 10-mile extension to Jockey Hollow and the excursion around the park (and any detour to Lewis Morris Park) are very hilly indeed. That is why the full 30-mile ride is designated a cruise. The shorter 20-mile option, bypassing Jockey Hollow, is a nice early-season ramble even for an out-of-shape novice.

When you are first pedaling through the forest and farm land, watching sheep graze in the meadows and turtles swimming in the swamp, you'll hardly believe that the grubby, noisy, crowded steel canyons of New York City are only 25 miles east of you. As in all wildlife areas, you'll see more animals in the spring and fall, especially at dawn or dusk. Pack a small pair of binoculars and tiptoe out on the wooden boardwalks to the bird blinds to watch great blue herons majestically standing in the marsh or swallows swooping for insects. Take along hiking boots and spend an hour or two midway through the ride to explore some of the marked but undeveloped trails. Listen, and in the late afternoon and early evening you will hear a chorus of peepers and frogs. Adjoining the Great Swamp to the east is the 425-acre Lord Stirling Park, home of the Somerset County Environmental Education Center (908–766–2489), offering another 8 miles of trails.

As for Jockey Hollow: You know the old joke about myriad out-of-the-way places trying to attract tourists by advertising "George Washington slept here"? Well, George Washington really did sleep here, along with 10,000 soldiers, who in 1779–80 nearly froze and starved in the sheltered hollows of Jockey Hollow during one of the snowiest winters of the Revolutionary War. There are many sites here preserved from those days, as well as historical restorations and mini-tours by guides in period costume, so take your time wandering through this park (which is open daily from 8:00 A.M. to 7:00 P.M.; for more information, call 201–543–4030). You'll also get a good aerobic workout on its rollercoaster hills.

Adjoining Jockey Hollow is the 1,154-acre Lewis Morris Park (201–326–7600); a county park at which you can pitch a tent for overnight camping. You might also want to pack a swimsuit for a dip in its Sunrise Lake; the sole disadvantage to refreshing yourself in the lake is that, after you're completely clean and relaxed, the only way back to Jockey Hollow is to grind up the very steep hill that you coasted down to the lake!

Because these are wildlife areas, services are few and far between. There are rest rooms and water for your water bottles at Loantaka Brook Reservation, at the parking lot for the wildlife observation area in the swamp, and at the visitor center at Jockey Hollow. There are only two delis near the swamp. On a Sunday you may want to play it safe and pack a lunch, as the Green Village Deli near the start of the ride is closed and Dom's General Store in Meyersville has limited hours. There are picnic tables and public barbecue grills at Loantaka Brook Reservation and at Lewis Morris Park, but eating within either Jockey Hollow or the Great Swamp is discouraged. Near the end of the ride, though, you can stuff your mouth with the blackberries growing alongside the road, ripe in late July.

The Basics

Start: Convent Station, in the Loantaka Brook Reservation at the parking area off Kitchell Rd. To get to the start, take local Rte. 24—also called Main St.—to Convent Station and, opposite the western edge of Fairleigh Dickinson University, turn south (the only way you can go) onto Kitchell Rd.; 1 mile later turn right to enter the reservation. Here there are rest rooms, water, picnic tables, wooden playground equipment, and a lovely duck pond.

Length: 20.3 or 30.3 miles. Traffic is generally light, with some roads—especially those to Jockey Hollow—a bit more heavily traveled.

Terrain: Flat to gently rolling in the portion touring the Great Swamp; very hilly in the 10-mile stretch to Jockey Hollow.

Food: Only two places to buy snacks or lunch: Green Village Deli 3.7 miles into the ride (closed Sundays) and Dom's General Store 0.9 mile off the route 9.5 miles into the ride.

Miles & Directions

- 0.0 Start at the northern entrance to the Loantaka Brook Reservation parking lot. Ride straight across the narrow Kitchell Rd. onto the paved bike path—a lovely meander next to the Loantaka Brook through forest glades. At mile 0.7 test your brakes after riding through the shallow brook at the water crossing—or carry your steed across on the concrete stepping stones.
- 1.0 Turn right onto the intersecting paved bike path, and follow it as it bends left. At mile 1.5 cross the moderately busy

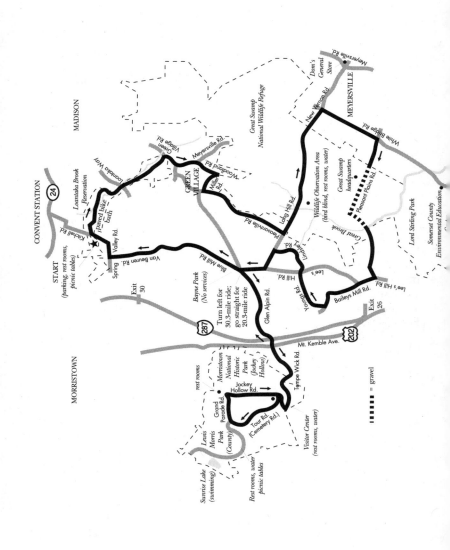

CONVENT STATION

(24)

MADISON

START
(parking, rest rooms,
picnic tables)

Kitchell Rd.

Loantaka Brook
Reservation

Paved bike
bath

Spring
Valley Rd.

Exit
30

Van Beuren Rd.

Blue Mill Rd.

Bayne Park
(No services)

Turn left for
30.3-mile ride;
go straight for
20.3-mile ride

Lombardy Way

Green
Village Rd.

GREEN
VILLAGE

Meyersville Rd.

Woodland Rd.

Miller
Rd.

Pleasantville Rd.

Lindsey
Rd.

Long Hill Rd.

Great Swamp
National Wildlife Refuge

Dom's
General
Store

Meyersville Rd.

MEYERSVILLE

New Vernon Rd.

White Bridge Rd.

Wildlife Observation
Area
(bird blind, rest rooms, water)

Great Swamp
headquarters

Pleasant Plains Rd.

Great Brook

Lord Stirling Park

Somerset County
Environmental Education

Lee's

Hill Rd.

Youngs Rd.

Glen Alpin Rd.

Lee's Hill Rd.

Baileys Mill Rd.

Exit
26

(287)

(202)

Mt. Kemble Ave.

MORRISTOWN

rest rooms

Morristown
National
Historic
Park
(Jockey
Hollow)

Jockey
Hollow Rd.

Grand
Parade Rd.

Tour Rd.
(Cemetery Rd.)

Lewis
Morris
Park
(County)

Tempe Wick Rd.

Visitor Center
(rest rooms, water)

Sunrise Lake
(swimming)

Rest rooms, water
picnic tables

= gravel

Loantaka Way and continue straight on the paved bike path.

- 2.9 Turn right at the end of the path onto Green Village Rd. Watch for cars.
- 3.7 Turn left onto Meyersville Rd. (Just before this turn on your right are a Sunoco gas station and the Green Village Deli, the first of the two chances on this ride to pick up snacks or lunch.) Now you're riding through pastoral farmland.
- 4.0 Take the first right (at the NO OUTLET sign) onto Woodland Rd. (Bird-watchers and hikers take note: If you continue straight here instead, in 1 mile the road will end in a small parking area, which is the trailhead for some of the nature trails into the northern unmanaged section of the Great Swamp.)
- 4.6 Take the first right (at the NO OUTLET sign) onto Miller Rd.
- 5.1 Turn left at the T intersection onto Pleasantville Rd.
- 6.8 Turn left at the T intersection onto Long Hill Rd. At mile 8.3 is the Wildlife Observation Area gravel parking lot on your right, where you can visit the boardwalks and bird blinds (and rest rooms) at the swamp. To resume the ride turn right out of the parking lot to continue on Long Hill Rd. (which eventually changes its name to New Vernon Rd.).
- 9.5 Turn right onto White Bridge Rd. (*Note*: For the second and last chance to buy snacks or lunch, continue straight through this intersection instead. In 0.9 mile, at the T intersection with Meyersville Rd., is Dom's General Store. This crossroads is the town of Meyersville, and the Mexican restaurant Casa Maya is well worth a dinner stop at the end of the day. Then retrace your route 0.9 mile to this intersection and turn left onto White Bridge Rd.)
- 10.7 Turn right onto Pleasant Plains Rd. to ride into the swamp itself. (*Note:* If you want to visit the Somerset County Environmental Education Center, continue straight ahead on White Bridge Rd. for another 1.3 miles and turn right just after the metal bridge. To continue the ride from there, retrace your route and turn left onto Pleasant Plains Rd. into the swamp.) At mile 11.0 on your right is the Great Swamp National Wildlife Refuge headquarters (908–647–1222), which is open Monday

through Friday from 8:00 A.M. to 4:30 P.M. and has public rest rooms. Just past the swamp headquarters, the road turns to gravel for the next mile, so ride carefully, following the road as it bends left. A third of a mile later, a gate blocks a bridge to cars. But the gate is designed in such a way as to admit pedestrians and bicycles—even those with a child seat on the back. After you cross this bridge over Great Brook, the road is paved once again.

- 13.6 Turn right at the T intersection onto Lee's Hill Rd. Watch for cars.
- 13.8 Bear left at the fork onto the quiet Baileys Mill Rd., and begin a gentle climb. Up to now the ride has been generally flat; now it becomes gently rolling.
- 14.8 Bear right onto Youngs Rd.
- 15.7 Turn right at the T intersection onto Lee's Hill Rd., and then make an immediate left onto Lindsley Rd.
- 16.4 Turn left at the T intersection onto Long Hill Rd.
- 16.8 Turn right at the T intersection onto Lee's Hill Rd.
- 17.2 Turn left at the light onto Glen Alpin Rd. toward Jockey Hollow.

For the shorter 20.3-mile ride, do not turn left; instead pedal straight through this light (at this intersection Lee's Hill Rd. changes its name to Blue Mill Rd.), and pick up the directions at mile 27.2.

This is where you'll start doing some serious climbing. At mile 18.9 you'll pass over I–287.

- 19.0 At the light at Rte. 202 (Mt. Kemble Ave.), keep heading straight and uphill onto Tempe Wick Rd.
- 20.4 Turn right at the entrance of Morristown National Historic Park. Keep pedaling uphill.
- 20.8 Just past the visitor center's parking lot, turn right to follow the one-way Tour Rd. (Cemetery Rd.) through the park. (The visitor center has literature, a short film about the park's history, and public rest rooms.) This road now becomes almost a rollercoaster, and you may find yourself screaming downhill faster than the posted speed limit of 25 mph.

- 22.1 Bear right at the parking lot for the soldiers' huts—which you can see up on the hill ahead of you—onto Grand Parade Rd. (If you wish to picnic or swim at the adjoining Lewis Morris County Park—a detour that will add a hilly 2 miles round-trip to your total—turn left instead and coast down to Sunrise Lake. Then return to this point to continue the main ride.)
- 22.6 Turn right at the yield sign to follow the one-way Jockey Hollow Rd. back to the visitor center. At this intersection is a cylindrical building with public rest rooms and a map of the entire park.
- 23.7 At the visitor center turn left at the stop sign onto the two-way road toward the park exit.
- 24.0 Turn left at the T intersection onto Tempe Wick Rd.
- 25.4 Cross Rte. 202 (Mt. Kemble Ave.) at the traffic light and continue straight onto Glen Alpin Rd.
- 27.2 Turn left at the traffic light onto Blue Mill Rd. At mile 27.3 on your left is Bayne Park, where you can relax on benches and watch geese and ducks in the pond and stream. This manicured park has no facilities or services, not even so much as a garbage can; if you open a snack here, take the remains with you when you leave.
- 28.2 Turn left onto Van Beuren Rd. where Blue Mill Rd. bends right.
- 29.8 Turn right at the T intersection onto Spring Valley Rd. Watch for cars, and ride single-file, as there is no shoulder. In July ripe blackberries dot the bushes on your right.
- 30.1 Turn left onto Kitchell Rd., braking carefully on the descent.
- 30.3 Turn left into the Loantaka Brook Reservation parking lot.

12

Stockton Mills Ramble

Mount Holly—Birmingham—Buddtown—
Vincentown—Mount Holly

For an easy ride with little traffic through the bucolic beauty of fields, farms, woods, and small towns of historical note, this exploration of Burlington County in southern New Jersey fills the bill. Devised and verified by Bert Nixdorf of Mount Holly, New Jersey, this lovely route is within the abilities of even the most casual cyclist.

After leaving Mount Holly, you'll pedal through Smithville, once the home of the H. B. Smith Works that made the Star bicycle, famous in the 1890s for its small wheel in the front and large wheel in the rear (just the opposite of the traditional pennyfarthing). Smithville is also where the bicycle railway—a treadle-type railroad—was built to carry commuting riders from Mount Holly to the factory at Smithville. On your ride take a moment to stroll through the Smithville Mansion, former home of H. B. Smith; in the summer the mansion's Victorian courtyard is abloom with the profuse, multicolored plantings of a century past.

As you ride through sleepy Birmingham, you'll find it hard to believe that this town was once the site of a large tourist hotel in the 1890s, catering to the wealthy of northern New Jersey who escaped to the "seclusion in the fresh, aromatic, and healthful air of the pinelands," according to a local history book. Today, however, there are no remnants left. Stockton Mill, the nominal destination of this ride, is the former location of one of the many sawmills in southern New Jersey a century or two ago.

About two-thirds of the way through the route, a perfect lunch stop is Mill Dam Park in Vincentown, where you can gaze out at a pretty dam and pond. According to Bert Nixdorf, there are several nice places on Vincentown's Main Street to buy food: The Village Cafe and a pizza parlor offer choices for a spring or summer picnic lunch. On fall or winter days, the hearty homemade soups at Main Street Deli are satisfying—and the restaurant is open on Sundays.

At the end of the ride, when you return to Mount Holly, there are a number of twists and turns; just follow the directions carefully and you'll do fine.

The Basics

Start: Mount Holly, at the corner of Rte. 541 (High St.) and Ridgley St., near the Trenton Savings & Loan and the vacant storefront that was formerly the Acme Super-Saver market in the Fairground Plaza shopping center. Park behind either Acme or Trenton Savings & Loan. To get to the start, take the New Jersey Turnpike to exit 5, and take Route 541 (Burlington–Mt. Holly Rd.) 2 miles south into Mount Holly. This road becomes High Street.
Length: 25 miles.
Terrain: Mostly flat.
Food: Convenience and grocery stores, some restaurants.

Miles & Directions

Note: Follow directions carefully, as not every small street is shown on the map.

- 0.0 From the front of the vacant Acme Super-Saver market, head south on Rte. 541 (High St.).
- 0.8 Turn right onto Rancocas Rd., at the Mount Holly Pharmacy and office buildings. Make an immediate left at the Bank of Mid-Jersey to ride through the bank's parking lot and over the bridge. Make a quick left at the log cabin onto Park Dr.
- 1.0 Turn left at the T intersection onto Washington St.

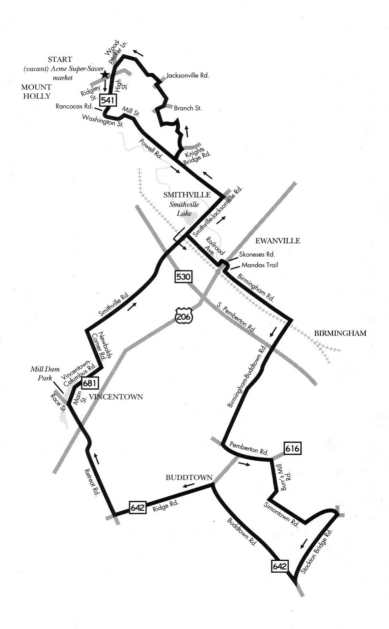

(Collective Federal Savings & Loan is on your right). In a couple of blocks, Washington St. becomes Mill St. and later Powell Rd. at Northumberland Dr. (on your left). If you still want a snack, you have your choice of the Wawa Market or the 7-Eleven along the way.

- 3.2 Turn right onto Smithville-Jacksonville Rd. Shortly you will pass the Smithville Mansion on your right. If the mansion is not hosting a wedding reception or other function, take a moment to stroll through the blooming courtyard, refill your water bottles at the water fountain, or use the public rest rooms off the side entrance.
- 4.0 Turn left onto E. Railroad Ave., just before the railroad bed (tracks have been removed). Now you're riding alongside the railroad bed, which is to your right. Follow the road as it bends sharply left at the end.
- 4.8 Turn right onto Rte. 206, and then make a quick left to cross the busy highway onto Skoneses Rd. You're now in the tiny burg of Ewanville. In 1 block turn right at the T intersection onto Mandas Trail. In another block turn left at the T intersection onto Birmingham Rd. at the sign INDIAN TRAIL. At mile 5.4 cross the railroad bed by bearing right.
- 6.2 At the post office in Birmingham, turn right onto Birmingham-Buddtown Rd. In 0.5 mile watch for traffic while crossing busy Rte. 530 (S. Pemberton Rd.), and continue straight.
- 8.3 Turn left at the T intersection onto Rte. 616 (Pemberton Rd.).
- 9.1 Turn right onto Burr's Mill Rd.
- 9.7 Just after the road bends right, turn left onto Simontown Rd. at the sod farm. This road will bend sharply left, then gradually right.
- 10.9 Turn right onto Stockton Bridge Rd.
- 12.1 Turn right at the T intersection onto unmarked Rte. 642 (Buddtown Rd.).
- 14.0 Turn left at the T intersection in Buddtown to stay on Rte. 642 (the unmarked name changes to Ridge Rd.).
- 15.5 Turn right to stay on Rte. 642 (the name changes to Re-

treat Rd.). At mile 17.0 cross Rte. 206 and continue straight into Vincentown.

- 17.5 In Vincentown turn left at the library onto unmarked Race St. to the town's Mill Dam Park for a snack or lunch al fresco at the Village Cafe. Leave Vincentown by heading north on Main St., passing Stokes Cannery. After you leave town, the road becomes Rte. 681 and changes its name to the unmarked Vincentown-Columbus Rd.
- 18.1 Turn left onto Newbolds Corner Rd.
- 18.9 Turn right onto Smithville Rd. At mile 20.4 use caution in crossing busy Rte. 530. At mile 21.2 you'll pass the Smithville Mansion again, where once more you can refresh yourself and enjoy the flowers. After crossing the railroad bed, Smithville Rd. becomes Smithville-Jacksonville Rd., and you'll be retracing a brief section of the outbound route.
- 21.5 Turn left onto Powell Rd.
- 22.4 Turn right onto Knights Bridge Rd. into the Vista's residential development. Now come some quick turns. Take the third left onto Nottingham Way. At the T intersection turn right onto Stonegate Dr., which horseshoes around. Turn right onto Brook Run Rd. At the T intersection turn left onto Dawn Dr. Turn right onto Parkview Dr.
- 23.8 At the T intersection, turn right at the stop sign onto Branch St. At the wide intersection bear left to cross Branch St., keeping the Ashurst Mansion on your left. Now for some more quick turns over the next mile: Take the first left onto Ashurst Ln., the first left onto Thornton Rd., and an immediate right onto Stevens Dr. When you reach Jacksonville Rd. at mile 24.1, jog right to cross it and continue straight on Walton Rd. At the T intersection turn left onto Front St. A block later turn right onto Randolph Dr. In 2 blocks bear left onto Tinker Dr.
- 24.9 Turn left at the T intersection onto Woodpecker Ln. Then turn right into the parking lot of the former Acme Super-Saver market or Trenton Savings & Loan at the start.

13

Heart of the Pines Cruise

Atsion—Chatsworth—Green Bank—Batsto—Atsion

The Pine Barrens in the southern part of New Jersey (Burlington County) is a wilderness area covering nearly a quarter of the state. Federal and state regulations protect most of it from development or abuse, thus making it a popular destination of cyclists. Its virtually flat expanse, the backwoods remoteness, sandy soil, and stark scrubby pines and oaks are reminiscent of swamps in the Deep South.

On this ride through Burlington County (and parts of Atlantic and Camden counties), you will see areas of specialized agriculture (blueberry fields and cranberry bogs), pass cedar-lined streams, and cross over three major rivers (the Batsto, the Mullica, and the Wading). Canoeing is popular in this area, and midway through the route at Chatsworth, you can take a break and rent all the equipment you'll need for paddling.

You'll also ride through some settlements that feel like ghost towns. When you reach Batsto, a former nineteenth-century bog-iron community, take half an hour to walk around the restored gristmill, general store, threshing barn, post office, and the Richards' Mansion, once the home of bog-iron baron Jesse Richards. In the summer and fall Batsto sponsors special events; for more information call the ranger's office at (609) 561–0024.

This ride is thoroughly delightful in any season, according to Bert Nixdorf of Mount Holly, New Jersey, who devised it for the Youth Environmental Society (YES) at Rutgers University and verified it for this edition. Bert's own favorite season is the autumn, especially the third week of October when the flaming reds and golds of the leaves are at their peak. (Note, however, that the third weekend in October is the annual Chatsworth Cranberry Festival, and traffic and crowds are very heavy on that Saturday and Sunday.) If your taste runs more to blooming mountain laurel—an ancient relative of the rose—choose to ride the second week in June. Because the ride has precious little shade, it can be blazing hot at the height of summer; on the other hand, the euphoria of sluicing off the sweat and grime by jumping into the refreshing swimming pool at Atsion Lake Camp may make it worth the hot dusty miles. On Tuesday the pool is open free of charge; all other days there is a fee.

For cyclists wishing to sleep out under the stars, there are two campgrounds along the route. One is Atsion Lake Camp on Atsion Rd. (also known as Lake Shore Rd.) at the start; apply for a permit at the Atsion ranger's office (609–269–0444). The other is Godfrey Bridge Camp midway through the ride on Washington Rd. at Jenkins. For that campground you must apply for a permit at the Batsto ranger's office (609–561–0024); if you're interested in that one, you might want to start the ride from the public parking area in Batsto instead of from Atsion.

Because there are so few paved roads in this region, automobiles can be of concern. Traffic can be heavy, especially on weekends. The best time to ride is during the week. Take special care watching for cars along busy Route 206; Bert notes, however, that the shoulders have been widened and repaved, and many cyclists use this road. (By the way, Route 206 is notable in that it can take you all the way from High Point to Hammonton without going over any major hills, and sections of it are popular with cyclists all along New Jersey's length.)

The Basics

Start: Atsion ranger's station near Atsion Lake Camp in Wharton State Forest, on Rte. 206, 10.3 miles south of the junction with Rte. 70. Park in the field immediately to the north of the ranger's office.
Length: 51 miles.
Terrain: Mostly flat. Traffic can be heavy on Rte. 206 but is light to moderate elsewhere.

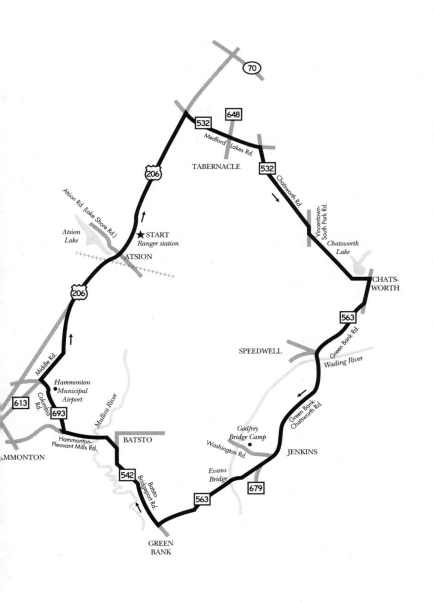

Food: Farm stands, grocery stores, and occasional small restaurants are at the major settlements; there can be 10 or more miles between water stops, so take the opportunity when it comes.

Miles & Directions

- 0.0 Turn right out of the parking lot at the Atsion ranger station to head north on Rte. 206; at mile 7.2 you'll see the sign TO TABERNACLE.
- 8.4 Turn right at Meridian Bank (traffic light) onto Rte. 532 (Medford Lakes–Tabernacle Rd.). At mile 8.4 there is an open-air farm market on the right where you can buy fresh fruit. Nixon's general store and deli at mile 8.5 is excellent. Eventually, Rte. 532 changes its name to Chatsworth Rd. (unmarked).
- 18.1 Turn right at the firehouse onto Rte. 563. You're now in the heart of Chatsworth. In 0.2 mile, at the cemetery, bear right to stay on unmarked Rte. 563. At mile 22.0 you'll cross over the Wading River at Speedwell, the northern terminus of a popular canoeing route. You'll cross the Wading River again at mile 28.5.
- 27.7 Just beyond Mick's Canoe Rentals, bear right at the major Y intersection to stay on Rte. 563 (Green Bank Rd.).
- 32.9 In the town of Green Bank, turn right (west) at the stop sign onto Rte. 542 (Batsto-Bridgeport Rd.) at Green Bank Inn. Now you're paralleling the Mullica River on your left.
- 37.0 Turn right into the public parking area of Batsto Historic Village, which has a picnic area, water, refreshment stands open in the summer, and public rest rooms. Ask at the park office about the self-guided and -conducted tours; there you can also buy topographic maps of the area. When you leave the park entrance, turn right to continue west on Rte. 542, which changes name at mile 38.8 to Hammonton–Pleasant Mills Rd. when you leave Burlington County and enter Atlantic County. At mile 41.4 Farmer John's Food Market in the village of Nesco is excellent.
- 42.4 Turn right onto Rte. 693 (Columbia Rd.).

- 45.1 Just after passing the Hammonton Municipal Airport on your right, bear right at the Y intersection onto unmarked Rte. 613 (Middle Rd.).
- 46.5 Turn right at the end of Rte. 613 (Middle Rd.) onto Rte. 206N. *Watch for cars!*
- 50.8 Turn right into the parking lot at the Atsion ranger station.

New York

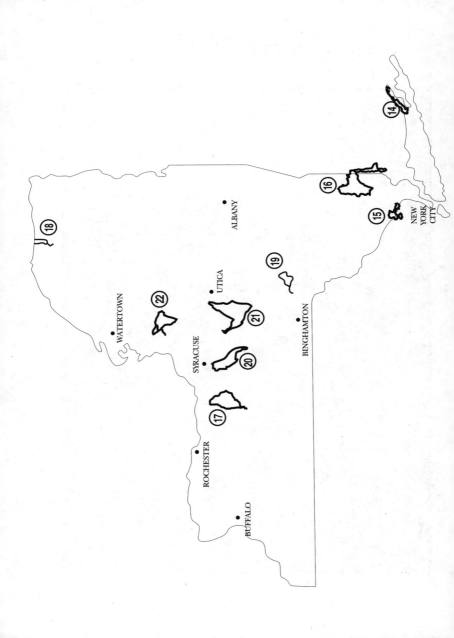

New York

14

Strawberries and Wine Cruise

Mattituck—Greenport—Orient Point—Mattituck

This flat ride, which is one of my personal favorites, is based in part on the traditional annual "Strawberry Ride" of New York City's American Youth Hostels and was verified by Larry Sturm of Shoreham. It starts at the town of Mattituck on the north fork of Long Island, which each June holds a strawberry festival in the fields of Mattituck High School. (For the date of the festival each year and also a possible change in venue, call the Greenport-Southold Chamber of Commerce at 516–477–1383.)

If after all that strawberry shortcake you can manage to swing your leg over your bicycle saddle, the route will take you through some of Suffolk County's best wine country. You'll pedal right past half a dozen vineyards, many of which offer public tours and wine tasting—Peconic Bay Vineyards, Pugliese Vineyards, Bedell Cellars, Pindar Winery, and Lenz Winery—and you can visit more by looking for signs with the symbol of grapes directing you down local side roads. Just use good judgment in sampling the wares: It's even more dangerous to bicycle than to drive under the influence of alcohol, as you are not surrounded by a ton of protective steel.

The midpoint of the ride—perfect for lunch—is a favorite destination for cyclists: Orient Beach State Park, with its refreshment stand, seafood cafe, bathhouse, and pebbly beach overlooking the sparkling Atlantic. This is also the trailhead for a 2-mile hike out to the bird sanctuary at the very tip of Long Beach Point. The park is friendly to cyclists, complete with bike lane on the highway (although it compels you to ride at least part of both directions facing traffic), and is open every day of the year excepting Tuesdays.

Elsewhere on the ride you'll pass some churches and houses dating back to the American Revolution, plus an old lighthouse commissioned by George Washington and now turned into a marine museum. Amateur astronomers might try to time their visit for one of the Saturday observing nights at the Custer Institute Observatory in Southold (516–765–2626), the only astronomical observatory on Long Island to allow the public to look through its telescopes.

Those wishing to make a long weekend of the visit can stay in one of the lovely bed-and-breakfast inns on Shelter Island (for a listing call the Shelter Island Chamber of Commerce at 516–749–0399), a detour that's just a five-minute ferry ride from Greenport. Shelter Island's rolling hills and beaches and lightly traveled roads offer superb cycling—a nice change of pace from the flat terrain of the basic tour on Long Island's north fork.

Although you'll be pedaling on some main roads on this ride (because some places on the north fork are so narrow that there is only one road), Long Island is civilized in offering wide paved shoulders. Just be careful: In some places the shoulder is an inch below the pavement of the main road, and brushing that lip with your tire could cause a spill.

A word about Long Island weather: The eastern tip of Long Island is the last place in the New York City tri-state area for the seasons to linger. Thus, the chill of winter lasts into mid-April, but summer's warmth lingers past the end of September. After Labor Day is perhaps the best time for cycling: You miss the frenetic summer crowds but can swim in the ocean still bathwater-warm from the summer's heating of the Gulf Stream.

The Basics

Start: Mattituck, in the parking lot of the station of the Long Island Rail Road. Take the Long Island Expressway to its very end (exit 73) and then take Rte. 25 farther east to Mattituck. In town turn left at the traffic light onto Love Ln. and then left into the parking lot of the train station.

Length: 51 miles.

Terrain: Virtually flat, although you are likely to run into substantial headwinds while traveling in one direction (usually eastward). Traffic ranges from light on the side roads to moderate on the main roads.

Food: Widely available in the various towns and at the concession and restaurants at Orient Beach State Park. But best of all are farm stands: Take advantage of the fresh local produce!

Miles & Directions

- 0.0 Turn left out of the parking lot of the Mattituck station of the Long Island Rail Road, making an immediate right onto Love Ln.
- 0.1 If you're going to the strawberry festival, turn left at the T intersection onto Rte. 25E (Main Rd.) until you reach the Mattituck High School; otherwise turn right onto Rte. 25W.
- 0.2 Turn left at the Handy Pantry convenience store onto New Suffolk Ave.
- 3.2 Turn left at the four-way flashing stop light onto 5th St., which becomes New Suffolk Rd. At this intersection, Olsson's Deli is very bicycle-friendly; it has decent food and rest rooms.
- 5.0 Turn right at the light onto Rte. 25E (Main Rd.). You'll now stay on Rte. 25E through all its incarnations for the next 15 miles. In the next 3 miles, you'll pass half a dozen wineries. At mile 9.3 you can turn right onto Corwin Ln. and make an immediate right onto Bayview Rd. to visit the Custer Institute Observatory. At mile 13.3 you'll enter the village of Greenport, where the traffic gets heavier. If you want to visit Shelter Island, at mile 14.1 turn right onto 5th St. and left at the next block (Wiggins St.) to reach the ferry dock. Otherwise continue to follow Rte. 25E (now called Front St.) straight into Greenport. Watch for car traffic!

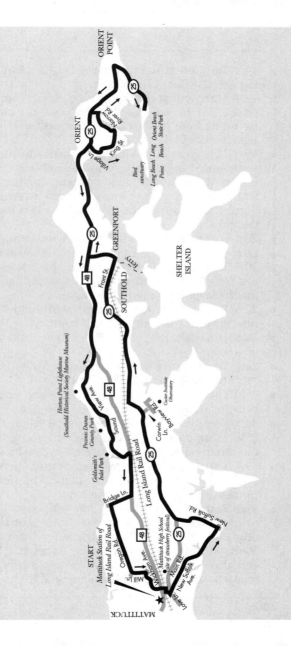

- 14.4 Turn left at the flashing red signal (T intersection) to follow Rte. 25E out of Greenport.
- 15.4 Turn right at the flashing red signal (T intersection) to stay on Rte. 25E toward Orient Point. There is a nice wide shoulder, for riding from here to Orient Point; this is the beginning of a signed official bike route.
- 19.6 Turn right onto Village Ln., marked with a grassy triangle surmounted by a small obelisk resembling a miniature Washington Monument. You are now entering the village of Orient, with its sparkling bay views and many wonderful centuries-old homes. Stop to read the historical markers to steep yourself in the mood.
- 20.1 Follow the road as it bends left and becomes King St.
- 20.4 Bear right at the Y intersection to stay on King St.
- 20.7 Turn left at the end (yield sign) onto Narrow River Rd. This is a truly lovely stretch past the swaying tall grasses of a salt marsh. Savor it through all its curves.
- 22.5 Turn right at the end (stop sign) onto Rte. 25E, which is now the only road out to Orient Point.
- 24.5 Turn right into Orient Beach State Park, taking the labeled bike route.
- 26.7 You've arrived! When you're ready to leave, retrace your route back out the park access road.
- 29.0 Turn left at the T intersection onto Rte. 25W, and keep pedaling straight west for the next 11 miles.
- 36.5 Keep heading straight where the yellow flasher marks Rte. 25W's turn back into Greenport; now you're on Rte. 48W. Use caution in riding on the shoulder, which is broken-up blacktop.
- 39.9 Turn right onto unsigned Sound View Ave., which is bumpy but beautiful, with little traffic. This turn is the first right turn after the Soundview Restaurant.
- 41.1 Bear left at the fork to stay on Sound View Ave. (If you want a little historical detour, bear right instead; the road dead-ends at Horton Point Lighthouse, now the home of the Southold Historical Society Marine Museum. It is open on weekend afternoons in July and August.) Go straight through two four-way stops. At mile 44.1 follow Sound View Ave. as it makes

an abrupt left (Goldsmith's Inlet Park will be on your right) and becomes Mill Rd.

- 44.4 Turn right to rejoin Rte. 48W (here called Middle Rd.).
- 45.8 Turn right onto Bridge Ln.
- 46.5 Turn left at the end onto Oregon Rd., where you'll be cycling past farms and vineyards for the next 3 miles.
- 49.4 Turn left onto unsigned Mill Ln., an old concrete road (not many concrete roads are in this area).
- 50.0 Turn right onto Wickham Ave., following it as it curves left through suburbs.
- 50.7 Turn left at the T intersection to stay on Wickham Ave.
- 51.1 After crossing Rte. 48 at the light, turn right onto Pike St. and follow it to Love Ln. and the Mattituck station of the Long Island Rail Road.

15

New Croton Reservoir Ramble

Teatown Lake Reservation—Lincolndale
Yorktown Heights—Croton Dam
Teatown Lake Reservation

The New Croton Reservoir, which is part of New York City's water supply, is a favorite of New York City cyclists because this wooded section of lower Westchester County is only 25 miles north of the city. Despite its proximity to what Frank Sinatra immortalized in song as "the city that never sleeps," Westchester County is characterized by wonderfully secluded backroads—in part because the county's affluent citizens would rather have their restful homes passed by dirt tracks than paved thoroughfares. The result is a cyclist's dream.

One of the route's highlights is a ride across the top of the Croton Dam overlooking the Croton Gorge Park below. Because for the most part the route hugs the shore of the reservoir, much of it is level to gently rolling, with lovely views of the sparkling water. The sections away from the water give you a chance to get a cardiovascular workout on somewhat steeper roads.

In fact, the inland terrain is so reminiscent of West Virginia or Vermont that Westchester County boasts one of the East Coast's two mountain-bike schools: Croton Mountain Biking Center (10 Sunset Trail, Croton-on-Hudson, NY 10520, 914–271–2640), run by Mike Zuckerman. This route leads you on a few of these peaceful roads, ruts and all, so you may find a fatter-tire bike more comfortable than a thin-tire racing bike. *Note:* In this area, street signs seem to be battered, twisted, or missing altogether. Follow descriptions carefully. This area also abounds in dry stone walls; enjoy examining them.

Should you wish to make a weekend of your visit, you may well enjoy the luxury of a night at the rambling Alexander Hamilton House bed-and-breakfast inn, just a couple of miles from this route at 49 Van Wyck Street in Croton-on-Hudson (914–271–6737). The owner is Barbara Notarius, author of a book on running a bed and breakfast. It was Barbara who suggested the basic route around the New Croton Reservoir and the more challenging but beautiful optional loop.

Teatown Lake Reservation is a wildlife preserve and environmental education center, with hiking trails as well as a small museum and gift shop. "This would be a good ride for those who feel guilty about leaving the [nonriding] family behind," notes the ride's verifier, Jim Yannaccone of Watsontown, Pennsylvania. "Anyone with an interest in the outdoors could find enough to do at the reservation to keep busy while waiting for the rider(s)," for the ride can easily be completed in two or three hours.

The Basics

Start: Teatown Lake Reservation parking lot. To get there from the Taconic State Pkwy., exit at ROUTE 134 OSSINING; drive on Rte. 134W to the second right (which comes fast); turn right onto narrow Spring Valley Rd.; drive more than a mile to Teatown, choosing left at every fork along the way. Turn right into the reservation parking lot.

Length: 20 or 24 miles.

Terrain: Gently rolling to moderately hilly. Traffic ranges from almost nonexistent on the true backroads to moderate on Rte. 129 around the north side of the New Croton Reservoir.

Food: Bring a full picnic lunch, as there are few services on any of these routes. Teatown Lake Reservation has a soda machine and a couple of hotdog trucks have their regular sites at dusty intersections as noted.

Miles & Directions

- **0.0** Turn left out of Teatown Lake Reservation Environmental Education Center onto Spring Valley Rd.
- **0.1** Turn left onto narrow Blinn Rd., which becomes Applebee Farm Rd.
- **1.6** Turn right at the T intersection onto Quaker Ridge Rd. At mile 1.8 bear slightly right onto Yorktown Rd. where Croton Dam Rd. heads left. Shortly, the road will bend to the right and then to the left as it goes downhill. In about half a mile, the bumpy, broken pavement ends and the road becomes hard-packed dirt; go slowly, for there are many ruts. At miles 3.8 and 4.1, you'll pass under the southbound and northbound lanes of the Taconic State Pkwy.
- **4.3** Bear right at the Y intersection onto unmarked Arcady Rd., which at mile 5.0 begins climbing. As you are climbing, and have the time to look about you, check out the ancient stone walls. Near the end, the road becomes Aqueduct St.
- **5.8** At the T intersection, just across from the entrance to IBM's famous Thomas J. Watson Research Center, turn left onto the moderately busy Rte. 134.
- **7.5** After crossing a paved bicycle path, turn left at the T intersection onto the moderately busy Rte. 100. At this intersection on your left, sometimes there is a hot dog truck. Ride with caution, for the next 1.3 miles has no shoulder. Have faith; it gets better. At mile 8.8 head straight at the first light to stay on the lane-wide painted shoulder of Rte. 100 over the bridge across the New Croton Reservoir.
- **9.3** Turn left at the traffic light onto Rte. 118; at this intersection there may be another truck selling snacks.
- **11.1** At the flashing yellow light, keep heading straight onto Rte. 129 where Rte. 118 goes right.
- **13.3** Turn right onto Underhill Rd. (which is marked with a very large green sign) and begin climbing; you have now begun the rather challenging optional loop of rutted road and quiet beauty circling an inlet of the New Croton Reservoir.

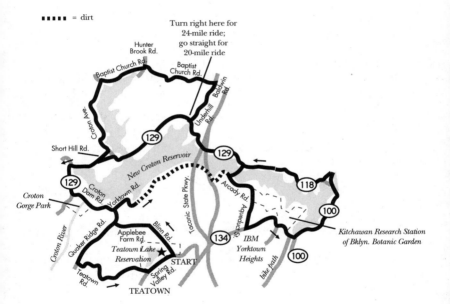

= dirt

Turn right here for
24-mile ride;
go straight for
20-mile ride

Hunter
Brook Rd.

Baptist Church Rd.

Baptist
Church Rd.

Baldwin Rd.

Croton Ave.

Underhill Rd.

Short Hill Rd.

129

129

New Croton Reservoir

118

129

Croton
Gorge Park

Croton
Dam Rd.

Yorktown Rd.

Arcady Rd.

100

Croton River

Quaker Ridge Rd.

Blinn Rd.

Taconic State Pkwy.

Aqueduct St.

134

100

Applebee
Farm Rd.

Teatown Lake
Reservation

★
START

IBM
Yorktown
Heights

Kitchawan Research Station
of Bklyn. Botanic Garden

Teatown Rd.

Spring
Valley Rd.

bike path

TEATOWN

For the 20-mile ride, do not turn right, but instead continue straight on Rte. 129 and resume following the directions at mile 18.1.

- 13.7 Turn left onto Baldwin Rd. Watch carefully for this inter-section, as it is easy to miss. Continue climbing, noting the nice stone walls on both sides.
- 14.0 Turn left onto Baptist Church Rd. Now you're plunged into a very bumpy but gorgeous, forested rollercoaster ride. Be prepared also for a sharp downhill turn to the right halfway along.
- 15.7 At the stop sign make a quick jog left onto Hunter Brook Rd. (unmarked) and then immediately right to continue on unmarked Baptist Church Rd.
- 16.4 At the yield sign turn left onto Croton Ave., noting the is-land in the inlet on your left. This narrow section of road is level and smooth, with very few cars.
- 18.0 Turn right at the T intersection onto Short Hill Rd. Be care-ful at this turn, as traffic from the left has a yield sign, not a stop sign. True to the road's name, you'll climb up a short, steep hill.
- 18.1 Bear right at the stop sign onto Rte. 129, *rejoining the 20-mile route.*
- 19.2 Turn left onto Croton Dam Rd. (shortly after the big intersection with Batten Rd.). Watch carefully for this almost hidden intersection after Rte. 129 starts descending. In a few moments you've climbed up to pedal across the top of the New Croton Dam. Very dramatic.
- 20.1 Turn right at the T intersection onto unmarked Quaker Ridge Rd. (You'll recognize the intersection from the beginning of the ride, as Yorktown Rd. goes to the left.)
- 21.3 Turn left onto the beautiful Teatown Rd., taking note again of the stone walls. The last section of this one-lane, wind-ing road descends in tight switchbacks, almost like San Fran-cisco's famous Lombard St., to end abruptly at a stop sign.
- 23.1 Turn left at the T intersection onto unmarked Spring Valley Rd. Soon you'll pass Teatown Lake on your left.
- 23.7 Turn left into Teatown Lake Reservation parking lot.

16

A Taste of New England Challenge

Bedford—Ridgefield—North Wilton—
Pound Ridge—Bedford

This ride, a somewhat abbreviated version of the 60-mile Bedford Silver Spring Sally of the Long Island Bicycle Club, Inc., is a tour of places reminiscent of New England. In fact, some of it is technically in New England, as part of the route dances back and forth across the New York border into Fairfield County, Connecticut. But most of it takes you through some of the hills in the eastern part of New York's Westchester County.

The shorter version of the ride is a brisk cruise for cyclists in moderately good condition; the rollercoaster terrain is challenging enough that the longer version should appeal to strong cyclists. The starting point in Bedford is close enough to New York City that the route can make a good one-day ride for city-dwellers who own or rent cars; but the forest is so quiet that you will be tempted to linger overnight as a momentary respite from city life.

If you want to make a weekend of it, that's easily done. You may luxuriate at a number of noted bed-and-breakfast inns in Ridgefield, Connecticut. Among them are the West Lane Inn (203–438–7323) and The Elms Inn (203–438–2541), Ridgefield's oldest continuously functioning inn, taking in guests since 1799.

For those preferring the wide open spaces, try camping at one of Westchester County's beautiful parks. At the 4,700-acre Ward Pound Ridge Reservation 6 miles north of Bedford, you can rent an open-faced lean-to cabin large enough to shelter eight sleeping bags

(914–763–3493). Farther north try one of the rustic cabins or tent sites at the 1,000-acre Mountain Lakes Campground, where some of the campsites also have showers (914–593–2618 or 669–5793).

This route, verified by Gil Gilmore of Norwalk, Connecticut, is perfect for a crisp autumn ride to gaze at the golden and fiery leaves. But please note that on nice weekends the traffic on some stretches can be moderate to moderately heavy. Also, this section of the world seems to have very sandy soil, and a fair amount of sand finds its way onto the road shoulders. Please, ride with caution.

The Basics

Start: Bedford, New York, at the village green (intersection of Rtes. 172 and 22). To get to the start, take exit 4 off I–684 onto Rte. 172E, and follow Rte. 172E into Bedford's village green.
Length: 34 or 52 miles.
Terrain: Moderately hilly to hilly. Traffic ranges from light to moderately heavy. *Please watch for sand.*
Food: Available in Bedford, New York, and Ridgefield, Connecticut, and at widely spaced convenience stores as noted; if in doubt, stock up.

Miles & Directions

- 0.0 Head north on busy Rte. 22 (you'll have done it right if, after leaving the village green, you immediately pass the Bedford Playhouse on your right).
- 0.3 Bear right at the triangle onto Rte. 121N.
- 2.0 Turn right onto Rte. 137.
- 3.0 Take the first left onto the secluded Honey Hollow Rd., following it as it eventually makes a sharp left.
- 6.0 Turn right at the T intersection onto Rte. 121N. In 0.75 mile you'll pass the entrance to Ward Pound Ridge Reservation. If you ride into the park, there are public rest rooms with water in the building on your right, just before the guard's kiosk.
- 6.9 Turn right at the T intersection where Rte. 121N joins Rte. 35E. Here are a deli and market.

- 7.5 Turn left at the light to stay on Rte. 121N; at this intersection are a gas station and deli—the last opportunity for food or snacks until Ridgefield in another 14 miles.
- 12.0 Turn right onto Hawley Rd. at the blue sign for Mountain Lakes Camp. This road climbs continually for the next mile.
- 13.2 Follow the road as it bends sharply left and becomes unmarked Oscaleta Rd. Take care, for the road descends quite steeply, and there may be cars behind blind corners. In 0.3 mile on the left pass the entrance to Mountain Lakes Camp.
- 14.5 Bear left at the Y intersection to stay on Oscaleta Rd. (Benedict Rd. heads right).
- 15.0 Turn left onto Old Oscaleta Rd., just before the stop sign at Main St. Use caution on this turn and don't overshoot. Old Oscaleta Rd. is a lovely rollercoaster ride that takes you across the border into Connecticut.
- 15.8 Turn left at the T intersection onto unmarked New Oscaleta Rd.
- 16.1 Make the first right onto Oscaleta Rd., which plunges down (if you erroneously stay on New Oscaleta Rd., you'll continue to climb).
- 17.6 Turn right at the T intersection onto unmarked Rte. 102 (Barry Ave.), which leads you into the town of Ridgefield.
- 20.6 Turn right at the T intersection to stay on Rte. 102 (here called High Ridge Ave.).
- 20.7 Turn left at the stop sign to stay on Rte. 102 (here called Catoonah St.).
- 21.0 Turn right at the light to stay on Rte. 102 (here called Main St.), which joins Rte. 35. There are many places to stop to eat along this stretch. Watch carefully for auto traffic.
- 21.4 Keep heading straight on Rte. 35 where Rte. 102 turns left.
- 21.6 Keep heading straight at the fountain onto Rte. 33, where Rte. 35 (here called West Ln.) bears right.

For the 34-mile cruise turn right at this fountain instead to stay on Rte. 35 (West Ln.), passing West Lane Inn on your right. In 0.6 mile, where Silver Spring Rd. comes in from the left, pick up the directions at mile 39.8 below.

The next 5 miles along Rte. 33 is a net downhill, although it is broken up by several rises. The road changes its name from W. Wilton Rd. to Ridgefield Rd. at the border of Wilton Township, but remains Rte. 33. The road is narrow but has a good surface; however, watch for sand. At about 5 miles, near the top of one rise, prepare to stop.

- 26.9 At the stop sign turn right onto Drum Hill Rd. Make an immediate right onto quiet Cheese Spring Rd., which becomes Mariomi Rd. at the border of New Canaan Township.
- 30.1 Turn right at the T intersection onto Valley Rd.
- 31.4 Shortly after crossing a small concrete bridge, turn right onto Benedict Hill Rd.
- 31.6 Turn left onto S. Bald Hill Rd.
- 32.4 Jog right at the T intersection onto the unmarked N. Wilton Rd., and make an immediate left onto the one-lane N. Bald Hill Rd.
- 32.6 Bear left at the Y intersection to continue on N. Bald Hill Rd. This is a beautiful stretch. As you reenter New York State, the road becomes graded dirt, which has many sharp stones that could work mischief on narrow tires. Ride slowly.
- 33.7 Turn left at the T intersection onto unmarked Silver Spring Rd. Although it starts out as graded dirt, it becomes paved again as you reenter Connecticut.
- 36.0 Bear left at the Y intersection to stay on Silver Spring Rd., and ride to the end.
- 39.8 Turn left at the T intersection onto unmarked but busy Rte. 35 (West Ln.). *This is where the 34-mile ride rejoins the 52-mile route.* If you were to turn right instead, you would pass two antiques stores, a pizza/deli, and the West Lane bed-and-breakfast inn. At mile 41.6, after Rte. 35 changes names several times, you'll reenter New York for the final time. At mile 41.8 keep riding straight through the light to stay on Rte. 35.
- 42.1 Turn left onto Ridgefield Ave. (Watch carefully, for it's easy to miss!) Eventually it changes its name to Highview Rd.
- 43.9 Turn left at the T intersection onto Rte. 124 (Salem–High Ridge Rd.).
- 46.7 Turn right onto Rte. 137N in Pound Ridge.

- 49.5 Turn left at the T intersection onto Rte. 121.
- 51.2 Turn left at the T intersection onto Rte. 22S.
- 51.5 You're back at Bedford's village green.

17

Great Finger Lakes Wineries Challenge

Watkins Glen—Ovid—Interlaken—
Reynoldsville—Burdett—Watkins Glen

The Great Finger Lakes are so popular for cycling that at least one publisher has devoted an entire guidebook to them for cyclists (*20 Bicycle Tours in the Finger Lakes,* by Mark Roth and Sally Walters, Backcountry Publications, third edition, 1990).

The Finger Lakes are eleven long and thin bodies of water gouged out by glaciers umpteen thousand years ago during the Ice Age in what is now western New York State. Seneca Lake, whose shore is hugged by the initial part of this ride, is the second largest of the lakes: 40 miles long, 4 miles wide, and so deep that its bottom is 200 feet below sea level. The southern end of Seneca Lake, where this ride guides you, is tucked between forested high hills relieved by valleys that cradle dairy farms, vineyards, and orchards.

This ride begins and ends at Watkins Glen State Park (607–535–4511), which has a splendid gorge featuring rock caverns and nineteen cascading waterfalls—and an Olympic-size swimming pool for sluicing off the road grime. You can make the park your base of operations for both rides by setting up camp at one of its cabins or tent/trailer sites (Watkins Glen KOA 607–535–7404) just 0.5 mile west of the park's lower entrance on Route 329. Alternatively, if your idea of roughing it is making do with black-and-white television, you might prefer to stay in one of Watkins Glen's bed-and-breakfast inns. For a brochure listing the many lovely inns in the area, contact the Finger Lakes Association (309 Lake Street, Penn Yan, NY 14527; 315–536–7488 or 800–KIT–4–FUN; World Wide Web: http://embark.com/FingerLakes).

The cycling through Schuyler, Seneca, and Tompkins counties is moderately rolling to undeniably hilly, although the traffic outside of the town of Watkins Glen is generally light. As upstate New York is the largest wine-producing area in the United States outside of California, this route passes a number of vineyards. You'll have the chance to stop in at Rolling Vineyards Farm Winery, Chateau La Fayette Reneau Winery, Poplar Ridge Vineyards, Hazlitt 1852 Winery, Wagner Vineyards, Wickham Vineyards Ltd., and other wineries, all of which allow visitors to sample their fare. (If you choose to do so, be sparing: Remember that cycling under the influence of alcohol is even dumber than driving while intoxicated, since you have no protection of a metal shell.)

The village of Ovid, the northernmost point of the ride not quite halfway through, holds a strawberry festival the second Saturday in June. An attractive village square with surrounding stores and churches makes this town a perfect rest or lunch stop any time of the bicycling season.

This route is from the Great Finger Lakes Bicycle Tour, held annually by Southern Tier Bicycle Club, Inc. (STBC). Each May or June the two-day tour, which can be joined by any cyclist for a modest fee, features different routes; this route is the day 1 portion of the 1991 tour, devised and verified by Augie Mueller of Vestal, New York. (If you wish to join the group for its annual Great Finger Lakes Bicycle Tour, call Augie Mueller at 607–722–6005.)

The Basics

Start: Watkins Glen, at the lower entrance to Watkins Glen State Park on Rte. 14. To get to the start, take Rte. 17 to Elmira and then Rte. 14N to Watkins Glen.
Length: 54 miles.
Terrain: Rolling to moderately hilly. Traffic is generally light except in Watkins Glen.

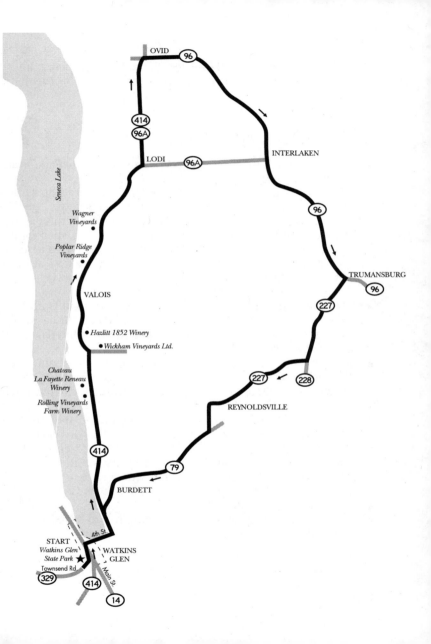

Food: Several stores in Watkins Glen, Burdett, Trumansburg, Inter-laken, and Ovid but nowhere else, so plan carefully for this long ride.

Miles & Directions

- 0.0 From the lower entrance to Watkins Glen State Park, head left to ride north on Rte. 14 (Main St.).
- 0.4 Turn right at the light onto 4th St., following Rte. 414N. In 500 feet you'll pass Tobe's Coffee Shop and Bakery.
- 2.0 Bear left to stay on Rte. 414N. Now you just cruise along here for the next 21 miles, with Seneca Lake (renowned for its trout fishing) off to your left. Along the way you'll pass a number of vineyards and wineries, and the Ginny Lee Cafe at mile 14.3 ("Excellent!" exclaims Augie Mueller) and the village of Lodi (mile 18.0). Continue north on Rte. 414/96A.
- 23.0 Just north of the Ovid village center, turn right onto Rte. 96S. Continue through the village of Interlaken (mile 31.0), passing Rte. 96A and bearing left a mile south of Interlaken to stay on Rte. 96S.
- 36.4 Just before the village of Trumansburg, turn right onto Rte. 227. Or if you feel like a pleasant rest stop, continue 100 yards and visit the village known locally for its unique architecture, good food, and friendly residents.
- 40.3 Turn right at the intersection of Rte. 228 to stay on Rte. 227, continuing on toward Reynoldsville and Watkins Glen.
- 46.1 Merge right onto Rte. 79W where Rte. 227 ends. After entering the village of Burdett, veer left to stay on Rte. 79, carefully braking on the steep downhill to Seneca Lake.
- 52.2 Continue straight onto Rte. 414 as Rte. 79 ends.
- 54.0 Turn left onto Rte. 14S.
- 54.2 You are now back at the lower entrance to Watkins Glen State Park.

18

St. Lawrence River Church Cruise

Canton—Morley—Madrid—Waddington
Chipman—Canton

With 2,800 square miles, St. Lawrence County is the fifth largest U.S. county east of the Mississippi and the largest county in New York, equal in area to Rhode Island and Delaware combined. Its gently rolling terrain crossed by scenic roads in excellent condition with little traffic makes it a haven for cyclists; yet so few people (114,000 in 1990) live in the county that it has never really been discovered by the bicycling world. This gentle 46-mile cruise will give you a chance to sample this lovely area for yourself.

This route was developed by Dale Lally, secretary of the Canton NY Bicycle Club. Since its introduction for the League of American Bicyclists' GEAR (Great Eastern Rally) in 1992, it has remained a popular tour for visiting cyclists. Originally called the Church Ride, the route takes you near no fewer than ten beautiful and historic churches in Canton, Morley, Madrid, Waddington, and Chipman. Lally recommends devoting a whole day to the ride: "Even though the tour is only 46 miles long, your pace will be slowed by the scenery, the churches, and various eateries along the way."

The ride starts from Canton, the county seat, which lies 75 miles south of the Canadian capital of Ottawa. Despite its remote location, Canton is part of an academic oasis, home to both St. Lawrence University (whose 1,000-acre campus makes up most of the southeast side of the village) and the Canton campus of the

State University of New York (SUNY); moreover, a mere 10 miles away lies Potsdam, with Clarkson University and SUNY's Potsdam campus. What does this mean for touring cyclists? As a result of several thousand college students getting around by bicycle, local governments have become increasingly sensitive to the potential of bicycle touring.

The ride's destination, the village of Waddington on the St. Lawrence River, is worth exploring as its majestic Victorian homes make it appear as though time has stood still since about 1890. There are several excellent restaurants (some open on Sunday), antiques shops, and even a delightful hardware store. Another local attraction for sweaty cyclists is the Waddington town beach at the western edge of the village. With a covered shelter, rest rooms, and changing rooms, it's perfect for a picnic or a swim in the clear water of the St. Lawrence River. ("Over the past several years, the water has been cleaned up by the zebra mussels, which eat everything but people!" Lally notes.)

Because Canton is so far north, the best time to visit is June through September; snow has been known to hang around until late April, and May can be rainy. But the summer and early autumn are quite pleasant and the tree-lined back roads around Canton are simply gorgeous. Those wishing to gaze at the spectacular fall foliage may prefer to try the tour in the brisk air of late September or early October, before the first snow falls. The biggest problem for cyclists in this area is the infamous black flies, which can be a pest unless you slather yourself with an effective insect repellent such as Cutter's. "And oh, yes, keep your mouth shut while riding," Lally advises, "or you might end up with bugs for dessert."

Canton has several motels: the University Best Western (315–386–8522), the Comfort Suites (315–386–1161), the St. Lawrence Inn (315–386–8587), and the Cascade Inn (315–386–8503). A lesser-known possibility for accommodations is the university dorms: During the summer months, SLU will put up traveling cyclists and provide three meals for a very reasonable rate. To make dorm arrangements, contact the SLU Conference Service office at St. Lawrence University at (315) 379–5232 during normal business hours.

For further information about the churches or touring in St. Lawrence County, contact the St. Lawrence County Chamber of Commerce, Municipal Building, Canton NY 13617 (315–386–4000). The Canton NY Bicycle Club, host of GEARs 92 and 97, may be contacted at P.O. Box 364, Canton NY 13617.

The Basics

Start: The village square of Canton. From the west (the Syracuse area), take I–81 north to exit 48 just north of Watertown. After exiting the interstate, take Rte. 342 east for about 5 miles. Turn left (north) onto Rte. 11 for the remaining 60 or so miles to Canton. From the east (through Lake Placid), take Rte. 3 west; at Sevey's Corners, turn right (north) onto Rte. 56; at Colton, turn left (west) onto Rte. 68 for another 12 miles to Canton. Both Rte. 11 and Rte. 68 will take you directly to Canton's Main Street and to the village square.

Note: The New York State Department of Transportation has designated the entire length of U.S. Route 11—all the way from its beginning on the Canadian border in Rouse's Point to the Pennsylvania border—as New York State Bike Route 11.

Length: 46 miles.

Terrain: Flat to gently rolling—so sedate that even a five-speed cluster should suffice.

Food: Many choices in Canton, Madrid, and Waddington, from fast food to sit-down restaurants.

Miles & Directions

Note: Follow directions carefully, as not every small street is shown on the map.

■ 0.0 In Canton's village square, face the Canton Free Library (Park St.) and look to your left. You will see the rather imposing First Presbyterian Church, built between 1876 and 1883 by Ogdensburg architect James Johnston in the style of parish Gothic design. When you've completed your examination of it, turn right onto Park St. After crossing Main St., Park St. changes name to Court St.

- 0.1 Turn left onto Chapel St. and glide downhill.
- 0.3 Turn right onto Riverside Dr. (St. Lawrence County Rte. 27—abbreviated CR 27). For the next 12 miles, you will be playing tag with the Grasse River.
- 6.1 Turn left (south) onto CR 14. In about 200 yards stop, for on the left side of the road is Trinity Chapel, an exact replica of a thirteenth-century English parish church, complete with graveyard. This early Gothic revival chapel was designed by New York architect Charles C. Haight, built in 1868 but closed in 1976 due to high maintenance costs. Now it is opened only for special occasions such as weddings. After viewing it, *retrace your route* to the intersection of CR 27 and proceed straight through the intersection to continue north on CR 14 toward Bucks Bridge.
- 9.4 Bucks Bridge. Follow CR 14 around to the left and stop. On your left is Bucks Bridge Community Church, which appeared on the cover of the September 1992 issue of *Bicycle USA*, the magazine of the League of American Bicyclists (until 1994, the League of American Wheelmen). Bucks Bridge's second claim to fame is the historical marker to your right, next to an old stone foundation. According to several local history buffs, that foundation allegedly is the remains of the first Seventh Day Adventist Church. After your examination, continue straight on CR 14.
- 12.8 Madrid. At the Atlantic gas station, go straight onto North St. (where CR 14 curves right). In 1 block, at the intersection of Church St., you will find Madrid's oldest and most imposing edifice, St. John the Baptist Catholic Church, on your left. (Another interesting church is the United Church, about a block away at 39 Main Street.) From St. John's, turn right onto Church St. and go 1 block to the intersection of CR 14 and Rte. 345. That intersection is the center of the village of Madrid and features a couple of restaurants and a convenience store.

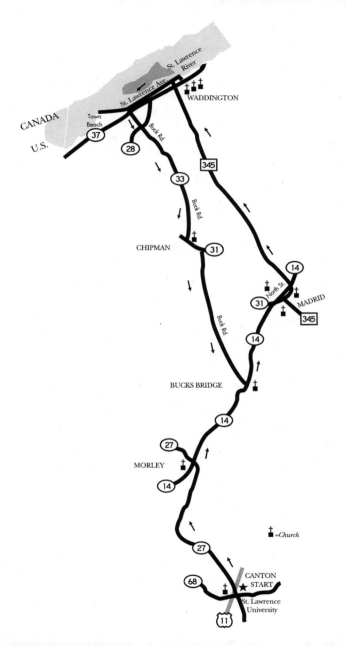

- 13.0 Turn left onto the combined CR 14/Rte. 345.
- 13.6 Bear left to follow Rte. 345, where CR 14 heads straight.
- 22.8 Waddington. At the blinking light (the only traffic light in Waddington) at the intersection with Rte. 37, stop and immediately look to your right to see St. Paul's Episcopal Church; built in 1818, it is the oldest stone church in northern New York. Just a block beyond stands St. Mary's Roman Catholic Church, built first in 1854 and then rebuilt in 1924, retaining the original walls and foundation. Just beyond St. Mary's is a third "bonus" church, the First Presbyterian Church, dating from about 1887. According to an undocumented local tradition, it was built by Isaac Johnson, a former slave from Kentucky, who lived in Ontario and St. Lawrence County and distinguished himself by building a number of bridges and churches. After examining these churches, continue north another 2 blocks on Rte. 345 to the St. Lawrence River.
- 23.0 Turn left onto St. Lawrence Ave. In about 2 miles, the Waddington town beach will be on your right. After a picnic and a dip, turn left out of the beach to retrace your route about 50 yards to Buck Rd.
- 24.2 Turn right (south) onto Buck Rd., crossing Rte. 37 (at mile 24.6) and CR 28 (at mile 25.1).
- 26.2 Continue straight at the stop sign onto CR 33 (which is still also Buck Rd., but not so marked). Get ready for the most scenic part of the whole tour! For the next 10 miles, Buck Rd. is in generally good condition, and several segments are absolutely superb, with shade trees, babbling brooks, and very few cars. At mile 30.8, you'll reach Chipman, home of the final ecclesiastical jewel on this tour: a beautiful Scottish Presbyterian church on the right side of the road just north of the intersection with CR 31. In the late eighteenth and early nineteenth centuries, this area was settled by a group of Scottish immigrant dairy farmers. They formed a congregation early on, although the current Chipman church dates from the 1890s (several of the older original stone homes, however, have survived to this day). If possible, go inside the church and check out the wood inlay interior. When leaving the church, turn right to continue south on CR 33 (Buck Rd.) for another few yards.

- 30.9 Turn left onto CR 31.
- 31.2 Turn right onto the continuation of Buck Rd.
- 36.5 Turn right onto unmarked CR 14. You may notice that you are back at Buck's Bridge Church, which you passed earlier in the day. Follow CR 14 around to the right.
- 39.3 Morley. Turn left onto CR 27.
- 45.7 Canton. Turn left onto Main St. (U.S. Rte. 11) and ride up the hill.
- 45.8 Arrive at the village square.

Note: If you wish to see more of the village, go into the Canton Free Library on Park St. in the village square and ask for the brochure describing the walking and cycling tours of Canton. The walking tour was created by Dale Lally and the cycling Tour de Canton by fellow Canton Bicycle Club member Don Peckham.

19

Cannonsville Reservoir All-Class Challenge

Deposit—Walton—Trout Creek—Deposit

The names Ashokan, Cannonsville, Cross River, Hemlock, Kensico, Neversink, New Croton, Pepacton, or Roundout may not mean much to the average New York City resident, but these are some of the many reservoirs that assure the Big Apple of having some of the best drinking water in the world. These far-off locations are all patrolled by the New York City Police Department—and on the reservoirs that allow fishing, one must obtain a special permit issued by New York City. One of the farthest from the city—a good 150 miles distant—is the Cannonsville Reservoir on the West Branch of the Delaware River in Delaware County. This ride aournd it is one of three in this book contributed by Augie Mueller of Vestal, New York.

The 10-mile-long section along Route 206 between Walton and Trout Creek is undeniably hilly; the whole route ridden as a loop as described should appeal to cyclists in excellent condition who do not mind busier car traffic. (For a challenge that's 1.3 miles shorter with somewhat less traffic, take Delaware County Route 47 from Route 206, bypassing Trout Creek; although the surface tends to be less smooth than the main route, it is a quiet, pretty road that is a net downhill.)

The many parking areas along Route 10, however, allow this lovely 54-mile challenge to be customized for all riding levels—great for a club or family ride. The trip along Route 10 from Deposit to Walton is gently rolling terrain, always near water, with light traffic and good shoulders; an out-and-back round-trip just between these two towns is 52 relatively flat miles. That cruise can be made as short as 35 miles by starting from the junction of State Route 10 and County Route 27. Moreover, the 8.4-mile section between the junction of Routes 10 and 27 and Trout Creek is also "extremely rewarding, with the babbling of the creek and vistas of sharp hills adding to the enjoyment of gliding down the extra-smooth, quiet valley road," notes Mueller—a round-trip of this stretch making a good ramble of 17 miles. For a longer cruise, join the ramble and the shorter cruise together: start from the junction and ride to both Walton and Trout Creek along Routes 10 and 27, retracing your path for a total round-trip of 52 miles. Everyone has a great time without getting lost and can talk about much of the same scenery.

Every season has its unique beauty, but in Mueller's opinion "early spring (May and June) with the water high and trees greening competes with the fantastic fall colors (late September and all of October)."

The Basics

Start: Deposit, 25 miles east of Binghamton. From New York State Rte. 17, the Southern Tier Expressway, take exit 84 onto Rtes. 8 and 10 north to Deposit, less than a mile north of the highway. Park anywhere on the streets of Deposit or along Rte. 10.

Length: 54 miles (the full loop), or anything shorter (17, 35, 52 miles), depending on how you customize the ride.

Terrain: Level to gently rolling between Deposit and Walton and between Deposit and Trout Creek, with light traffic. Rte. 206 between Walton and Trout Creek, however, is quite hilly and can also be busy.

Food: Deposit and Walton both have good restaurants and grocery stores. Trout Creek has a convenience store. *There are no other services along the route,* so pack all the water, food, and tools you think you will need. *Note:* On Sundays between May 1 and October 30, from 8:00 A.M. to 1:00 P.M., various groups serve a pancake breakfast for a few dollars at the White Birch Airfield, a grass-strip airport 3.2 miles off State Rte. 10 up Sand Creek Rd. (County

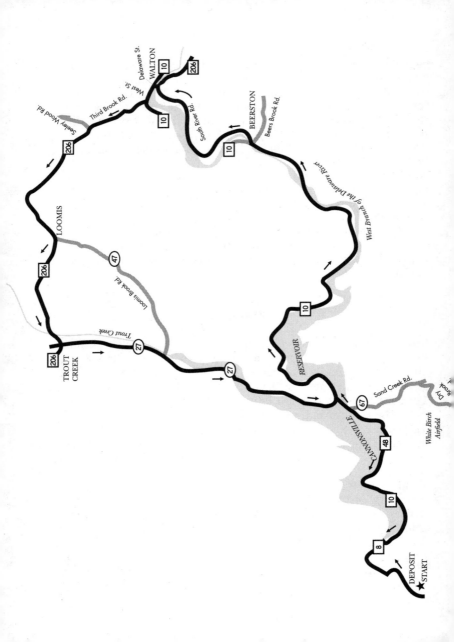

Rte. 67). It is a tough, steep climb on a bicycle, but one could drive there and then leave the car on Rte. 10 near Sand Creek Rd. Once on Sand Creek Rd., the way to the airport is well signed.

Miles & Directions

- 0.0 Leave Deposit on Rte. 10N.
- 1.5 Turn right to stay on Rte. 10 at the junction of Rtes. 10, 8, and 48. At mile 7.5, you'll pass Sand Creek Rd. on your right (heading toward the White Birch Airfield with its Sunday pancake breakfasts).
- 8.2 Just after crossing over the reservoir, bear right at the Y intersection to stay on Rte. 10 where County Rte. 27 (with the sign to Trout Creek) comes in from the left. You'll pass over the West Branch of the Delaware River several times in the next 10 or 12 miles. At mile 21.0, look to your left to see the Beerston District Police Division headquarters of the New York City Police Department. Pass Beers Brook Rd. on your right 0.1 mile later; although it looks inviting, it leads to the land of regrets—huge hills and unpaved roads. Stay on Rte. 10. Beers Brook Rd. is a convenient landmark, though, heralding the next turn 0.1 mile later.
- 21.2 Turn right onto South River Rd.
- 25.8 Turn left onto Rte. 206, cross the river again, and enter Walton.
- 26.0 Turn left onto Walton's main street, Delaware St., which is also Rtes. 10 and 206. Watch for traffic.
- 26.5 Turn right just past a Getty gas station onto West St., just across from the TA Restaurant. After passing the Agway, the Big M Market, and the local fire station, West St. becomes Lower Third Brook Rd. and then Third Brook Rd.
- 28.2 Bear left at the fork to stay on Third Brook Rd. (where Seeley Wood Rd. heads right).
- 28.6 Bear right onto Rte. 206. Watch for traffic. At mile 32.7, you'll pass the left turn for County Rte. 47 (Loomis Brook Rd.), which you could also take should you wish to have a slightly

shorter return, bypassing Trout Creek (and the only remaining convenience store on the route).

■ 36.2 Trout Creek. Turn left onto County Rte. 27. At mile 39.2, pass the terminus of Rte. 47 coming in from your left.

■ 44.4 Turn right onto Rte. 10.

■ 52.0 Turn left at the stop sign to stay on Rte. 10.

■ 53.5 Enter Deposit.

20

Skaneateles Lake Cruise

*Skaneateles—Borodino—Scott—
New Hope—Skaneateles*

Hill-climbers who love rural areas are certain to enjoy this rolling and scenic route circling Skaneateles (pronounced "skinny-atlas") Lake. The second easternmost of the eleven Finger Lakes, Skaneateles Lake offers lovely vistas of sailboats for the first half of this route, as well as fishing and swimming. The lake's water is the purest in the state of New York—so pure, in fact, that it is the source of drinking water for the city of Syracuse. The lightning class of sailboat was developed on its waters, and today the lake hosts many races and regattas. The lake also supports one of the few remaining water-borne mail delivery routes, which leaves every morning at 10:00 A.M.; for a modest fare you can catch it for a three-hour tour (call Mid-Lakes Navigation at 315–685–8500).

This ride, one of three in this book contributed and verified by Peter C. Lemonides, cartographer for the Onondaga Cycling Club, Inc., of Syracuse, New York, begins in the town of Skaneateles and passes through Onondaga, Cortland, and Cayuga counties. The town, which calls itself the Eastern Gateway to the Finger Lakes, has many wonderful nineteenth-century buildings, along with some world-class (and expensive) restaurants. Of local fame is Krebs (founded in 1899), which serves family-style dinners and a Sunday brunch. "Don't miss Doug's Fish Fry!" exclaims Pete Lemonides. The eatery is at the municipal parking lot where you start.

If you wish to stay overnight, you can rest your bones at the Sherwood Inn (315–885–3405), which you pass near the end of the route. Its sixteen guest rooms are decorated in a variety of nineteenth-century styles. A stay at the inn, which traces its origin to a building that fed and housed travelers on Isaac Sherwood's stagecoach line as long ago as 1807, includes a continental breakfast.

The Basics

Start: Skaneateles, at the municipal parking lot on Rte. 321 (State St.) just off Rte. 20 (Genesee St.). To get to the start, take I–81 to exit 15 just south of Syracuse and then take Rte. 20W into Skaneateles.

Length: 47.8 miles.

Terrain: Hilly. Traffic is light on Rte. 41 and very light on the rest of the roads.

Food: Readily available in Skaneateles; not available elsewhere, so load up on lunch and snacks.

Miles & Directions

- 0.0 Turn right out of the municipal parking lot onto Rte. 321 (State St.).
- 0.1 Turn left (east) onto Rte. 20 (Genesee St.).
- 0.6 Turn right onto Rte. 41S (E. Lake Rd.). Now just enjoy your cruise down the eastern shore of Skaneateles Lake for the next 19 miles. At mile 8.4 you'll pass through the village of Borodino.
- 19.5 In the village of Scott, turn right onto Glen Haven Rd.
- 22.5 Turn left to stay on Glen Haven Rd. and begin climbing a big, long hill. At mile 28.5 in the town of New Hope, continue straight where the road changes its name to New Hope Rd.
- 29.5 Turn left onto Old Salt Rd.
- 30.3 In the village of Kellogsville turn right onto Globe Rd. At mile 31.2, after you cross Rte. 38A, the road changes its name to Twelve Corners Rd.
- 36.5 Bear slightly right onto unmarked Cemetery Rd., where Twelve Corners Rd. bears left.

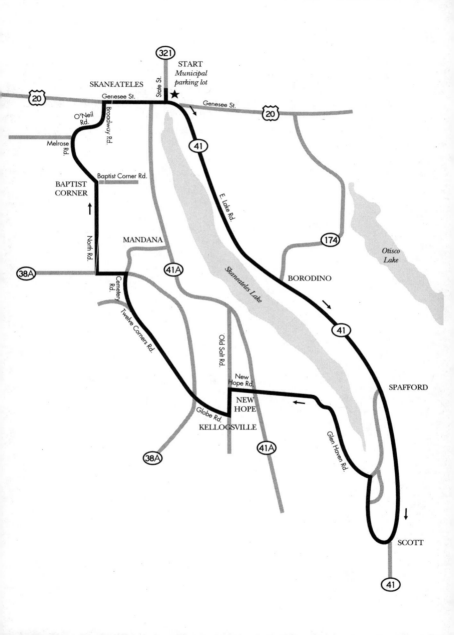

- 37.2 Turn left onto Rte. 38A.
- 38.1 Turn right onto North Rd.
- 41.5 In the village of Baptist Corner turn left onto Melrose Rd.
- 43.3 Turn right onto O'Neil Rd., which is stony and bumpy.
- 44.4 Turn left onto unmarked Broadway Rd.
- 45.4 Turn right onto Rte. 20E (Genesee St.). Soon you'll pass Krebs and the Sherwood Inn.
- 47.7 Turn left onto Rte. 321 (State St.).
- 47.8 Turn left into the municipal parking lot.

21

Pratts Falls Half-Century-Plus Challenge

Pompey—Truxton—Erieville—Fabius—Pompey

Light traffic, hills, farms, hills, quaint villages, and more hills combine to make the Pratts Falls Half-Century-Plus a pleasant yet challenging day ride. Passing through Onondaga and Madison counties, this ride is a real retreat from automobiles and people: Rolling acres of farms and four-corner towns don't offer much to tourists seeking typical tourist attractions, but they will refresh the spirit of a cyclist seeking solitude and good, scenic, challenging terrain.

The Pratts Falls Challenge is one of three rides in this book contributed and verified by Peter C. Lemonides, cartographer for the Onondaga Cycling Club, Inc., of Syracuse, New York. It begins at Pratts Falls Park, a county-run recreational park offering plenty of parking, covered picnic areas, rest rooms, hiking trails, and a beautiful view of Pratts Falls. (Swimming and overnight camping are not permitted.) The first opportunity to pick up provisions for the road is in the village of Pompey, 3 miles into the ride.

Beginning about 10 miles into the ride, you will be pedaling along Route 91 as it passes through the exceptionally scenic Labrador Hollow and the Labrador Mountain Ski Center. A natural lunch stop is DeRuyter, nearly halfway (26 miles) into the 58-mile loop. DeRuyter is a quaint village dotted with charming bungalows (one of which is an antiques shop). You'll have your choice of grocery stores, several small restaurants, and an ice cream parlor. Three-quarters of the way through the ride is another nice stop:

Highland Forest, a county park with picnic areas, hiking trails, bridle paths, and some challenging mountain-bike trails.

The Basics

Start: Three miles north of Pompey, at Pratts Falls Park on Pratts Falls Rd. Take I–81 to exit 15 just south of Syracuse and follow Rte. 20E into Pompey. Take Henneberry Rd. north to Pratts Falls Rd. and then turn right to the park entrance.
Length: 58 miles.
Terrain: Rolling to very hilly in stretches. Traffic is light in the villages of Pompey and Fabius and extremely light everywhere else.
Food: Occasional convenience stores and neighborhood bar-and-grill restaurants, with some long stretches between.

Miles & Directions

- 0.0 From Pratts Falls Park parking lot, turn right onto Pratts Falls Rd.
- 0.6 Turn right onto Henneberry Rd., and make an immediate left to stay on Pratts Falls Rd.
- 1.3 Turn left onto Sweet Rd.
- 3.5 In the town of Pompey, bear right at the stop sign onto Cherry St. In 1 block cross Rte. 20 and continue straight and slightly left onto Berwyn Rd.
- 5.8 Bear right onto Collins Rd. At mile 9.4 continue straight as the road becomes Berry Rd.
- 9.6 In the village of Apulia, turn left at the T intersection onto Rte. 80.
- 9.9 Turn right onto Rte. 91.
- 18.3 In the town of Truxton, turn left at the T intersection onto Rte. 13. At mile 22.7 continue on Rte. 13 through Cuyler.
- 26.6 In the town of DeRuyter, turn left to stay on Rte. 13.
- 31.8 In Sheds continue straight onto unmarked Dugway Rd. (where Rte. 80E heads right and Rtes. 13W/80W head left).

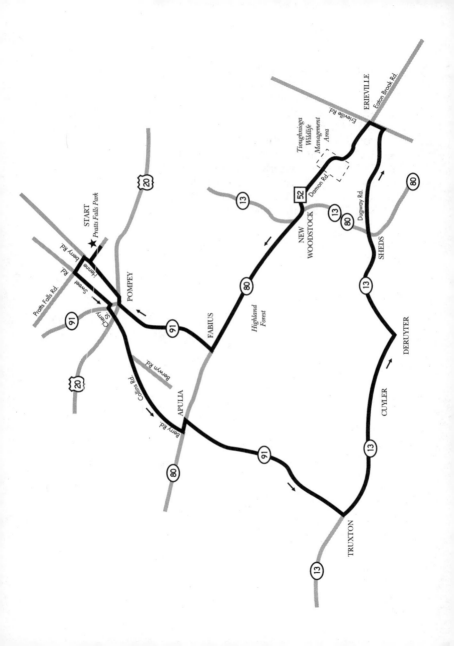

- 37.0 Turn left at the T intersection onto Erieville Rd.
- 37.4 In Erieville turn left at the Erieville Post Office onto unmarked Damon Rd. Now you'll begin climbing.
- 43.1 In New Woodstock continue straight onto Rte. 80W (Rtes. 13E/80E head left and Rte. 13W heads right). In a few miles you'll pass the Highland Forest on your left.
- 50.2 In Fabius turn right onto Rte. 91.
- 55.3 In Pompey turn right onto Rte. 20.
- 55.5 Turn left onto Henneberry Rd.
- 57.5 Turn right onto Pratts Falls Rd.
- 58.1 Turn left into Pratts Falls Park.

22

Salmon River Cruise

Altmar—Orwell—Redfield—Ricard—Altmar

The rural countryside of this ride is known primarily for its hunting and fishing. You'll pedal over green rolling hills troubled by few cars, catch isolated glimpses of the reservoir, and pass many spots tempting you to stop and picnic and let your spirit catch up to your body. Although there are no bed-and-breakfast inns or campgrounds in the area, there are fishing lodges for those desiring such accommodations; if you enjoy fishing or swimming as well as cycling, this is definitely the tour for bringing your portable rod and reel or swimsuit. You may also want to pack your own picnic lunch before embarking, as the only food anywhere along the route is the fare offered by convenience stores.

This Oswego County ride, one of three in this book contributed and verified by Peter C. Lemonides, cartographer for the Onondaga Cycling Club, Inc., of Syracuse, New York, begins in Altmar; its main attraction is the large Salmon River Fish Hatchery (315–298–5051), which offers informative tours.

Perhaps the most scenic spot is just off the route about 5 miles into the ride: Turn right onto Falls Road and 1 mile later you will behold a waterfall with a greater vertical drop than Niagara Falls. To see the falls at their best, visit in early spring when the river is swollen from the runoff from winter's snows. But even in the drier summer, the sight of the narrow pencil of water plummeting into the gorge below is dramatic.

The Basics

Start: Altmar, at the public parking lot near the Salmon River at the intersection of Bridge St. and Pulaski St. Altmar has two bars, a

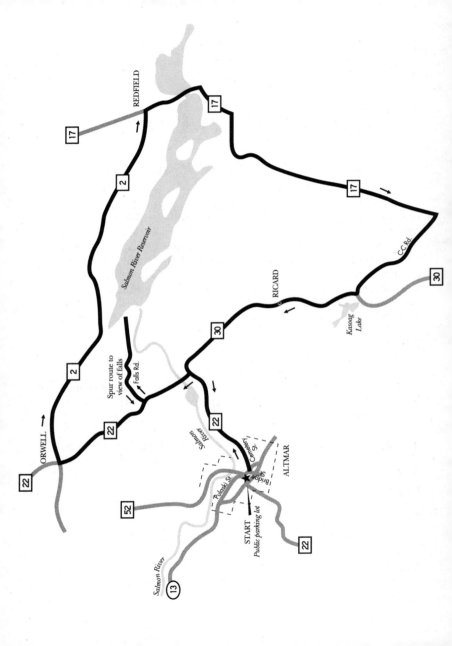

gas station, and a convenience grocery store. To get to the start, take exit 36 off I–81 north of Syracuse, and then take Rte. 13 southeast to Altmar.

Length: 37 miles.

Terrain: Rolling (no long hills or steep climbs). Traffic is very light and reasonably polite, if somewhat above the posted speed limits.

Food: Isolated convenience stores.

Miles & Directions

- 0.0 From the public parking lot, ride away from the river up the hill along Bridge St. Three blocks later turn left onto Cemetery St. At mile 1.3 Cemetery St. becomes Rte. 22.
- 3.6 Bear left to stay on Rte. 22. In a short distance you'll cross over the Salmon River, although unfortunately you will not be able to see it. In another couple of miles, Falls Rd. heads right to a view of the high waterfall.
- 7.5 In the rural village of Orwell, turn right onto Rte. 2, and stay on it for the next 9 miles. Eventually you will pass the Salmon River Reservoir, although it will remain unseen behind the trees. You may also want to stop to take a swim.
- 16.6 Turn right at the T intersection in Redfield onto Rte. 17.
- 18.2 Turn right to stay on Rte. 17.
- 19.2 Turn right to stay on Rte. 17.
- 25.4 Turn right onto C-C Rd. (A historical note: C-C Rd. was originally C.C.C. Rd., named after the Civilian Conservation Corps's camp there during the 1930s; somewhere along the line the last C was dropped.)
- 28.3 Turn right at the T intersection onto Rte. 30.
- 33.1 Bear left to stay on Rte. 30.
- 33.4 Bear left onto Rte. 22. As you enter Altmar at mile 36.0, Rte. 22 becomes Cemetery St.
- 36.8 Follow Cemetery St. as it turns right onto Bridge St. Continue straight for another 3 blocks to return to the public parking lot.

Pennsylvania

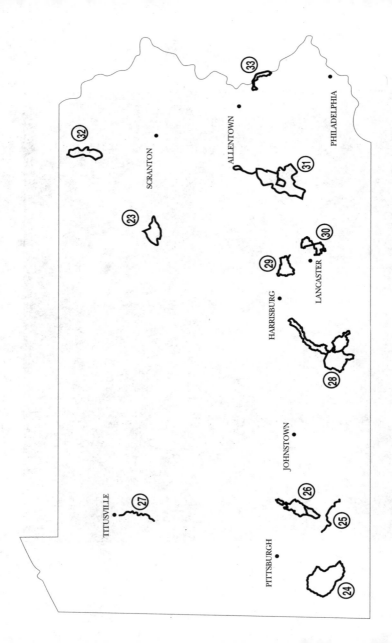

Pennsylvania

23

Montour
Preserve Challenge

Montour Preserve—White Hall—Muncy—Dewart—
Warrior Run—Turbotville—Montour Preserve

This ride has wildlife, beautiful scenery, exceptionally light traffic, and hills—even a 40-mile-per-hour downhill. It also has history, as the area is dotted with sites that were used as forts during the Indian wars before and during the Revolutionary War (Fort Muncy, Fort Brady, Fort Freeland, Fort Boone, and Fort Rice to name a few), although most of the sites now are nothing more than a marker or a name.

The route, devised by Jim Yannaccone of the nearby burg of Watsontown, passes through three counties: Montour, Lycoming, and Northumberland. It starts at the Montour Preserve, a nature preserve and outdoor recreation area centered around the 165-acre artificial Lake Chillisquaque. The preserve makes it possible to combine the ride into a general outing with noncycling family, who can spend the ride time at the preserve digging for fossils in the fossil pit, fishing, boating, bird-watching, hiking, enjoying the exhibits on wildlife, Indian culture, and land management at the visitor center, or just relaxing in the shade with a good book. (The preserve office and visitor center are open all year Monday through Friday, 9:00 A.M. to 4:00 P.M., and on weekends May through September from 12:00 noon to 4:00 P.M.; for more information, call 717–437–3131 during weekday office hours.)

According to Yannaccone, this ride is particularly lovely in October, when the leaves are changing color. The first weekend in October there is an annual Heritage Days festival held at the old Hower-Slote House near the high school in Warrior Run, three-quarters of the way through the ride (mile 29); the farmhouse, as well as the site of nearby Fort Freeland, saw battles during the Indian wars of the eighteenth century. Warrior Run is also worth visiting the second Sunday in June, the usual time for an annual strawberry festival held at Warrior Run Church. And on the second Sunday of each month (except June and July), a few dollars will buy you brunch at the monthly fund-raising breakfast of the fire company of Turbotville, served until 12:30 P.M. in the firehouse building (mile 32).

The Montour Preserve is nestled in the broad Central Susquehanna Valley, surrounded by two long, rolling ridges: the Montour Ridge to the south and the Muncy Hills to the north. As this ride climbs the steep side of the latter, the terrain is undeniably vertical. The ride's lowest point, near the West Branch of the Susquehanna River, is about 500 feet above sea level, while its highest point on the ridge of the Muncy Hills (at mile 6.3) is 1,226 feet. As a result, despite the modest distance of under 40 miles, "I don't know how to categorize the ride—a difficult cruise, or an easy challenge," Yannaccone notes. There are so many side roads from this ride that, with a good set of county maps, topographic maps, or a gazetteer, a cyclist can create many variations.

As roads in this part of the world are poorly signed, Yannaccone has indicated some of the intersecting roads along the mapped route where a person could be confused about the route. A note on his terminology: State routes are generally indicated by small ($10'' \times 10''$ or $18'' \times 10''$) white signs along the road; the route number is a four-digit number prefixed by *SR*. Township road signs have many variations. Most are green but there are a few white ones. Generally the green signs have a township road number. The white signs are mixed—some have a road number and some don't. The township road number is usually a three-digit number that may or may not be prefixed with *TR*, *RT*, or *T*. "When I give township road numbers I try to give them as they are shown on the road signs the cyclist actually sees, not on the maps," Yannaccone cautions. "Note that different sections of the same township road may have the same number but different names." Moreover, maps from different sources often disagree about the road numbers. For these reasons, follow the cue sheet and mileages very carefully.

The Basics

Start: The parking lot of the Montour Preserve. From I–80, take exit 33 for Danville and Pennsylvania State Rte. 54. Drive north on Rte. 54 to Washingtonville, 4.6 miles north of I–80. At the blinking traffic light, turn right onto Rte. 254E and drive 0.5 mile, following the brown road signs to the Montour Preserve. Turn left onto SR 1003 and drive 3.7 miles (after a mile, you will pass the Montour Steam Electric Station of the Pennsylvania Power and Light Co. on your right). Turn right onto SR 1006 and drive 0.5 mile; turn left into the parking lot of the preserve's office—housed in a restored Victorian farmhouse—and separate visitor center.
Length: 39 miles.
Terrain: Mostly rolling hills, except for a steep climb over the Muncy Hills both to and from Muncy. Some township roads are gravel or oiled-and-chipped (gravel laid on oil and pressed into the road by the weight of passing vehicles). For comfort, Yannaccone recommends a wider-tire cross, hybrid, or mountain bike, although the ride can also be done on a thin-tire road bike. Traffic is generally light except near the towns.
Food: At exit 33 off I–80 and in Washingtonville before you get to the preserve, and in Muncy on the ride route. Pack plenty of water and snacks for the actual ride, however, as the route does not pass any convenience stores (or public rest rooms); off the route, however, there is an ice cream parlor in Dewart and a mini-mart in Turbotville. *Note:* The second Sunday of the month (except in June and July) is the fund-raising breakfast at the Turbotville firehouse, and the second Sunday of June is the annual strawberry festival at the Warrior Run Church. Neither is low-fat, but both are scrumptious.

Miles & Directions

- **0.0** From the parking lot access road of the Montour Preserve's office and visitor center, turn left onto unsigned SR 1006.
- **0.4** Bear left onto TR 423 (Sportsman Rd.). At mile 1.1, pass the preserve's fossil pit on your right, where collecting is allowed.
- **2.2** Turn left at the T intersection onto PA 44.
- **3.0** Bear right onto T 360 (Shupp Rd.) where PA 44 heads left; Shupp Rd. is paved here, but soon becomes gravel. By mile 4.2, the road you are on has changed names from Shupp Rd. to Walburn Rd. Although the number on the sign indicates that the road is now TR 431, on many maps this section of road is still shown as T 360.
- **4.9** Bear right at the T intersection onto oiled-and-chipped Fairview Church Rd., whose road number is back to T 360.
- **6.2** Just past Fairview Church on your left, bear right onto SR 1003. In 0.1 mile, you'll reach the highest point on the ride. At mile 8.6, you'll leave Montour County and enter Lycoming County, so change maps. Note the white road sign on the Lycoming County sign—the road you are on changes number from SR 1003 to SR 2009. *Stop at the crest to read ahead about the deceptive intersection at mile 9.5 so you won't be distracted as you go zipping downhill.*
- **9.5** Just after passing T 608 (Swank Hill Rd.) on your right, bear left onto SR 2009 just past two large silos on your left. This is also an intersection with T 596 (Kepner Hill Rd.), which comes in on your right. This junction is deceptive: As you approach the intersection it appears as though your road continues straight ahead, up a slight rise; that is really Kepner Hill Rd. It is not until you reach or pass the silos that it becomes apparent that SR 2009 is going downhill to the left. At mile 11.2, follow SR 2009 as it makes a sharp turn to the left, crossing the creek Glade Run. In just another 0.1 mile, follow SR 2009 as it makes a sharp turn to the right. Soon I–180 will be paralleling your course on your left.
- **12.6** Turn left at the T intersection onto SR 2061 and ride under

I–180. At mile 13.0, follow SR 2061 as it makes a sharp turn to the right as you enter Muncy. You are now on New St., although it will be several blocks before you see a sign identifying the street.

- 13.4 Turn right at the T intersection onto Main St. (SR 2014, also known as the Susquehanna Trail), and then make an immediate left onto Pepper St., which you'll follow through and out of Muncy. (*Note:* If you make any detour in Muncy to look at lovely old homes or to grab a snack, remember to account for your mileage as you follow the cue sheet.) At mile 14.2, follow Pepper St. as it makes a sharp left, a sharp right, and then another sharp left. At this point you are following the West Branch of the Susquehanna River at the lowest elevation of the ride.
- 14.8 Turn right at the T intersection onto SR 2007 (Musser's Ln.). (*Note* that Pepper St. had become McKay's X-Rd. [T 432].) At mile 16.3, as you leave Lycoming County and enter Northumberland County, your road SR 2007 becomes SR 1001. For the next few miles, as the route dances back and forth across the county line, the township route numbers are confusing. Yannaccone uses the numbers that actually exist on the road signs that you will see.
- 16.9 Bear right onto TR 511 (Orchard Rd.), which on different maps is also variously shown as Peach Orchard Rd., T 471, and T 667. At mile 17.1, look to your right; that peak is Bald Eagle Mountain. In 0.5 mile, stay on Orchard Rd. as it turns downhill to the right; at the crest, the elevation is about 1,000 feet above sea level—the second highest point on the ride. Around mile 19, the pavement ends and you are on a gravel road. *Caution!* This gravel road is steep in places; at one point you will drop more than 300 feet over a distance of less than a mile.
- 20.0 Turn right at the T intersection onto unsigned PA 54. This end of the road you have just traveled is signed Grittner Hollow Rd. (T 632); it was Orchard Rd. at the other end.
- 20.1 Turn right at the T intersection onto PA 405, and almost immediately turn left onto TR 630 (River Rd.). In 0.1 mile,

follow River Rd. as it makes a sharp turn to the left.

- 24.0 Immediately after passing beneath PA 405, bear left to stay on River Rd. where T 628 (Russells Rd.) comes in on the right.
- 24.2 Turn left at the T intersection onto Main St. in Dewart. Continue east on Main St. passing through Dewart; eventually Main St. becomes Springtown Rd. (T 715). Follow Springtown Rd. through its various turns.
- 26.7 Turn right to stay on Springtown Rd.
- 27.5 Follow the paved road right to stay on Springtown Rd., where TR 650 (Hickory Grove Rd.) heads left. Follow Springtown Rd. as it makes two sharp left turns, followed by another to the right.
- 28.3 Turn right at the T intersection onto unsigned Church Rd. (T 700); the only sign is one to your left identifying the road you have been on as Springtown Rd. (T 715).
- 29.4 Turn left at the T intersection onto unsigned 8th St. Dr. (T 705 and SR 1006) and pass under I-180. In 0.1 mile, you'll pass the historic Warrior Run Church, which is the home of an annual strawberry festival, usually the second Sunday in June.
- 29.6 Turn right at the T intersection onto the unsigned Susquehanna Trail (SR 1007); you crossed this earlier as Main St. in Muncy.
- 29.7 Turn left onto SR 1006 (an extension of Eighth St. Dr.) and immediately cross the Conrail tracks. At mile 30.9, follow SR 1006 as it curves left.
- 31.5 Ride straight through the intersection with PA 44 onto Pine St.; you are now in the borough of Turbotville. At the stop sign at mile 31.7, continue straight ahead on Pine St. (A left turn here onto Church St. will take you to a water fountain near the flag pole of the community center. For the breakfast the second Sunday of the month excepting June and July, also head left onto Church St. and 1 block later turn right onto Broadway to the Turbotville firehouse.)
- 31.9 Turn right at the T intersection onto SR 1015 (Paradise St.). (To get to the mini-mart, turn left instead onto Paradise St., turn right onto Main St., and continue to the end of town.)
- 32.6 Make the first left onto T 617 (Schuyler Rd.). At mile 32.9,

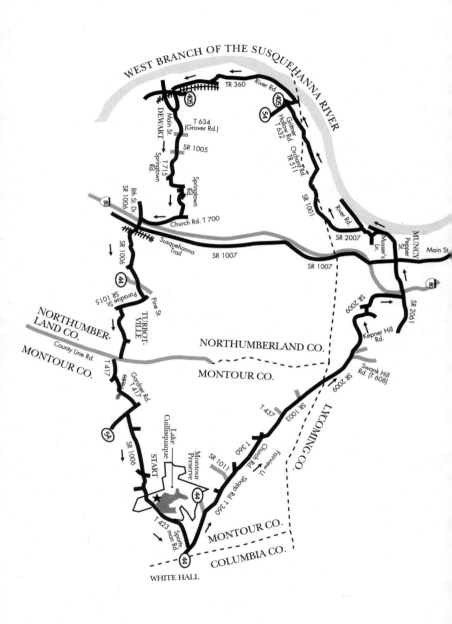

follow Schuyler Rd. as it makes a sharp right and then a sharp left, followed by a more gentle right.

- 34.2 Turn right at the T intersection onto SR 4001 County Line Rd.).
- 34.4 Make the first left onto unsigned T 417; you are now back in Montour County. At mile 34.9, follow T 417 as it curves to the right.
- 35.0 Turn left onto an unsigned gravel road, which is a continuation of T 417 (Gardner Rd.).
- 36.2 Turn right at the T intersection onto unsigned PA 54.
- 36.5 Make the first left back onto SR 1006, at the brown road sign pointing to the Montour Preserve.
- 38.8 Turn left into the Montour Preserve.

24

Prosperity Covered Bridges Cruise

Prosperity—West Finley—Rogersville—Prosperity

A marvelous old club ride of the 1,000-member Western Pennsylvania Wheelmen (WPW) bicycle club, this route will take you near no fewer than nine covered bridges. Back in the nineteenth century, of course, bridges were covered in part to prevent the accumulation of snow, which could not be plowed, and to minimize wetting of the main structure, thus prolonging a bridge's life by minimizing rot. Time your visit for mid-September and you may be able to take in the crafts, food, live entertainment, and other activities of the Covered Bridge Festival, held every year since 1971 on-site at many of the bridges. For exact dates, events, and bridge locations, call the Washington–Greene County Tourist Promotion Agency at (800) 531–4114 or (412) 228–5520.

Although the basic ride route does not take you through these bridges, directions are given for a few short side trips to visit them. You may want to do this ride on a cross (hybrid) or mountain bike, as some of the roads on the main route (and on some of the side trips to covered bridges) are dirt—shown on the map as dashed lines. But the payoff is very light automobile traffic and the back-to-nature romance of recalling an earlier age, notes contributor Noel P. Grimm, board member of the WPW. (The ride was verified by Bill Ingalls of Arlington, Virginia.) By the way, these side trips add up: If you visit all nine bridges, you add another 24.0 miles to the route, turning this 51.4-mile cruise into a 75.4-mile classic.

The ride begins about 1 mile south of Prosperity, Pennsylvania, which is about 10 miles south of Washington, Pennsylvania. This tour through Washington and Greene counties heads north through the tiny town of Prosperity, where a stop at the town grocery store provides a glimpse back in history because of its old wood floors, old display cases and shelves, and antique lighting. Then you'll warm up on flat to rolling farm land, paralleling Ten Mile Creek on your left.

About 4 miles into the ride, you'll begin a climb up a 10 percent grade to the top of a ridge—the steepest climb of the entire basic route (although not of the side trips). Once up there you'll pedal along the ridge for the next 12 miles, enjoying expansive views of the farm valleys on your right and left.

After riding through the town of West Finley, you'll coast down into the valley, where there are some good choices for a roadside picnic. The last 20 miles, which parallel railroad tracks, are a slight uphill grade. As this beautiful loop is accessible to most average fit cyclists, it is a favorite club ride and no. 63 in the packet of 150 rides in western Pennsylvania available from the Pittsburgh-based WPW. "Keep your eyes open for old one-room school houses that have been converted to homes," notes Ingalls. "There are also a lot of dogs that are unleashed that can startle you." It is also *very* important not to wander off the roads during hunting season in the fall.

A few notes about road designations in this part of Pennsylvania: The highways prefixed *PA* have a keystone-shaped sign with a one-, two-, or three-digit number. The PA highways are also marked with State Route (SR) numbers as well as the keystone sign. Four-digit SR roads—which are also county roads—are the less traveled access roads preferred by cyclists; they can be marked either by black letters on white signs or even by small numbers on reflective tape on a 5-foot-high pole about every 0.5 mile. Roads marked with a *T* followed by three digits are township roads that have little traffic and are usually very narrow; when the roads are marked—and often they are not—the *T* designation appears on a green city street sign with white letters. Having noted all this, "the local people will not know the T route numbers and they usually don't know the SR route numbers even though they are signed," remarks Grimm, so pay close attention to the cue-sheet mileages and the map. With the advent of 911 service and its requirement for street names and signs, however, direction-finding is a little easier, notes Ingalls. Still, one route number may incorporate several names.

The Basics

Start: One mile south of Prosperity, in Washington County, at the intersection of PA 221 and PA 18. To get there take I–79 south from Pittsburgh and then I–70 west. Drive about 6 miles on I–70, passing exits to Washington, Pennsylvania, and take exit 3, marked as Route 221/Taylorstown. Turn left at the end of the off-ramp, and make another left onto PA 221S. Then drive about 7 miles to Prosperity, a town with a population of about 200. Here PA 221S and PA 18S share the same road through town. Drive another mile to the south to the starting point where the two routes separate. Park on the right (south) side of the road in the gravel parking lot (used for road maintenance).

Length: 51.4 miles (75.4 miles with all the side trips to the covered bridges).

Terrain: Flat to rolling, with a couple of stiff climbs. Traffic is light for most of the ride, although it is moderate on PA 21 and PA 18.

Food: Sparse. Stock up at Jim's Stop & Shop, the only store in Prosperity; other convenience stores are in West Finley (mile 16.4), Graysville (mile 23.3), and Rogersville (off the route at mile 37.5, near Waynesburg restaurant). There is also a bank ATM in Rogersville. *Note:* On this ride, make sure to drink only *bottled* water; there has been a history of bad water in some of this area.

Miles & Directions

- 0.0 Turn left (north) out of the parking lot onto PA 18/221 (Prosperity Pike) toward Prosperity.
- 1.0 Turn left onto PA 221N (South Bridge Rd.) in Prosperity, leaving PA 18.

- 3.9 Turn left onto SR 3029W (Pleasant Grove Rd.) toward Pleasant Grove. At mile 5.4 don't blink, or you'll miss your passing through Pleasant Grove.
- 8.3 At the stop sign where the road intersects with PA 231, make a quick jog left and then an immediate right to keep heading straight ahead on SR 3029 (Burnsville Ridge Rd.).

Side trip to three covered bridges (11.8 miles round-trip): Turn left instead onto PA 231 (East Finley Rd.). After 2.5 miles turn right onto T 414 (Templeton Run Rd.). After another 0.2 mile follow T 414 as it turns right to Brownlee Bridge (spanning 31 feet over the Templeton fork of Wheeling Creek). From here the rest of this detour to the next two bridges will take you on dirt roads. Ride through the Brownlee Bridge and continue on T 414 for 2.0 miles. Turn left onto T 408 (Hickory Rd.) to Plants Bridge (spanning 24.5 feet over the Templeton fork). Ride through that bridge on T 408 (now called Sky View Rd., and eventually Fairmount Church Rd., Sky View is a very steep climb and descent on gravel and dirt, giving you an idea of the climbs on the other side trips) for 0.9 mile, and turn right onto SR 3035 (Rocky Run Rd.). After 0.3 mile turn left onto T 450 (Newland School Rd.) to Sprowls Bridge (built in 1875, spanning 27.5 feet over the Rocky Run branch of Wheeling Creek). Return to the main ride by retracing this detour route.

- 12.6 Continue straight at the junction with SR 3025 (Good Intent Rd.), to stay on SR 3029. At mile 12.6 you have your next chance to visit a covered bridge.

Side trip to one covered bridge (4.2 miles round-trip—very steep): Turn right onto SR 3025 (Good Intent Rd.) and ride 0.7 mile to Good Intent. Turn right at the T intersection to stay on SR 3025. After another 1.4 miles turn right onto T 379 (Dogwood Hill Rd.) to Danley Bridge, spanning 39 feet across the Robinson fork of Wheeling Creek. Return to the main ride by retracing this detour's route.

- 15.8 Go straight to stay on SR 3029 (Burnsville Ridge Rd.).
- 16.4 Turn left at the T intersection onto SR 3037 (West Finley

Rd.) in West Finley, heading toward Graysville. At this intersection is a pay phone and Scherich's Store, where verifier Ingalls bought "two peanut butter with applebutter sandwiches. They were yummy!"

Side trip to two covered bridges (4.0 miles round-trip): Turn right instead of left at the T intersection onto SR 3037 (West Finley Rd.). In 0.2 mile turn right to stay on SR 3037. Use caution, as this steep descent has hairpin turns with loose gravel. *In 0.7 mile turn left onto T 307 (Crawford Rd.) to Crawford Bridge, spanning 39 feet across the Robinson fork of Wheeling Creek. Return to SR 3037 and continue north. In 0.8 mile turn right onto T 360 (Robinson Run Rd.). Ride 0.3 mile to Wyit Sprowls Bridge, spanning 43 feet across the Robinson fork. Return to the main ride by retracing this detour route.*

- 18.7 The road you are on becomes SR 4007 (Ackley Creek Rd.) as you enter Greene County.
- 18.9 Bear right at the base of the downhill to stay on SR 4007 toward Graysville. At this curve the road heading left is SR 4016 (Enon Church Rd.).

Side trip to one covered bridge (1.8 miles round-trip): Turn left onto SR 4016 (Enon Church Rd.). After 0.6 mile, turn left onto T 414 (Miller Crossing), a gravel road. After 0.3 mile you'll see Longdon Bridge spanning a remarkable 67.5 feet across the Templeton fork of Wheeling Creek. Return to the main ride by retracing this detour route.

Continue straight at the junctions at miles 21.9 and 22.1 to stay on SR 4007 (now called Main St.). At mile 23.4 is Shriller's Country Store, where you can have a sandwich, buy hardware, or rent a movie. "Good ole hardwood floors," notes verifier Ingalls.

- 23.5 Head straight onto PA 21E (Roy Furman Hwy.; also SR 0021), watching carefully for traffic. At mile 27.4 PA 21E will take you through the village of Rutan. *At mile 28.5, opposite SR 4017, look right: You'll see Scott Bridge, built in 1885; it spans 41 feet across Ten Mile Creek on T 424.* At mile 30, you'll pass Stewart's Groceries.

221

221   18

Pleasant Grove Rd.
3029
PLEASANT
GROVE

Prosperity Pike
PROSPERITY

Burnsville Ridge Rd.
231
East Finley Rd.

Danley
Covered Bridge   379
3029

Good
Intent Rd.
3025

GOOD
INTENT
3029

Templeton Run Rd.
414
Brownlee Covered Bridge

Plants Covered Bridge
403   3035

Sprowls Covered Bridge

Wyit Sprowls
Covered Bridge

West Finley Rd.

Crawford
Covered
Bridge   3037

Presbyterian Church
(rest rooms)
WEST
FINLEY

Longdon Covered Bridge
Enon Church Rd.
4016

221   18
START ★   18

18
339
Day
Covered
Bridge

WEST
UNION

221

DUNNS
STATION
3039

DEERLICK

W. & W. Rail Rd.

SWARTS

18

Ackley Creek Rd.
4007

21

GRAYSVILLE

21

Roy Furman Hwy.

RUTAN

424
Scott
Covered
Bridge

21

18

ROGERSVILLE

21

4029

SYCAMORE

Albert's Restaurant
(rest rooms) and ice
cream store

18

21
WAYNES-
BURG

▪▪▪▪▪▪ = dirt

- **31.4** Bear left at the stop sign where PA 18N joins PA 21E. In 0.5 mile you'll pass through Rogersville, where there are pay phones, the only ATM on the ride, and Rush Grocery and Video. In another 0.3 mile is Center Township Park—a nice spot for a picnic. At mile 35.4 keep heading straight at the junction to stay on PA 21E/18N.
- **37.5** Turn left onto PA 18N (leaving PA 21E), following the PA 18N signs. (If at this intersection you continue straight on PA 21E instead, within 0.5 mile on your left are an ice cream store and Albert's Restaurant, where you can relax with an iced tea and visit the rest rooms. Then resume the main route on PA 18N.) At mile 39.6 continue straight at the junction to stay on PA 18N.
- **40.7** In the village of Sycamore, turn right onto SR 4029 (W. & W. Rail Rd.), heading north. At mile 42.9 you'll pass through the village of Swarts; keep heading straight at the junction, following the sign to Prosperity.
- **45.3** Bear right at the Y intersection in the village of Deerlick to stay on SR 4029. At mile 46.7, after passing through the village of West Union, you reenter Washington County, and SR 4029 becomes SR 3039.
- **48.5** Head straight at the junction onto PA 221N (Conger Rd.), leaving SR 3039.
- **49.3** Turn left at the stop sign to stay on PA 221N, heading toward Prosperity.
- **51.4** Bear right where PA 18 joins PA 221; then make a sharp left into the gravel parking lot at the start.

Side trip to one covered bridge (2.2 miles round-trip): Turn right out of the gravel parking lot and make an immediate right onto PA 18S. After 1.1 mile turn left onto T 339. There is Day Bridge, built in 1875 and spanning 36.5 feet across Short Creek. Return by this route to your starting point in the parking lot.

25

Youghiogheny River Trail Ramble

Ohiopyle—Ramcat Hollow—Ohiopyle

The Youghiogheny River Trail is the southern section of a multi-purpose trail for cyclists, hikers, and cross-country skiers that, when completed, will ultimately be 60 to 70 miles long. Located entirely within Ohiopyle State Park, straddling the border of Fayette and Somerset counties, the 8- to 12-foot-wide, hard-surfaced path of fine gravel runs through the scenic, forested gorge of the Youghiogheny (pronounced "YAHK-ah-gain-ee") River on the old Western Maryland Railway bed. The nearly level 18-mile out-and-back course from Ohiopyle to the Ramcat Hollow Launch area, near Confluence, is highlighted by magnificent river views, cascading feeder streams, and maturing forests. The trail was officially dedicated in 1986, after the Western Pennsylvania Conservancy acquired the abandoned railroad right-of-way from the Chessie System and transferred it to the Bureau of State Parks of the Pennsylvania Department of Environmental Resources.

Although Ohiopyle is nearly due west of Ramcat Hollow, the 900-foot-deep Youghiogheny River gorge carved through Laurel Ridge makes the bike path between the trailheads far from a direct route. Cyclists heading upriver from Ohiopyle, for example, will occasionally find themselves pedaling directly north or south as they make their way steadily eastward. Because it was originally designed as a railroad corridor, the bike trail never exceeds a 3 percent grade. The path appears level on the uphill first half toward Confluence, but the grade becomes apparent after you turn around and

---

gradually descend back to Ohiopyle. The gentle slope and smooth trail surface allow easy access to remote sections of the Yough Gorge that were once enjoyed only by white-water rafters, railroad travelers, and determined hikers, hunters, and anglers.

Although cyclists generally prefer loop trails over out-and-back courses because they do not like recrossing the same territory, the scenery on this trail is so varied and breathtaking that you are certain to notice new features from the different perspective of the return ride. Moreover, take the time to venture off the trail for a short distance to visit the riverbank, tributary valleys, waterfalls, and other hidden wonders just off the beaten track. "The trail becomes almost secondary and a simple highway to the wilder and isolated nooks and crannies of the Yough Gorge," remarks Paul g. Wiegman, director of natural science and stewardship of the Western Pennsylvania Conservancy, who contributed this ride (note that the lowercase *g* is not a typo). The route was verified by James Yannaccone of Watsontown, Pennsylvania, who recommends that cyclists also try the northern section of the trail, which extends about 17 miles north to Connellsville.

Each season has its own appeal. Riding in April and May reveals migrating warblers, blooming woodland wildflowers, and the river swollen with runoff from winter snows. Summer outings are highlighted by field flowers in the meadows, a river temperature that invites swimming, and the pleasant, pervasive fragrance of hay-scented fern. In the autumn the northern and southern hardwoods on the gorge's high, wooded ridges are ablaze with vibrant reds and golds. For full enjoyment, take a wildlife guide to help you identify flowers, birds, and insects.

Note: As you're heading for the start, on Route 381 just north of Ohiopyle you may want to stop to see Fallingwater, the most famous private house designed by Frank Lloyd Wright (412–329–8501). For information on camping at one of the 223 sites at Ohiopyle State Park, call (412) 329–8591; in summer, reservations are highly recommended.

The Basics

Start: Ohiopyle, at the bike trailhead parking lot of the single-story frame building that was once Ohiopyle's railroad station. To get to the start, take the Pennsylvania Turnpike (I–76) to exit 9 (Donegal, Ligonier, and Uniontown). Turn left at the T intersection onto Route 31E. Drive a bit further than 2 miles to Route 381S, and turn right. *(Note:* This turn comes quickly on a downhill after a blind curve to the left; it is just before Sarnelli's Market.) Stay on Route 381 to Ohiopyle. As you enter Ohiopyle, cross the concrete bridge over the Youghiogheny River and make an immediate left just before the gas station, following the signs for BIKE/HIKE TRAIL. Make another left into the bike trailhead parking lot immediately off the bridge. By the way, you can rent bicycles in Ohiopyle, in which case, you might want to park at one of the lots in town and pedal back 200 yards to the trailhead. A visitor center is 1 block up the street in an old train station building on the left.

Length: 18 or 22 miles.

Terrain: Flat. No automobile traffic unless you ride into Confluence.

Food: In keeping with the gorge's rugged, natural character, there are no drinking fountains, rest rooms, or eating facilities along the trail. Carry all your own water and snacks. There is a deli in Ohiopyle at the western end and in Confluence at the eastern end (open April 1 to October 10). The Ohiopyle volunteer fire company, about 100 yards from the trailhead, sells sandwiches, fries, and drinks on Saturdays from 11:00 A.M. to 6:00 P.M. in the summer. There are clean pit toilets at the Ramcat Hollow parking lot.

Miles & Directions

Note: Throughout the trail's length, mileage posts have been placed on the river side of the path. On both the trip to Ramcat Hollow and the return to Ohiopyle, the mileposts are numbered 1 through 9. Because there are no turns off the trail on this trip, the narrative descriptions below are indications of the scenery you will enjoy at different mileposts.

- 0.0 From the single-story frame building that was once Ohiopyle's railroad station, take the trail down through a 150-yard tunnel of trees. Soon (mile 0.6) it passes across the top of the wide dirt ramp that serves as a take-out point for canoes descending the river. The path then skirts the edge of a second gravel parking lot (for river take-outs only) and squeezes between four vertical wooden posts designed to keep out motorized vehicles.

  Just after this gate you will get your first unobstructed view of the Youghiogheny River. Trees along the left edge soon obscure the river, and your attention will be directed back to the path as you enter a mile-long straightaway. This wide open stretch allows time to scan the wooded ridges that tower over the river. All the rugged terrain visible from the trail is part of Laurel Ridge. The section of the Youghiogheny Gorge traversed by the bike path is a water gap carved through the ridge.

- Milepost 9 is at the midpoint of the long straightaway. Between mileposts 9 and 8, you can look into the mature forest for more than 100 yards in several places, even in midsummer.

- Milepost 8 or shortly thereafter is where the trail emerges back into the sunlight and reveals a panoramic view of a broad river bend interspersed with rapids. At mile 2.5 you'll cross a wide bridge at the apex of the bend over Long Run, your first tributary mountain stream.

- Milepost 7, like several other places along this portion of the trail, is marked by vertical cliffs of native stone where the former railroad cut into the hillside. Many have groundwater slowly seeping from the rock, thus keeping the exposed faces moist throughout the year. In spring these cliff faces are veritable hanging gardens, adorned with wild columbine and early saxifrage, growing from beds of bright green moss.

- Milepost 6 or just beyond presents a grassy side trail on the left, leading across the field to the river's edge, where a pond-size pool of calm, deep water is framed by rapids and wooded banks. You won't be able to ride a bike past the edge of the field, but the scenery is worth a short hike.

- Milepost 5 includes some sections immediately above the river and some out of the river's sight and sound.

- Milepost 4 is passed on a shaded section of path. About 0.2 mile later you cross an unnamed Youghiogheny tributary. An unmarked trail on the downstream side of the tributary will take you up to a terrace; a side trail from the terrace will lead you to half a dozen apple trees growing wild on the level patch of ground.

- Milepost 3 is just after some 15- to 20-foot cliffs towering above the path's right side. Wherever patches of soil have accumulated, moss, ferns, and columbine now grow on the damp rock. After passing this vertical wild garden, you'll have views of the Youghiogheny River's rapids and pools of calm water. As you round a bend (mile 7.7), the trail passes through a 150-yard-long railroad-carved canyon. The rock walls here rise for 12 feet on your left side and as high as 20 feet on your right. Young tulip trees share this narrows with the bike path, and when in leaf, their overlapping branches create a living tunnel.

- Milepost 2 is in a long straightaway, which is followed by the bike path's most impressive river scenery: a panoramic view of the white, water-filled bend known as Ramcat Rapids. This rock-and-moving-water obstacle course is a good example of the Class II rapids found on the Youghiogheny between Confluence and Ohiopyle. The steel cables (mile 8.2) strung across the river directly above these rapids are used to suspend gates in the foaming water for competitive slalom paddling. Just before the bend a wide, grassy area on the path's left edge offers a convenient place to pull off and watch canoeists and kayakers negotiate the tumbling water.

- At mile 8.5 is the Ramcat Hollow Launch Area, the gravel parking lot of the trail's eastern terminus in the Ohiopyle State Park. Cross the first paved road (mile 8.6) to continue straight on the trail for another mile. At the sign TRAIL END (mile 9.6), turn left onto the narrow paved road, following the sign CONFLUENCE 1 MILE. Turn left at the stop sign—the unmarked position for Milepost 0—to cross the bridge and immediately turn left into Confluence. Turn around and return the same way you came to get back to Ohiopyle.

To exit 9 of
Pennsylvania
Turnpike

Youghiogheny River

381

Fallingwater

Note: Trail also continues
another 17 miles north
along the river.

Ohiopyle Station

START

OHIOPYLE

381

*Ohiopyle
State Park*

Youghiogheny River

*Ramcat
Hollow*

CONFLUENCE

26

Ligonier Wildlife Challenge

*Ligonier—Darlington—Stahlstown—
Jones Mills—Rector—Ligonier*

If you love hills, wildlife, hills, beautiful wooded scenery, and more hills, this western Pennsylvania ride is for you. On the route you're likely to see deer, mallard ducks, Canada geese, black bear, wild turkey, pheasants, and other wildlife. Plus there are breathtaking panoramic vistas of the surrounding countryside from the tops of the climbs and colorful wildflowers even into the autumn. For those thrilled by rollercoaster rides, on one downhill stretch you can coast at up to 40 miles per hour!

The shorter 31-mile version is a cruise for those wanting to enjoy the best of the scenery while cutting off the worst of the climbs. But the 49-mile challenge will satisfy even the fittest, strongest cyclist, with a total of about 3,000 feet of hill climbing and grades ranging from 10 to 18 percent.

Yes, 18 percent, as measured by an inclinometer on the top tube of his bicycle, affirms Noel P. Grimm, board member of the Western Pennsylvania Wheelmen (WPW), who submitted this ride. (Eighteen percent would be the grade of a hill where you climbed 180 feet over a horizontal travel of 1,000 feet.) "This is a steep hill!" he exclaims. The steepest hills of 15 to 18 percent grade are seldom more than 0.25 mile long, but the climbs of 10 to 12 percent grade can be more than 1.0 mile long. "The hills on this ride are sharp, choppy ups and downs," Noel Grimm warns. "You need low gears on your bicycle. Also, on the downhills riders need well-adjusted brakes and some expertise on applying the brakes." (Verifier Jim Yannaccone of Watsontown, Pennsylvania, thinks "too much has been made of the climbs. Yes, some of them were steep" but only two or three were steep enough to require his 23-inch granny gear.)

This "Ligonier Wildlife" ride is no. 94 in the package of 150 western Pennsylvania rides available from the WPW, a Pittsburgh-based, 1,000-member bicycle club founded in 1969. The route explores the foothills between the Chestnut and Laurel ridges in Westmoreland County between Ligonier and Donegal. It also passes near the eighteenth-century Fort Ligonier, which is at the intersection of Routes 30 and PA 711.

A few notes about road designations in this part of Pennsylvania: "Road signs in this area are a joke," declares verifier Yannaccone. The highways prefixed *PA* have a keystone-shaped sign with a one-, two-, or three-digit number. The PA highways are also marked with State Route (SR) numbers as well as the keystone sign. Four-digit SR roads—which are also county roads—are the less traveled access roads preferred by cyclists; they can be marked either by black letters on white signs (which may have been crudely made out of 2-by-4s) or even by small numbers on 3- or 4-foot-high plastic pipes every so often. Roads marked with a *T* followed by three digits are township roads that have little traffic and are usually very narrow; when the roads are marked—and often they are not—the *T* designation appears on a green city street sign with white letters. Having noted all this, many roads are unmarked and "the local people will not know the T route numbers and they usually don't know the SR route numbers even though they are signed," remarks Grimm, so pay *very close attention to the cue-sheet mileages*, even more than to the map, whose scale is too small to show all the intersections that might be helpful landmarks.

The Basics

Start: Ligonier, in front of the National Guard Armory on Walnut St. north of Main St. Directions are from U.S. Rte. 30, heading east or west as appropriate. From the west, drive on Rte. 30 until the first traffic light in Ligonier, passing a Giant Eagle grocery store on your left (the north side of Rte. 30); turn left onto Walnut St. From the east, drive on Rte. 30 until the traffic light after the intersection of Rte 30 with PA 711; turn right onto Walnut St. Follow Walnut St. north to Main St. (1 block from Rte. 30); you have a stop sign. The armory is to the right on the north side of Main St. Cross Main St. and park on Walnut St. alongside the armory. Walk south to the Giant Eagle on Rte. 30, where you can provision up and, in the public rest rooms, fill your water bottles.

Length: 31 or 49 miles.

Terrain: Moderately hilly on the 31-mile cruise; very hilly with exceptionally steep climbs on the 49-mile challenge. Outside of Ligonier itself, Darlington, Stahlstown, and the crossing of Rte. 30, traffic is exceptionally light (maybe two cars in 10 miles).

Food: Several stores and restaurants in Ligonier. Stock up, because this ride is so rural that there are long stretches between convenience stores and public rest rooms.

Miles & Directions

Note: Follow directions carefully as not every small street is shown on the map. Because so few roads are marked with names or numbers, the narrative below notes the mileages of many intersections so you may cross-check your progress.

- 0.0 From your parking spot on Walnut St. north of Main St., head 1 block south to Main St.
- 0.1 Turn right onto Main St., heading west.
- 0.3 Turn right (north) onto SR 1021 just after crossing a small bridge over Mill Creek, which is just after an Exxon gas station. At mile 1.9, stay to the left and head uphill as some unnamed and unnumbered road goes to the right. Watch for deer.
- 2.1 Turn left to stay on unmarked SR 1021.
- 2.8 At this T intersection, the ride splits. For the 49-mile challenge turn right onto PA 259N.

For the 31-mile cruise turn left (instead of right) onto PA 259S, and ride 2.0 miles; resume following the directions below at mile 14.1.

After climbing a few hills, you'll reach a high plateau where Chestnut and Laurel ridges can be seen. You'll pass two intersections on the left (miles 3.1 and 3.4), one with Wood Rd. on the right (mile 4.1), Berkeley Rd. on the left (mile 4.4), Myers School Rd. on the right (mile 4.7), SR 1019 on the right (mile 4.9), and unmarked dirt Jinks Rd. on the left (mile 5.3).

- 6.3 Turn left onto SR 1008 at the top of the hill. This is a pleasant, narrow, tree-lined backroad dotted with a few infrequent houses. Follow SR 1008 as it bends left (mile 6.5). Pass TR 855 (Shirley Rd.) on the right (mile 7.0). Follow the SR 1008 as it makes a 90-degree turn to the left—where TR 980 (Fire Tower Rd.) is directly ahead of you and TR 981 (Pluto Rd.) is to the right—and head downhill. Although the downhill is paved, it is not smooth; despite the bumps, verifier Yannaccone hit 38 mph, and is "sure that it is possible to go even faster with less braking and a better tuck."
- 8.8 Continue straight onto Austraw Rd. where SR 1008 heads right and the other end of unmarked Jinks Rd. heads left. Pass unmarked McCurdy Trail on the left (mile 9.5); pass Red Arrow Rd. on the right (mile 10.8). At mile 11.1, the Latrobe Reservoir comes into view on the right; depending on the season, you should see mallard ducks or Canada geese on the water.
- 11.8 Turn right at the T intersection onto PA 259S. *Soon the 31-mile ride rejoins the main ride.* At mile 13.5, follow the road as it curves sharply left and unnumbered and unmarked Chrisner Rd. comes in from the right. At mile 14.0, pass Matson Rd. on the right.
- 14.1 Turn right at the T intersection onto Rte. 30, riding on the shoulder of this busy road. Fortunately, this heavy-traffic stretch lasts only about 300 feet.
- 14.3 Turn right onto Orme Rd. Now you're riding another loop of wooded area with summer and year-round homes.
- 15.6 Turn left onto unmarked Clark Hollow Rd. At mile 17.3, cross Rte. 30, *using extreme caution* both here and on the short, steep downhill that follows. Now you are on Darlington Rd.
- 17.6 Turn left at the T intersection onto SR 2043 in Darlington,

after crossing the bridge over Loyalhanna Creek. Now you can let 'er rip along a stretch of fast, flat riding. Use caution; this road has fast traffic and no shoulder. Continue through an intersection with two unnamed and unnumbered roads (left and right, mile 18.5), an unmarked gravel road on your right (mile 18.9), and Ross Rd. on your left (mile 19.1). By mile 19.7, you'll begin riding alongside a nice little stream on your right: Fourmile Run, which will be your companion now for several miles.

- 20.2 Bear right onto SR 2037, to continue the flat run. Now you'll pass three intersections with unmarked and unnamed roads at miles 21.9, 22.6, and 23.0.
- 23.2 Bear right at the Y intersection to stay on SR 2037 as SR 2008 comes in from the left.
- 24.1 Turn left at the T intersection onto SR 2033. At mile 24.8, pass an intersection with Hood's Mill Rd. on the right (the lettering on the wooden sign is worn). Pass twin unmarked roads on the right at mile 25.7. In another 0.1 mile, you'll enter the village of Mansville.
- 26.1 Continue straight and slightly downhill onto SR 2031 where SR 2033 heads left and uphill.
- 27.5 Turn right at the stop sign onto PA 711. You are entering Stahlstown. Ride with caution, as there is no shoulder and a lot of traffic. In 0.3 mile the 49- and 31-mile rides split again.

For the 31-mile cruise, in 0.3 mile turn left onto unmarked T 421. This corresponds to mile 18.6 of the 31-mile cruise. At mile 21.0 of the 31-mile cruise, turn right at the T intersection onto unmarked T 501. At mile 21.3 turn left onto unmarked T 329. At mile 22.1 turn right at the stop sign onto PA 381. At mile 22.6 turn left onto T 950 at the bottom of the hill. Here is where you rejoin the 49-mile challenge. Resume following the directions below from mile 40.7.

For the 49-mile challenge pass the left turn taken by the 31-mile cruise and pedal 0.2 mile farther.

- 28.0 Bear left onto the continuation of SR 2031 (unmarked). Continue straight past the Brass Duck restaurant in Stahlstown at the corner of PA 130 (mile 28.2). Pass Oak Rd. on the left (mile 29.2) and another unnumbered and unnamed road on the right (mile 29.7). Just after this second intersection, follow SR 2031 as it makes a sharp turn to the right, going uphill—a climb that is steep but mercifully short. Use caution on this twisting road, which is almost too narrow for two cars to pass each other. At about mile 29.0 is a great view to your left, sweeping down to the Pennsylvania Tpke. (I–76) several hundred feet below and then up again to the mountains in the distance.

- 31.0 Turn left at the T intersection to stay on SR 2031 where Ben Franklin Rd. heads right.
- 31.0 Turn right at the T intersection to stay on SR 2031 (Jones Mill/Stahlstown Rd.), and cross over the Pennsylvania Tpke. (I–76/I–70). Test your brakes, for now you'll drop down some fast hills. Follow the road as it makes a sharp curve to the right and then makes a sharp turn to the left (mile 31.6); just after the turn to the left, note that there are a few buildings near where a road comes in from the right. Continue straight through the stop sign (mile 32.2), crossing over Schoolhouse Ln. to stay on SR 2031 (Stahlstown/Jones Mill Rd.).
- 33.0 Turn left at the stop sign onto PA 31/PA 381N. Stay single-file on this road because the traffic is fast. A corner store offers food, drink, and an excuse for a rest.
- 33.7 Follow PA 381N as it turns left, leaving PA 31, and ride through the Mountain Streams Preserve. This road has little traffic and a lot of gravel crossroads and is a slight uphill all the way to the Pennsylvania Tpke. After crossing over the turnpike again (mile 37.9), you're in for the best downhill plunge of the entire ride—speeds of up to 40 mph are possible. Braking is required on downhills, and always be alert for uneven road surface and gravel. Soon after it flattens out, you'll pass through the Powdermill Nature Preserve; at mile 40.5, on your left there is a visitor center with public rest rooms.
- 40.7 Continue straight onto unmarked Weaver Mill Rd. (T 950), leaving PA 381N (which makes a sharp left). *Here the 31-mile cruise joins the route of the challenge.* This is another tree-lined, relatively flat road.

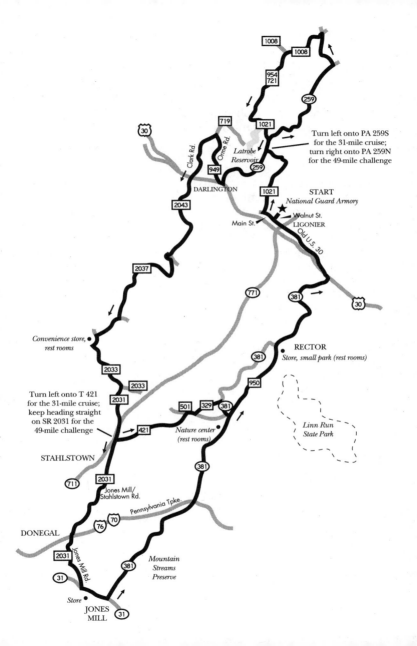

1008
1008
954
721
259
30
719
Clark Rd.
Orme Rd.
1021
Latrobe
Reservoir
949
259
DARLINGTON
2043
1021
Turn left onto PA 259S
for the 31-mile cruise;
turn right onto PA 259N
for the 49-mile challenge

START
National Guard Armory
Walnut St.
Main St.
LIGONIER
Old U.S. 30

2037

771
381
30

Convenience store,
rest rooms

RECTOR
Store, small park (rest rooms)
381

2033
950
Linn Run
State Park

2033
2031
501 329 381

Turn left onto T 421
for the 31-mile cruise;
keep heading straight
on SR 2031 for the
49-mile challenge

421
Nature center
(rest rooms)
381

STAHLSTOWN

711
2031
Jones Mill/
Stahlstown Rd.
76 70
Pennsylvania Tpke.

DONEGAL

2031
Jones Mill Rd.
381
Mountain
Streams
Preserve
31

Store

JONES
MILL 31

- 43.6 Turn right at the T intersection, rejoining PA 381N, and ride into Rector. If you want more snacks and drinks, there is a store on the right at the entrance to Linn Run State Park. Rest rooms are in the small park to the left of the store. Continue past the majestic maples and oaks of the Rolling Rock horse farms.
- 45.0 Turn left at the three-way stop to continue on PA 381N.
- 46.4 Turn left at the T intersection to cross Rte. 30 and make an immediate right onto unmarked Old Rte. 30, just past Marble Ave. Soon you'll reenter Ligonier.
- 48.1 Continue straight at the stop sign onto Main St. Now, you'll half-circle the gazebo in the center of town onto West Main St.
- 48.8 Turn right onto Walnut St. and 0.1 mile later you'll reach the starting point, the National Guard Armory on the right.

27

Paean to Petroleum Ramble

Oil Creek State Park—Titusville—Oil Creek State Park

Oil Creek State Park commemorates the booming oil industry that once filled the Oil Creek Valley. The Oil Creek Bike Trail, a 9.7-mile paved trail in Venango County that is very popular with families of cyclists of all ages, is built on an abandoned railroad grade. After beginning at the historic site of Petroleum Center, an oil-boom town of the late nineteenth century, the trail winds its way north through the scenic Oil Creek river valley to Drake Well Museum at Titusville, the site of the world's first commercial oil well.

With the discovery of rich oil fields in northwestern Pennsylvania in 1863, this area was suddenly transformed into a lively town of 5,000 people. By 1870 there were theaters, hotels, stores, saloons, a whiskey mill, and an oil refinery. But as the oil boom waned, the town began to die as rapidly as it sprang up, and a fire in 1878 reduced it to ashes.

Today the park's wooded hills look almost as they did before the boom. It is difficult to believe that the valley once supported as many as 20,000 people, that its hillsides were covered with oil derricks as far as the eye could see, and that its air was filled with the raucous noise of pumps and trains and the acrid odors of oil and smoke. Today, wildflower enthusiasts should enjoy the ride as there are dozens of varieties along the trail.

Petroleum Center has a park office with trail maps and literature, as well as displays and programs on the history of the park and the region. The Egbert Farm Day Use Area, across from the park office, has picnic tables, a pavilion, rest rooms, and a playground; also, there is a parking lot for the cars of bike trail users.

Opposite the lot is Oil Creek Outfitters, where you can get a cold drink and rent a bicycle between Memorial Day and Labor Day if you did not bring your own. Call (814) 677–4684 before your trip to confirm park office hours and to reserve a rental bike.

This ride is one of two contributed by Paul g. Wiegman, director of natural science and stewardship of the Western Pennsylvania Conservancy (the other is Ride 25). It was verified by Jim Yannaccone of Watsontown, Pennsylvania, and his mother, Dorothy Yannaccone.

The Basics

Start: Oil Creek State Park office parking lot at Petroleum Center. To get to the start, take I–80 to exit 3; then take Route 8N to Oil City. At Oil City take the Route 8 bypass. After the bypass continue on Route 8N past oil refineries and through Rouseville. Look for an Oil Creek State Park sign (about 3.7 miles from the end of the bypass) and a right turn just beyond. Follow this road about 3 miles to the park office at Petroleum Center.
Length: 19 miles.
Terrain: Mostly flat. No automobile traffic.
Food: Cold drinks can be purchased from Oil Creek Outfitters; rest rooms are at the park office and day-use area at the start; there are services also at the Drake Well Park Museum and in Titusville. There is *no water* along the trail.

Miles & Directions

Note: Because there are no turns off the trail on this trip, the narrative descriptions below are indications of the scenery you will enjoy at different mileposts.

■ 0.0   The bike trail begins beside the parking lot and is clearly marked. Swing right onto the trail and head into the cool valley. The trail heads upstream on the east side of Oil Creek, and a

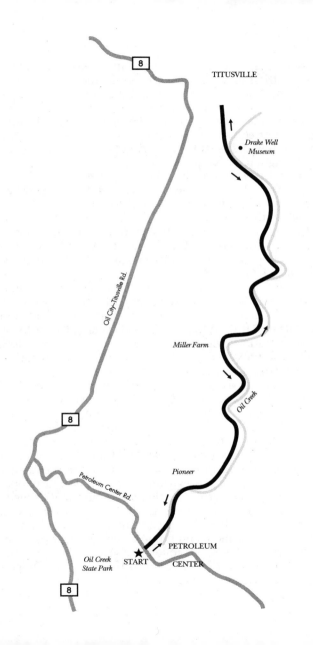

steep slope laced with hemlocks and tiny waterfalls immediately rises on the right. Watch for a fork in the trail (at mile 0.5) where the bike path bears left and descends gently to a sharp left. At this sharp bend—which can be slippery if the trail is wet—note the beaver pond on the right of the trail, with the stark, bare tree trunks surrounding it reaching skyward. From here the trail descends to the very edge of Oil Creek and turns sharply right under an iron bridge.

- Milepost 1.0 is followed by a brief rise that will bring you to a bridge over Oil Creek (mile 1.5). Here you have a good vantage point from which to take in the view of the steep-walled valley, a small upstream island, fish and frogs in the clear waters below, and the active tour railroad that runs along the east side of the valley. (You can take a 26-mile, two-and-a-half-hour round-trip ride on this Oil Creek & Titusville Railroad by making reservations at 814–676–1733.)

  As you leave the bridge, you may notice rusting, abandoned oil pipes on the left, nearly obscured by the underbrush—reminders, scattered all along the trail, of the booming oil industry that once thrived in the valley. A parking lot on the left at mile 1.8 marks Pioneer, the site of another oil-boom town of 2,000. The trail continues to follow Oil Creek upstream, now along its west bank.

- Milepost 2.0 is passed before you ride under some power lines. At mile 2.8, note the handsome shelter where visitors can rest on rainy days. Now you are pedaling on a mile-long straight-away past milepost 3.0 through shady hemlock forest.

- Near milepost 4.0 the trail passes through Shaffer Farm, which once functioned as a major transportation center in the valley. The floodplain on the west side of the creek broadens once again, and white-barked sycamores stand along the opposite shore. In midsummer this section of the bike trail is lined with blackberries ripe for picking; in the fall, with witch hazel in bloom. In 0.7 mile a clearing on the left offers picnic tables, under a large pavilion, and primitive pit toilets. If you're up for a strenuous hike, you can follow the yellow blazes, which start behind the pavilion, and climb to the top of the ridge for a magnificent view of the Oil Creek Valley.

- Milepost 5.0 is just after the location of historic Miller Farm, the terminus of the first successful oil pipeline, where oil was stored and transferred to rail cars. Shortly thereafter is a hiking trail upstream alongside Miller Run; the trail will bring you to a lovely waterfall.

  For the next few miles, Oil Creek snakes through the picturesque valley, cutting alternately into the east and west banks of the creek. The occasional ripplings in the water create a pleasant background sound in the otherwise quiet valley. Groundwater emerges from the steeper slopes, forming small waterfalls along the trail.

- Between mileposts 8.0 and mile 9.0 (the milepost marker is missing), rusted remnants of the oil boom become more prominent as the trail nears Drake Well Museum. At mile 9.3, the trail starts downhill, with a corner at the bottom. Drake Well marks the site where oil was struck on August 27, 1859, and both the oil industry and the oil boom in Oil Creek Gorge were born.

- The trail ends at mile 9.5 as the paved path bears right out of the forest and into sunshine and civilization in a parking lot; the museum is just a short ride across a bridge over the creek. To return, retrace the entire path back to Petroleum Center.

28

Hanover Horse Farms to Gettysburg Battlefield Century Classic

---

Hanover—Gettysburg—Rossville—Hanover

Although dubbed a classic, this route through Adams and York counties is actually a group of three rides that can be enjoyed by cyclists of almost any ability. As the terrain is flat to rolling farmland and the traffic mostly light, the 25-mile ramble is suitable even for novices early in the spring; the 50-mile cruise will delight stronger cyclists midseason; and the century classic will exercise the experts. Since the three rides overlap by a minimum of 20 miles, several cyclists of varying abilities can time their separation and reunion to spend some time riding together.

These three rides, devised and verified by Connie and Clair Bentzel, were originally used by their club The Hanover Cyclers for its annual Labor Day Century. All three routes first take you through the Hanover Shoe Horse Farms, the largest standardbred nursery in the world, which has produced champion harness-race trotters and pacers since 1926. You'll pedal past a few of the thirty sprawling farms totaling 3,000 acres in Adams and York counties; the main farm is open for self-guided tours Monday through Saturday from 8:00 A.M. to 3:00 P.M. For information call (717) 637–8931.

The 50- and 100-mile routes then go on to circle Gettysburg, allowing you to visit the national military parks and steep yourself in the memorial to the bloodiest battle in American history. Time your visit for the last weekend in June and the first week in July, and you may take in the city's annual commemoration of the battle as well as the annual Civil War Collectors Show and the Civil War Book Fair. Call the Gettysburg Travel Council at (717) 334–6274 for information.

Both Hanover and Gettysburg have many places to stay overnight. Aside from the usual chain hotels and restaurants, the seven-room Beechmont bed-and-breakfast inn (800–553–7009 or 717–632–3013) in Hanover offers afternoon tea and a full gourmet breakfast with—among other luxuries—the option of being served in bed. Right on the Gettysburg battlefield is the Doubleday Inn (717–334–9119), which features a candlelight country breakfast.

Those preferring to camp under the stars also have choices. Two miles southeast of Hanover on Route 216 is Codorus State Park (717–637–2816), with 3,320 acres of woodland and water offering boating, fishing, and hiking—and swimming in one of the nation's largest pools; the campgrounds are open from the second Friday in April to the third Sunday in October. Closer to Gettysburg is the Drummer Boy Campground at the junction of Routes 116 and 15; call (800) 336–3269 or (717) 334–3277 for information.

In this part of Pennsylvania, hardly any roads go straight for more than a few miles; thus, these directions have a fair number of turns. But be patient, for following them will allow you to explore some of Pennsylvania's most beautiful secondary roads. The 25- and 50-mile rides stay within Adams County; the century ride continues into York County.

The Basics

Start: McSherrystown, at South Street Recreation Park. To get to the start from Rte. 30, head south on Rte. 194 and then turn right onto Rte. 116 into McSherrystown. Turn south off Rte. 116 at the McSherrystown Fire Company, go 1.5 blocks on South Street, and turn left into the park's hidden entrance. Here there are public parking and rest rooms.

Length: 25, 50, or 100 miles. The 100-mile extension is long and skinny, and there are several cutoffs that, at your discretion, could shorten it as well.

Terrain: Flat to rolling farm land. Traffic is generally light to very light.

Food: In McSherrystown there is a Hardee's about 6 blocks from the start at the intersection of Rte. 116 and Elm St. There are also choices around Gettysburg. But elsewhere the territory is so rural that choices are limited; plan to carry snacks and lunch.

Miles & Directions

Note: Follow directions carefully, as not every small street is shown on the map.

- 0.0 Turn left out of the park onto S. 3rd St., which becomes Mt. Pleasant Rd.
- 1.7 Cross over Rte. 194 (Hanover Pike) and head straight onto Narrow Dr.
- 2.4 At the three-way stop, turn right onto unmarked Lovers Dr.
- 3.2 Cross Rte. 194 and head straight on Race Horse Rd. Here the main barns of the Hanover Shoe Horse Farms are on your left; visitors are welcome.
- 5.2 Turn left at the T intersection onto Hostetter Rd.
- 6.6 Bear left at the Y intersection onto Hoover Rd.
- 7.7 Turn right at the T intersection onto unmarked Sell's Station Rd.
- 7.9 At the stop sign, cross Littlestown Rd. and head straight onto Flatbush Rd.
- 8.6 Where Flatbush Rd. turns right, head straight onto Schoolhouse Rd.
- 9.3 Turn left at the T intersection onto Honda Rd.
- 9.4 Turn right onto White Hall Rd.
- 11.8 Turn left onto Two Taverns Rd. where Locust St. heads right.

For the 25-mile ramble turn right onto Locust St. instead. At mile 11.9 turn left onto Rte. 116 (Hanover Rd.). At mile 12.0 turn right onto N. Pine St., which becomes Granite Station Rd. At mile 14.3 turn right onto Low Dutch Rd. At mile 15.1 turn right onto Salem Church Rd. At mile 16.7 turn left onto Kilpatrick Rd. At mile 17.0 turn right onto Centennial Rd. Ride for 1.8 miles and then follow the directions from mile 91.5 to the end.

- 14.7 Turn left at the T intersection onto Rte. 97 (Baltimore Pike).
- 14.8 Turn right onto Hoffman Home Rd.
- 16.9 Turn right onto Orphanage Rd.
- 18.4 Turn right onto Furney Rd.
- 19.0 Cross Barlow–Two Taverns Rd. and continue straight onto White Church Rd.
- 20.9 Turn left onto Goulden Rd., which becomes Sachs Rd.
- 23.0 Turn right at the T intersection onto Rte. 134 (Taneytown Rd.).
- 23.1 Make the first left onto Wheatfield Rd. You have now entered the grounds of the Gettysburg Battlefield, through which you will be riding for the next 2.2 miles. At mile 24.3 cross Business Rte. 15 (Emmitsburg Rd.).
- 25.3 Turn right onto Black Horse Tavern Rd. On your left is the Eisenhower National Historic Site, where former President Dwight D. Eisenhower lived and farmed; for tickets call (717) 334–1124.
- 27.0 Turn right onto Rte. 116 (Fairfield Rd.).
- 27.1 Turn left onto Bream Hill Rd.
- 27.3 Turn left onto Herr's Ridge Rd. At mile 29.1 jog right to cross Rte. 30 (Chambersburg Rd.). Here on your right is the Eternal Light Peace Memorial.
- 30.1 Turn left onto unmarked Mummasburg Rd.
- 31.0 Turn right onto Russell Tavern Rd.
- 33.2 Turn right onto Goldenville Rd. At mile 33.5 you'll cross Rte. 34 (Biglerville Rd.).
- 35.5 Turn right at the T intersection onto Rte. 394 (Shrivers Corner Rd.). At mile 36.6 you may wish to refresh yourself at the Distelfink Drive-Inn Restaurant (closed Mondays). At mile 36.7 cross Business Rte. 15 and then Through Rte. 15.

ROSSVILLE

Carlisle Rd.

Carroll St.

Old York Rd.

WELLSVILLE

Community St.

Ridge Rd.

Main St.

Wellsville Rd.

Ridge Rd.

Kralltown Rd.

Creek Rd.

Red Mount Rd.

Poldiotown Rd.

Ridge Rd.

Lake Meade Rd.

Braggtown Rd.

Van Cleve Rd.

Cashman Rd.

Latimore Valley Rd.

Quaker Church Rd.

Gun Club Rd.

Wierman's Mill Rd.

Tape Wo

White Church Rd.

Turn left here for
100-mile classic;
head straight for

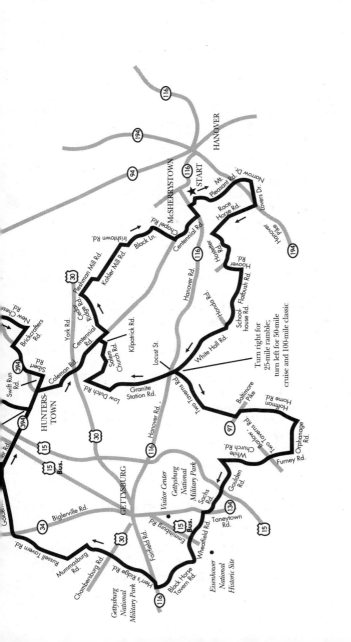

- 38.4 In Hunterstown, turn left onto Red Bridge Rd.

For the 50-mile cruise do not turn left. Instead, bypass Red Bridge Rd. to keep heading straight on Rte. 394 (now called Hunterstown-Hampton Rd.). At mile 39.0 turn right onto Coleman Rd. Ride for 1.7 miles and then follow the directions from mile 89.7 to the end.

- 42.3 Turn left onto Oxford Rd. At mile 43.7, after crossing Rte. 234, keep heading straight onto White Church Rd.
- 45.5 Turn right onto unmarked Wierman's Mill Rd.
- 46.0 Turn left onto Gun Club Rd. At mile 48.0, after crossing Rte. 94 (Carlisle Pike), keep heading straight onto Quaker Church Rd.
- 49.9 Bear left at Y intersection onto Latimore Valley Rd.
- 52.4 Make a sharp right onto Braggtown Rd.
- 54.8 At the five-road intersection, bear slightly left onto unmarked Pondtown Rd. Soon you will enter York County.
- 55.6 After crossing Rte. 194, keep heading straight on Ridge Rd. At mile 57.7 you'll cross Kralltown Rd.; at mile 59.4 you'll cross Rte. 74.
- 62.4 Turn right at the T intersection onto unmarked Old York Rd.
- 63.8 In the town of Rossville, turn right onto Rte. 74 (Carlisle Rd.). Across the intersection is a small store. About 3 miles away in Pinchot Park are campgrounds.
- 65.1 In the town of Wellsville turn right onto Carroll St. at the small grocery store.
- 65.3 Turn left onto Community St.
- 65.5 Turn left onto Rte. 74 (Main St.).
- 65.6 Turn right onto York St., which becomes Wellsville Rd.
- 68.6 Turn right onto Kralltown Rd.
- 69.1 Mark a sharp left onto Creek Rd., which eventually bends right.
- 71.5 Turn left onto Rte. 194.
- 71.9 Turn right onto Red Mount Rd. Now you have reentered Adams County. Red Mount Rd. changes its name four times in the next 10 miles. At mile 72.9, after crossing Braggtown Rd.

to your right and Stoney Point Rd. to your left, keep heading straight onto Lake Meade Rd. At mile 76.7 you'll cross Rte. 94 (Carlisle Pike). At mile 78.4, after crossing Rte. 234, keep heading straight on Van Cleve Rd. In 0.2 mile after crossing Cashman Rd., keep heading directly on Tape Worm Rd., which, like its namesake, writhes through many turns.

- 81.5 Turn right at the T intersection onto Plum Run Rd.
- 81.7 Turn left at the T intersection onto Oxford Rd.
- 82.3 Turn right onto Rte. 394 (Hunterstown-Hampton Rd.).
- 82.6 Bear left onto New Chester Rd.
- 83.8 Turn right onto Brickcrafters Rd.
- 84.5 Turn left onto Rte. 394 (Hunterstown-Hampton Rd.).
- 85.3 Turn left onto Sibert Rd.
- 86.6 Turn right at the T intersection onto Swift Run Rd.
- 88.0 Turn left onto Coleman Rd. *This is where the 50-mile cruise rejoins the century classic.*
- 89.7 Turn right onto Rte. 30 (York Rd.) and immediately turn left onto Centennial Rd. *This is where the 25-mile ramble rejoins the century classic.*
- 91.5 Turn left onto Cedar Ridge Rd.
- 93.2 Turn right onto Fleshman Mill Rd. At mile 93.7 cross Bon Ox Rd.
- 94.2 Turn left to stay on Fleshman Mill Rd. At mile 94.4 head straight onto Kohler Mill Rd. At mile 94.9 cross Poplar Rd. At mile 95.3 keep heading straight onto Irishtown Rd. At mile 96.1 keep heading straight onto Black Ln.; do not follow Irishtown Rd. as it turns right.
- 97.1 Turn right onto Chapel Rd.
- 98.0 Turn left at the T intersection onto Centennial Rd.
- 99.2 Turn left at the T intersection onto Rte. 116 (Hanover Rd.).
- 99.6 Turn right onto Academy St.
- 99.7 Turn left onto South St.
- 99.9 Turn right onto 3rd St.
- 100.0 Turn left into South Street Recreation Park. *Congratulations!*

29

Mount Gretna–Cornwall Cruise

Annville—Mount Gretna—Cornwall—Annville

The area south of Lebanon around Cornwall and Cornwall Iron Furnace includes some of the most beautiful and historic parts of Pennsylvania Dutch country. On this ride—contributed by the Lebanon Valley Tourist and Visitors Bureau and verified by David and Christine Cameron of Columbia, Maryland—you'll pass handsome old stone farm buildings still in use and ride along a part of the Furnace Hills ridge, affording you memorable vistas of rural Lebanon County. Although much of the terrain is gently rolling, the segment through Rexmont to the Lebanon Reservoir on Rexmont Road has a few short grades steeper than 10 percent that may prove too arduous for inexperienced cyclists. Much of the ride is or was known as the Tour D' Lebanon Valley, a ride sponsored by a local club.

The first part of this ride out of Annville is through level cornfields and dairy farms. Then you'll shift into lower gears as you ascend Mount Pleasant. The climb affords glimpses of the Lebanon Valley below through the cool forests of the low mountain. You'll then pedal through Colebrook and more beautiful forest to Mount Gretna, where you can gaze at the view of Conewago Lake on your left. As a special treat you'll pass on your right the renowned Jigger Shop Ice Cream Parlor, which is open during the summer.

The effort at the climb now pays off with an easy descent to historic Cornwall, a restored miner's village reminiscent of southwest England. The village was built around iron mining and manufacturing. The open-pit mine called Cornwall Banks, the greatest iron-ore deposit east of Lake Superior, was once the greatest source of iron in the eastern United States; now it is filled in with blue water that beautifully reflects the golds and reds of fall foliage. The village's heart was the Cornwall Iron Furnace, which fired and bellowed day and night from 1742 to 1883. During peacetime it produced pig iron, household goods, and stoves; during the Revolutionary War it supplied George Washington's army with cannon, shot, and shells.

Today the furnace is the only completely intact nineteenth-century charcoal–iron-making complex left in the country. Pay the nominal admission fee to walk in and gaze at the massive stone furnace and its steam-powered air-blast machinery (open Tuesday through Saturday 9:00 A.M. to 5:00 P.M. and Sunday noon to 5:00 P.M.; call 717–272–9711). Slake your thirst at the Minersvillage Store while you marvel at the statue of a miner that was sculpted with a chainsaw!

The final stretch of the ride brings you out of the hills and back into Pennsylvania's rich farmland. Return to Annville, where each December the Friends of Old Annville conduct candlelight tours through the historic town.

Note on automobiles: Traffic can be moderately heavy around Cornwall Iron Furnace during the summer when the facility is open to the public. On a Monday when it is closed, however, the tourists seem to desert the spot; you will miss seeing the furnace and exhibits, but as compensation the roads are delightfully quiet and car-free.

The Basics

Start: Annville-Cleona High School on Rte. 934, just south of Annville; park in the visitor spaces. To get to the start, take exit 29 off I–81 and drive 7 miles south on Rte. 934; after passing through the heart of Annville, turn left into the high school. Parking is also available at Cornwall Center, should you wish to start from there instead.

Length: 28 miles.
Terrain: Gently rolling, with some steep climbs. Traffic is light along most of the route, although there are brief sections of riding along the wide shoulders of busier roads. Be especially cautious about cars while entering Cornwall Center and the village of Rexmont on summer days when Cornwall Iron Furnace is open.
Food: Widely available at Annville if you ride about 0.75 mile north of the start; available in Cornwall Center and Rexmont and, between April and October, at Mount Gretna.

Miles & Directions

- 0.0 Exit Annville-Cleona High School following the one-way signs, and turn right onto the painted shoulder of Rte. 934N.
- 0.1 Turn left onto Reigerts Ln. You'll pass residences on your right, but the tone of the entire ride is set by the cornfields on your left.
- 0.9 Turn left at the T intersection onto unmarked Mt. Pleasant Rd., a delightful, narrow rural lane that curves past dairy farms.
- 3.8 Turn right at the T intersection onto Rte. 322W. Traffic is moderately heavy, but the shoulder is wide (although the pavement is rough). Watch for cars for the next 0.4 mile.
- 4.2 Make the first left to continue on Mt. Pleasant Rd. at the big blue sign for Thousand Trails. Soon you'll begin climbing along rough pavement and then you'll be coasting through forest.
- 6.7 Turn right at the T intersection onto unmarked Rte. 241.
- 7.0 Follow the main road as it bears left and joins Rte. 117S.
- 7.8 Turn left to continue on Rte. 117S (Mt. Gretna Rd.). At mile 10.1 look left for a view of Conewago Lake. At mile 10.4 is the Jigger Shop Ice Cream Parlor on your right; at mile 10.7 you can stop for refreshments at the Mt. Gretna Corner Deli on your left; the Mt. Gretna Inn bed-and-breakfast is on the right. Here the shoulder is wide but the pavement is rough.
- 13.1 After passing under the overpass for Rte. 322, keep heading straight onto unmarked Ironmaster Rd. (where the sign says END RTE. 117).

- 14.0 Follow the main road as it bends left and becomes Burd Coleman Rd. Now you're riding through a small development of multifamily stone houses.
- 14.4 Just after you pass the Cornwall Garage on your right, turn right onto Rexmont Rd. At mile 15.0 are the red stone buildings of the Cornwall Iron Furnace museum, where you can begin to explore the exhibit.
- 15.1 Past the museum bear right at the yield sign and the stop sign onto unmarked Boyd St. Pass the Cornwall Children's Center on your left. In less than 0.25 mile, gaze to the right to the lake of Cornwall Banks. At mile 15.4 you'll enter the miner's village with its stone buildings. At mile 15.7 at Shirk St. you'll pass the Minersvillage Store on the left; look for its chainsaw-carved statue. When you're done exploring, *turn around and leave the miner's village the same way you entered.*
- 16.3 Turn right at the T intersection and make an immediate right to stay on Rexmont Rd. At mile 16.7 keep heading straight at the yield sign, enjoying the view of the valley to your left.
- 17.5 Turn left at the brick firehouse and white clapboard church onto Store Ln. Now you'll begin a gentle downhill.
- 18.0 At the T intersection turn left onto unmarked Rte. 419. *Caution* for the next 0.25 mile—the traffic is moderate and the shoulder is below road level!
- 18.3 Make the first right onto S. Lincoln Ave.
- 18.7 Bear right at the T intersection to stay on S. Lincoln Ave. Be careful crossing the railroad tracks in 0.5 mile.
- 20.1 Turn left at the stop sign onto moderately busy Evergreen Rd., which immediately becomes Rocherty Rd. The shoulder is wide but gravelly. Keep heading straight through the traffic lights at miles 20.8 and 21.1 to stay on Rocherty Rd. After the second light the traffic becomes lighter and the shoulder narrower but smoother.
- 22.7 Turn right at the T intersection onto Rte. 241 (here called Colebrook Rd.), which is moderately busy but has a wide shoulder.
- 23.1 Turn left onto Royal Rd., which has no shoulder.
- 24.6 Turn right at the stop sign onto Oak St., following the sign TO ROYAL RD.

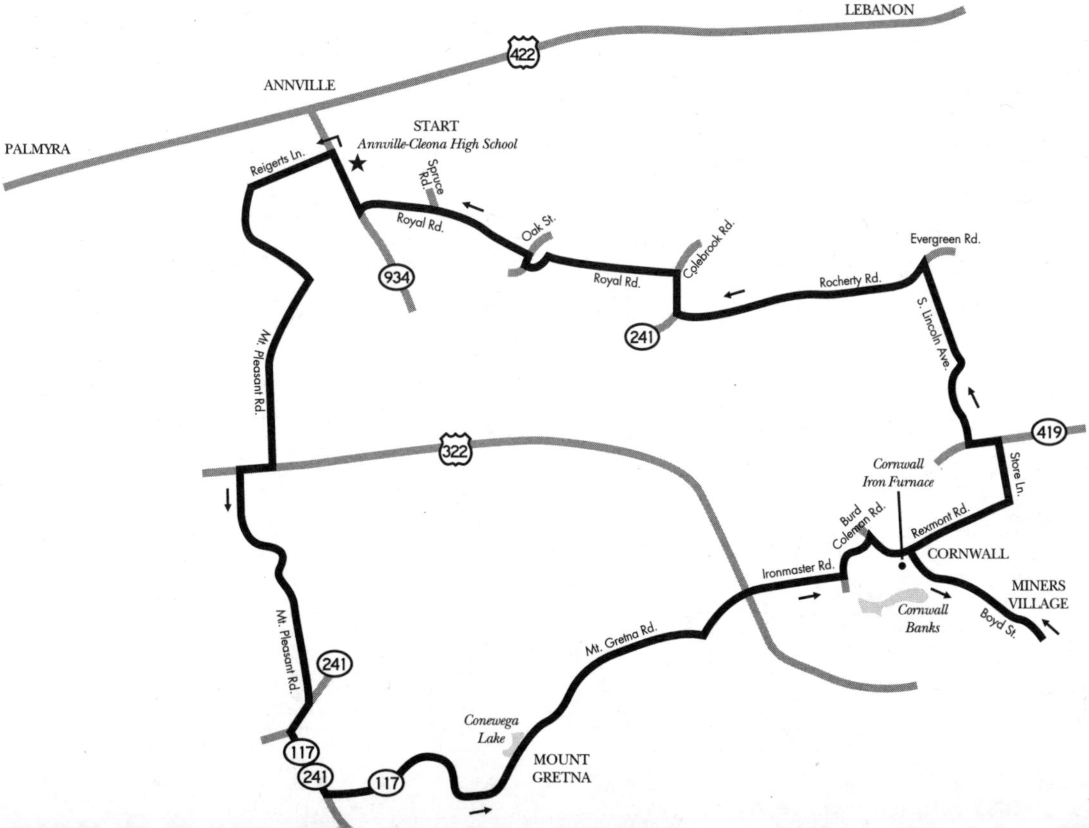
LEBANON
422
ANNVILLE
PALMYRA
START
Annville-Cleona High School
Reigerts Ln.
Spruce Rd.
Royal Rd.
Oak St.
934
Colebrook Rd.
Royal Rd.
Evergreen Rd.
Rocherty Rd.
241
S. Lincoln Ave.
Mt. Pleasant Rd.
322
419
Cornwall Iron Furnace
Store Ln.
Burd Coleman Rd.
Rexmont Rd.
CORNWALL
Ironmaster Rd.
MINERS VILLAGE
Cornwall Banks
Boyd St.
Mt. Gretna Rd.
Mt. Pleasant Rd.
241
Conewega Lake
MOUNT GRETNA
117
241
117

- 25.7 Turn left onto the continuation of Royal Rd. (which actually reads Royal Dr. at this end of the road). Pass the golf course on your right. At mile 26.7 keep heading straight through the stop sign to stay on Royal Rd. (where Spruce Rd. heads right).
- 26.6 Turn right at the T intersection onto Rte. 934N, another road that is fairly busy but has a wide shoulder.
- 27.1 Turn right into the parking lot of Annville-Cleona High School.

30

Pennsylvania Dutch Sampler Cruise

*Lampeter—Iva—Intercourse—
Weavertown—Strasburg—Lampeter*

On this ride it is likely that you will want to spend as much time off the bike as on, for you will be pedaling through some of the most beautiful Amish farmland in Lancaster County, near or through three of Pennsylvania's several hundred still-standing covered bridges, and past plenty of quilts and crafts boutiques.

The terrain varies from gently rolling in the northern half of the ride to longer and steeper hills south of Rte. 741. Because farm country is so open and there is little shade, riding could be hot on very warm summer days. Road surfaces are good, but there are occasional ruts left by the wheels of Amish buggies, pockmarks from horses' hooves, and "road apples" deposited by the horses. Although the secondary roads are narrow—usually less than 20 feet wide—the traffic is light.

Film buffs may appreciate the fact that near the beginning of the ride, the route passes the farm where much of the 1985 movie *Witness* (about an Amish family drawn into a murder case) was made; next the route goes through the town of Intercourse, where the fight scene was filmed. But anyone will enjoy the fact that this single bicycle trip will take the rider through most of what is famous about the Pennsylvania Dutch country, notes its contributor and verifier, Bill Hoffman of the Lancaster Bicycle Club.

Give yourself plenty of time to stop and explore, for in the area you will have opportunities for taking tours of the working Amish Farm and House (717–394–6185), wandering through the Amish Village (717–687–8511), and watching the animated re-creation of a class at the Weavertown One-Room Schoolhouse (717–768–3976). For more information about what to see in the area, call the Intercourse Tourist Information Center at (717) 768–3882 or the People's Place interpretive center at (717) 768–7171 (both of which you will pass on this route).

You can also eat your way through this tour, tasting the best of Pennsylvania Dutch smoked meats or shoofly pie at the Bird-in-Hand Farmers Market (717–393–9674) or other restaurants and shops along the way. Should you wish to stay overnight, there are three campgrounds right in the thick of things: Beacon Camping Lodge in Intercourse (717–768–8775) right on the route, Flory's Cottages and Campground in Ronks (717–687–6670), and Mill Bridge Village and Campground in Strasburg (717–687–8181). Moreover, there are numerous bed-and-breakfast inns in the area, as well as a few "farm vacation homes"—working farms licensed by the state to host overnight guests, who may help with the farm chores. Word to the wise: Book overnight accommodations six to eight weeks ahead, as they are very busy in the summer and fall.

The Basics

Start: Lampeter, at Lampeter-Strasburg High School. To get to the start, take Rte. 222S from Lancaster; turn left onto Rte. 741 (Village Rd.) into Lampeter; the high school is at the corner of Book Rd. and Rte. 741 (Village Rd.), 0.5 mile east of the traffic light in Lampeter. Park in the school parking lot on weekends. (This school is a starting point for several of the rides of the Lancaster Bicycle Club.)
Length: 37 miles.
Terrain: Rolling to hilly. Traffic is light except in the village of Intercourse and while crossing Rtes. 30, 340, and 741.
Food: A few farm stands with seasonal vegetables and baked goods; Amish restaurants in Intercourse and Strasburg. Take water, but save your appetite for the goodies en route.

Miles & Directions

Note: Follow directions carefully, as not every small street is shown on the map.

- 0.0 Turn right out of the school parking lot onto Book Rd.
- 0.2 Turn right at the T intersection onto Village Rd.
- 0.4 Turn left onto Bridge Rd.
- 1.3 Turn right at the T intersection onto unmarked Penn Grant Rd. (Before turning at this T intersection, look left to see the covered bridge through which you will ride at the end of the route.)
- 1.4 Make the first left onto Pequea Ln.
- 2.6 Turn left at the T intersection onto Lime Valley Rd. (If you were to turn right instead, in 0.3 mile you would see the second covered bridge near this route.)
- 3.0 Turn right onto unmarked Walnut Run Rd.
- 3.8 Make the first left onto unmarked Deiter Rd.
- 5.3 Turn right onto Bunker Hill Rd.
- 6.0 Turn right at the T intersection to stay on Bunker Hill Rd. At mile 6.5 on your right—although not visible from the road—are the farmhouse and barn filmed in the movie *Witness.*
- 6.8 Turn left onto Sandstone Rd.
- 7.6 Turn left at the T intersection onto Old Rd.
- 8.0 Turn left onto Winter Hill Rd.
- 9.1 Turn left at the T intersection onto Stively Rd.
- 9.2 Turn right to continue onto unmarked Winter Hill Rd.
- 9.8 Head straight onto Weaver Rd. (which joins from the left).
- 10.8 Cross May Post Office Rd., at the stop sign, onto unmarked Lantz Rd.
- 11.1 Turn left at the T intersection onto Strubel Rd.
- 11.3 Bear right onto unmarked Girvin Rd.

- 12.3 Turn left at the T intersection onto unmarked Summit Hill Rd.
- 12.5 Turn left at the T intersection onto unmarked Iva Rd.
- 12.9 Turn right at the T intersection onto Paradise Ln.
- 13.2 Jog across unmarked Rte. 896 (Georgetown Rd.) to stay on Paradise Ln. *Caution!* This intersection has poor visibility. (If you were to turn left at the next intersection—Rte. 741—you could visit the Railroad Museum of Pennsylvania.)
- 15.2 Bear right to stay on Paradise Ln. where Fairview Rd. angles in from the left.
- 15.3 Bear right at the Y intersection to stay on Paradise Ln.
- 16.8 Follow the main road left onto Singer Ave. Cross busy Rte. 30.
- 17.1 Turn left at the T intersection onto Leacock Rd.
- 17.7 Turn right onto Vigilant St.
- 17.8 Bear left at the T intersection onto E. Gordon Rd.
- 18.9 Turn left at the T intersection onto Belmont Rd.
- 19.2 Turn right at the T intersection onto Harvest Dr.
- 19.7 Turn left at the T intersection onto Queen Rd.
- 20.1 Turn left at the T intersection onto Rte. 772 (E. Newport Rd.) and then immediately bear left onto Rte. 340 (Old Philadelphia Pike). Here are the Intercourse Tourist Information Center and the People's Place. If you're hungry now that you're a bit more than halfway through the ride, in 500 feet you can turn right for a stop at the Kitchen Kettle Shops. You may prefer to walk your bike, as the heavy traffic includes tour buses. But forego dessert for a little later in the route.
- 20.4 Turn right onto Rte. 772 (W. Newport Rd.). Soon you'll pass the Beacon Camping Lodge on your right.
- 21.0 Bear left at Centerville Rd. to stay on Rte. 772.
- 21.5 Turn right onto Groffdale Rd.
- 22.1 Turn left onto Scenic Rd.
- 22.7 Turn right at the T intersection onto Rte. 772 (W. Newport Rd.).
- 23.1 Turn right at N. Harvest Dr. to stay on Rte. 772 (W. Newport Rd.).
- 23.4 Turn left at Hess Rd. to stay on Rte. 772 (Newport Rd.).

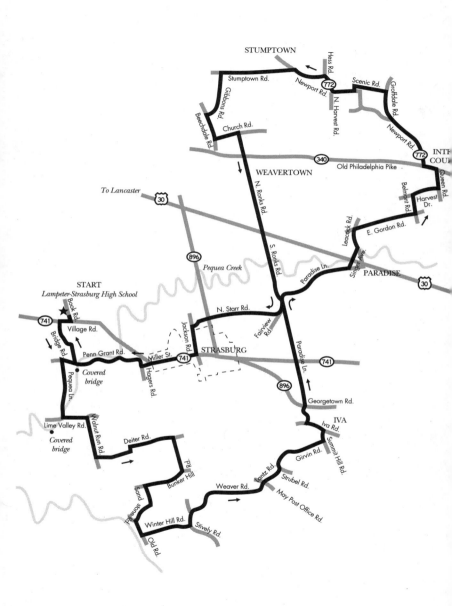

- 24.0 Turn left onto Stumptown Rd. The Mascot Roller Mill at this corner is open from May through October, Monday through Saturday 9:00 A.M. to 4:00 P.M.
- 25.4 Turn left onto Gibbons Rd. At mile 25.8 you can now pick up dessert at the Bird-in-Hand Bake Shop on your right.
- 26.4 Turn left at the T intersection onto Beechdale Rd.
- 26.9 Turn left onto Church Rd.
- 27.3 Turn right onto N. Ronks Rd. Cross Rte. 340 (Old Philadelphia Pike). The Weavertown one-room schoolhouse is to your left but cannot be seen from the road). Cross Rte. 30 onto S. Ronks Rd.
- 30.7 Turn right onto unmarked Fairview Rd.
- 30.8 Bear right to stay on Fairview Rd.
- 31.0 Turn right onto unmarked North Star Rd. (SR 2038).
- 32.6 Turn left onto Jackson Rd.
- 33.2 Turn right onto W. Main St. and immediately bear left at the Y intersection onto Rte. 741 (Miller St.). At mile 34.0 keep heading straight onto Lime Valley Rd. where Rte. 741 heads right.
- 34.2 Turn right at the T intersection onto Hagers Rd.
- 34.5 Turn left at the cemetery onto Penn Grant Rd.
- 35.6 Pass through the covered bridge over Pequea Creek and turn right onto Bridge Rd.
- 36.5 Turn right at the T intersection onto unmarked Village Rd. and then left onto Book Rd. Turn left into the parking lot of Lampeter-Strasburg High School.

31

Hopewell–Daniel Boone Classic

*Kutztown—Oley—Birdsboro—French Creek
State Park—Hopewell Furnace National
Historic Site—Daniel Boone Homestead—
Stowe—Earlville—Kutztown*

Berks County, although barely an hour from Philadelphia, is overwhelmingly rural. Undoubtedly, that is due to the influence of the German immigrants who settled the area in the late 1600s and became known as the Pennsylvania Dutch. On many of these country roads, the traffic is light, and it is not uncommon to see Mennonites driving horse-drawn carriages, as they have for more than a century. In late June and early July, tiger lilies are in bloom, adding a bright splash of orange to the landscape. Several of the roads are positively rollercoaster rides, swooping downhill past farms selling corn or apples and cider (depending on the time of year).

You will pedal through rolling farmland dotted with covered bridges and grazing sheep, interspersed with stone barns and houses dating back two centuries. In fact, one of this ride's charms is the way a road may suddenly narrow and then wind and squeeze between the buildings of a farm. The lovely valleys are separated by wooded hills, some of which will challenge the most seasoned cyclist. And throughout the ride keep your ears open for the musical splashing of water in stony creek beds.

Time your visit for Independence Day, and near the start you can listen to some of the nation's best folk and country-and-western singers at the annual Kutztown Folk Festival. And any Saturday in Kutztown, take a moment to stroll through Reninger's Antiques Market to survey the offerings of the area's largest collection of antiques dealers.

Take your camera, as this ride features a special treat: It takes you through two 150-year-old covered bridges whose main structures are supported by curved wooden beams—a method known as the Burr Arch Construction, named after Theodore Burr, a renowned nineteenth-century designer of covered bridges.

The Daniel Boone Homestead, settled in 1730, is the birthplace and boyhood home of Daniel Boone, one of America's best-known pioneers. For a modest admission fee, you can learn about the saga of the region's settlers; you can also refill your water bottles at the public rest rooms in the visitor center. The homestead is open Tuesday through Saturday from 9:00 A.M to 5:00 P.M. and Sunday from noon to 5:00 P.M.; it is closed Mondays and all but summer holidays. For more information call (610) 582–4900.

If you are an American history buff, you should particularly enjoy this ride, for a bit less than halfway through the route you can stop at Hopewell Furnace National Historic Site (215–582–8773), an iron-making village that cast cannon and shot for the Revolutionary War and then reached its peak making everything from kettles to machinery during the Industrial Revolution. You can wander around the reconstructed buildings and gaze at the restored anthracite furnace that blew day and night from 1771 to 1883. Stop at the visitor center not only to browse through its excellent selection of books on early iron making but—as a bonus in autumn—to get a permit to pick your own apples at orchards near the site.

This ride starts from the campus of the university at Kutztown (with the *u* pronounced as a short "oo," as in *cook*). Kutztown University was the site of the 1993 League Of American Wheelmen rally, hosted by the Lehigh Wheelmen Association, Inc. This ride, devised for the rally, is based on two cue sheets designed and contributed by Mark Scholefield of Birdsboro. The combination was designed and verified by Rick and Wendy Davis of Reading.

For those desiring fewer miles in a day, the 95-mile classic can be broken almost in half into two cruises by camping overnight in one of the 310 sites at French Creek State Park. The route takes you through the campground, which is 42 miles through the route (and 3 miles before Hopewell Furnace). French Creek also offers swimming in its three lakes and 32 miles of hiking trails; for information and reservations call (215) 582–1514.

Alternatively, this classic can be shortened to 73 miles by starting south of Kutztown in Oley, a town listed on the National Register of Historic Places for having the largest concentration of stone architecture in the country.

One special note: Directions are given for two alternative routes out of Birdsboro to French Creek State Park. The main route takes you over a hill by Cocalico (pronounced "co-CAL-i-co") Road. But Mark Scholefield's original cue sheet for the 1993 LAW rally included an option along a 2-mile stretch of abandoned road outside of Birdsboro that was partly washed out by flooding in the early 1980s and has been blocked off to cars ever since. According to local residents, the reason the road has not been repaired is primarily that people in the area don't want it to be: They too much enjoy jogging, walking, and cycling along its quiet, forested, pine-scented length. Despite the gates locking out cars, it is still a public road open to pedestrians and nonmotorized vehicles. If you choose to pedal this traffic-free stretch of abandoned road (thus subtracting a mile from the mileage of either route), *ride with caution at your own risk:* Stick close to the road's center double line, as in several sections the edges of the road, along with the guardrail, have slumped into the river below.

The Basics

Start: Kutztown, at Kutztown University. To get to the start from I–78, take exit 12 onto Rte. 737S directly into the heart of Kutztown; from Rte. 222 take the exit for Rte. 737S. Turn right onto Main St. and drive straight to the entrance of the university. Turn right onto College Blvd. and immediately left into the Student Union parking lot.

The alternate start is at King's IGA at the intersection of Friedensburg Rd. and Memorial Hwy. (Rte. 73) in Oley. Please park at the far end of the lot, which is covered by gravel. To get to this starting place, continue south from Kutztown by following the directions below for the first 14.5 miles, which is the most direct route.

Length: 73 or 95 miles; subtract 1 mile from either if you take the alternative route on the section of abandoned road at the edge of Birdsboro.

Terrain: Rolling to moderately hilly. Traffic is generally moderately light to very light, except it is heavier in Kutztown, Oley, and Stowe (a suburb of Pottstown) and at the crossings of major highways.

Food: Plenty of options in Kutztown, Oley, and Stowe; elsewhere there are convenience stores about every 10 to 15 miles along the route.

Miles & Directions

Note: Follow directions carefully, as not every small street is shown on the map.

The directions below start from the Student Union parking lot at Kutztown University. If you are starting instead from King's IGA at Oley for the 59-mile ride, turn right out of King's onto Friedensberg Rd., and you're already on the main route. Continue the directions below at mile 16.6 (the left turn onto West School Rd., 1.7 miles from King's).

- 0.0 Turn right out of the Kutztown Student Union parking lot onto College Blvd.
- 0.1 Head straight through the traffic light onto Normal Ave., passing the university's main entrance. Normal Ave. is a gentle downhill that will take you through four stop signs and past the Kutztown Elementary School.

- 1.2 After crossing over the railroad tracks, keep heading straight onto Kohler Rd. Now just follow this road's double yellow line through all its ninety-degree turns until you encounter the first stop sign.
- 5.0 Turn right at the stop sign onto Old Bowers Rd.
- 5.3 Turn left at the T intersection onto Bowers Rd. at the Bowers Hotel. At mile 5.4 continue straight at the stop sign to stay on Bowers Rd. and begin climbing.
- 6.7 Turn left at the stop sign at the end onto unmarked Lyons Rd.
- 7.0 Turn right onto Forgedale Rd. At mile 9.1 head straight at the stop sign to stay on Forgedale Rd.; Boyer's Market is a convenience store at this intersection. At mile 11.1 continue straight at the stop sign to stay on Forgedale Rd.
- 11.5 Bear left onto Hoch Rd.
- 12.1 Bear right onto Jefferson St.
- 12.5 Turn right at the T intersection onto Mud Run Rd., and then make an immediate left to continue on Jefferson St. Soon you will enter Oley.
- 14.3 Turn right at the stop sign onto Main St. in Oley.
- 14.7 Turn left at the stop sign onto Friedensburg Rd. At mile 14.9, you will pass King's IGA on your right. *The 73-mile classic joins the 95-mile classic at this point.* In Oley you will find rest rooms, food stores, water, and restaurants; the next opportunity is in 15 miles.
- 16.6 Turn left onto School Rd.
- 17.1 Turn right at the T intersection onto West School Rd. (where Moravian School Rd. heads left).
- 17.6 Follow the main road right (where Quarry Rd. goes straight) onto the continuation of School Rd.
- 18.1 Turn left at the T intersection onto Limekiln Rd. ·
- 19.2 Turn left at the T intersection onto Oley Turnpike Rd.
- 19.3 Turn right onto the continuation of Limekiln Rd.
- 19.7 Turn right onto Oley Line Rd. In 0.3 mile you'll pass a stone marker on your right on the grounds of the Hidden Valley Farm noting that this is the original site of the log cabin of George Boone III, Daniel Boone's father.

- **20.6** Turn left at the T intersection to stay on Oley Line Rd. (where Loder Rd. heads left). In less than 0.4 mile, you'll pass a deli on your right.
- **21.5** Head straight at the stop sign (crossing Rte. 562) onto Old Tulpehocken Rd.
- **21.7** Turn right onto Friends Rd., exercising care on the rough pavement. Soon you'll pass under high-tension power lines.
- **22.4** Turn left at the T intersection onto Daniel Boone Rd.
- **22.5** Turn right onto Pineland Rd.
- **22.8** Turn right onto Troxel Rd.
- **23.4** Turn left at the T intersection onto Schoffers Rd.
- **24.4** Bear left at the Y intersection, following the double yellow line onto Rugby Rd. (where Schoffers Rd. continues straight).
- **24.7** Bear right to stay on Rugby Rd. (where Stonetown Rd. goes straight).
- **25.3** Turn left onto Lincoln Dr. into the modern housing development. Immediately turn left at the T intersection onto Diane Ln. Now you'll circle halfway around the development and then out the other side. At the end of Diane Ln., turn right onto Fairway Dr., and then turn left at the continuation of Lincoln Dr.
- **25.8** Head straight through the traffic light (crossing Rte. 422) onto Lincoln Rd. (There are a number of food places at this intersection.) Keep following the double yellow line of Lincoln Rd. through all its ninety-degree turns. Now you're riding through industrial suburbia, with somewhat more traffic.
- **28.8** Turn right at the stop sign onto Rte. 82S, taking the bridge over the railroad tracks. Watch for potholes!
- **29.1** Continue straight through the traffic light to stay on the former Rte. 82, now called Furnace St. Watch while passing over the railroad tracks at mile 29.4. After passing through downtown Birdsboro, the road becomes Haycreek Rd.
- **29.7** Bear right at the Y intersection onto Cocalico Rd. *(If instead you want to ride the stretch of abandoned road—the alternative shown as a dashed line on the map—bear left at the T intersection instead to stay on Haycreek Rd. At mile 30.2 you can stop for a snack at the Birdsboro Rustic Picnic Area on your right. Just beyond the picnic area, walk your bike around the gate to continue on the closed*

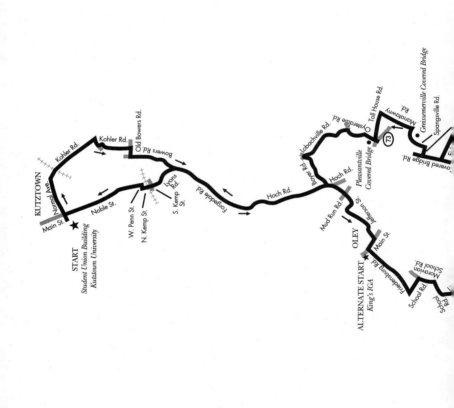

KUTZTOWN

Kohler Rd.

Kohler Rd.

Old Bowers Rd.

Bowers Rd.

Normal Ave.

Main St.

START
Student Union Building
Kutztown University

Noble St.

W. Penn St.

N. Kemp St.

S. Kemp St.

Lyons Rd.

Faggedde Rd.

Hoch Rd.

Lobachville Rd.

Oysterdale Rd.

Toll House Rd.

Monatawny Rd.

Greissemerville Covered Bridge

Spangsville Rd.

Covered Bridge Rd.

73

Boyer Rd.

Hoch Rd.

Pleasantville
Covered Bridge

Jefferson St.

Mud Run Rd.

OLEY

Main St.

Friedensburg Rd

ALTERNATE START
King's IGA

Moravian School Rd.

School Rd.

School Rd.

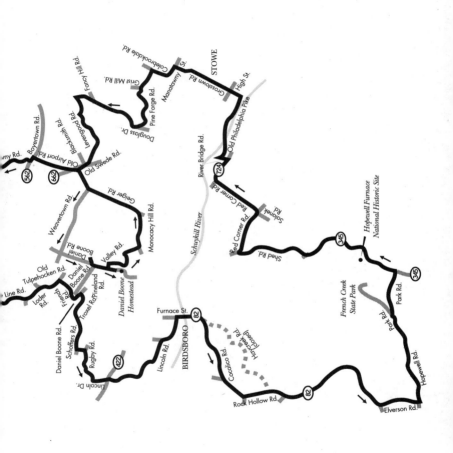

*road. **Ride carefully, as some sections of this abandoned road may be treacherous.** At mile 31.6 walk your bike around the second gate to resume riding on opened road. At mile 32.6 turn left to stay on Rte. 82 where Rock Hollow Rd. heads right; here you resume riding on the main route. At various turns keep following all the signs for Rte. 82. Pick up the directions below at mile 38.7—the left turn onto Elverson Rd.)*

- 30.0 Bear right at the Y intersection (stop sign) to stay on Cocalico Rd.
- 30.3 Bear left at the Y intersection to stay on Cocalico Rd. Gear down for this steep climb.
- 32.5 Turn left onto Rock Hollow Rd. for a steep, curvy downhill.
- 33.6 Head straight at the stop sign onto Rte. 82S.
- 33.7 Turn right at the T intersection to stay on Rte. 82S.
- 38.7 Turn left at the stop sign onto Elverson Rd. to stay on Rte. 82S. *(If you took the stretch of abandoned road, resume following the directions at this turn.)*
- 39.0 Bear left at the Y intersection onto Hopewell Rd.
- 41.4 Head straight onto Park Rd. (where Pineswamp Rd. heads right). At mile 42.1 you'll pass a sign for French Creek State Park. At mile 42.4 keep heading straight past the sign for Hopewell Furnace National Historic Site. At mile 42.6 you'll enter French Creek State Park. The park headquarters will be on your right; there you'll find soda machines, drinking water, and rest rooms. Take some time to see the park, which has picnic grounds, swimming beaches, and campsites. When departing, backtrack 0.2 mile to the sign for Hopewell Furnace National Historic Site.
- 42.9 Turn left at the sign for Hopewell Furnace National Historic Site onto unmarked Park Rd.; watch for potholes!
- 44.1 Turn left at the T intersection onto Rte. 345N, leaving French Creek State Park. A tenth of a mile up this road is French Creek General Store, which is open in the summer. At mile 45.5 is the Hopewell Furnace National Historic Site on your left; the visitor center is about 0.25 mile up the road. When you leave the site by this entrance, turn left to continue the ride on Rte. 345N.

- 46.4 Turn right at the top of the hill onto Shed Rd. Now you'll begin a long, gentle descent.
- 48.5 Turn right at the T intersection onto Red Corner Rd. Continue descending.
- 49.8 Turn left to stay on Red Corner Rd. (where Salanek Rd. heads right). In 0.75 mile you'll pass the Blackwood Golf Course clubhouse and driving range. At the clubhouse is a restaurant, along with water and rest rooms. Continue the long, gentle downhill.
- 51.3 Turn right at the T intersection onto Rte. 724. Soon you'll be paralleling the Schuylkill River.
- 52.0 Turn left onto unmarked River Bridge Rd. following the sign to Douglassville, to cross the bridge over the Schuylkill River.
- 52.2 Just after the bridge turn right onto unmarked Old Philadelphia Pike.
- 54.1 Turn left onto S. Grosstown Rd., crossing the bridge over the railroad tracks.
- 54.4 Continue straight through the traffic light (across High St.) onto Grosstown Rd.
- 56.2 Turn left at the T intersection onto Manatawny St.
- 56.7 Turn right onto Colebrookdale Rd.
- 57.2 Turn left onto Pine Forge Rd. Be careful on the downhill—there's a stop sign at the bottom of the hill.
- 57.8 Turn left at the T intersection to stay on Pine Forge Rd. (Grist Mill Rd. goes right). Cross the bridge over beautiful Manatawny Creek.
- 59.0 Turn right at the T intersection onto unmarked Douglass Dr. Now you're riding through open fields and apple orchards.
- 60.2 Turn left onto Fancy Hill Rd.
- 60.6 Turn left onto Levengood Rd., past dairy farms.
- 61.0 Turn left to stay on Levengood Rd. (where Worman Rd. goes straight). Now you'll descend steeply into the forest, cross a bridge over Manatawny Creek, and climb back out.
- 62.7 Turn left at the T intersection onto Blacksmith Rd.
- 62.8 Turn right at the T intersection onto Rte. 662 (Old Swede Rd.) and then bear left onto Weavertown Rd., which at mile

65.8 becomes Daniel Boone Rd. Keep heading *straight* on the main Daniel Boone Rd. where a smaller Daniel Boone Rd. heads right (yes, there is indeed a signpost showing the intersection of Daniel Boone Rd. and Daniel Boone Rd.). At mile 67.3 on the right is the entrance to the Daniel Boone Homestead. After your visit turn left out of the homestead to retrace 0.5 mile back along Daniel Boone Rd.

- 67.8 Turn right onto Valley Rd.
- 69.0 Turn left at the T intersection onto Monocacy Hill Rd.
- 69.6 Turn left onto Limekiln Rd. and make an immediate right to continue on Monocacy Hill Rd. At mile 70.0 begin climbing into the forest of Monocacy Hill.
- 70.6 Turn left at the T intersection onto Geiger Rd. Now you're at the crest and will begin descending out of the forest and into rolling farmland.
- 72.1 Turn right at the T intersection onto Weavertown Rd.
- 72.7 Turn left onto Old Airport Rd. In 0.1 mile continue straight at the traffic light to stay on Old Airport Rd. At this intersection is a convenience store (not open on Sundays), the first food stop in 20 miles.
- 74.1 Turn left at the T intersection onto Rte. 562W (Boyertown Pike), and then make the first right onto Manatawny Rd.
- 74.8 Bear left at the Y intersection to stay on Manatawny Rd., keeping Manatawny Creek on your left.
- 76.5 Turn left onto Fisher Mill Rd.
- 77.2 Turn right at the T intersection onto Covered Bridge Rd. You will now be rolling through flat farm fields.
- 78.2 Turn right onto Church Rd. This is past the second church on your right.
- 78.5 Turn left at the T intersection onto Spangsville Rd. Get your camera ready for a good picture of the Greissemerville Covered Bridge, a striking red-painted bridge with a double Burr arch and an entrance graced by a large hex sign. Ride through the bridge and up the hill.
- 79.2 Turn left onto Manatawny Rd. There is a candy store on the right, open from September until Easter.
- 80.3 Turn left onto Toll House Rd.

- 81.2 Turn right at the T intersection onto Covered Bridge Rd. At mile 83.5 the road delivers on the promise of its name as you approach Pleasantville Covered Bridge (blocked to cars but accessible to bicycles and pedestrians). *Walk your bicycle through the bridge.*
- 81.6 Head straight at the traffic light across Rte. 73 onto Oysterdale Rd. There is a sandwich shop and restaurant at this intersection.
- 82.4 Bear right at the Y intersection to stay on Oysterdale Rd.
- 82.7 Make the first left onto unmarked Lobachville Rd. at the sign LOBACHVILLE 1 and begin climbing. Follow the main road as it bends left to stay on Lobachville Rd. (where Mill Rd. continues straight). Continue straight through the stop sign at mile 83.3 to stay on Lobachville Rd.
- 84.4 Turn left onto Boyer Rd.
- 85.4 Turn right at the stop sign onto Bortz Rd.
- 85.5 Bear right onto Hoch Rd., which in 0.25 mile becomes Forgedale Rd.

To end the 73-mile classic, turn left onto Water St. In 2.5 miles, turn left at the T intersection onto Main St. In 0.2 mile, turn right at the stop sign onto Friedensberg Rd. and then turn right into the parking lot of King's IGA.

- 90.1 Turn left at the T intersection onto Lyons Rd. for a long downhill into Lyons.
- 91.4 Go straight at the stop sign (following the sign KUTZTOWN 3) onto unmarked S. Kemp St., which becomes N. Kemp St. after you cross the railroad tracks. Follow the road as it bends right and becomes W. Penn St.
- 91.8 Turn left at the stop sign (following the sign KUTZTOWN 3) onto Main St., which at mile 92.7 becomes Noble St.
- 94.2 Turn left at the stop sign onto Normal Ave.
- 94.6 Continue straight through the traffic light onto College Blvd., passing the main entrance to Kutztown University.
- 94.8 Turn left into the Student Union parking lot.

32

Endless Mountains Challenge

Lenox-Susquehanna—Lanesboro—Starrucca—
Thompson—Elkdale—Clifford—Lenox

Green valleys, scenic overviews, excellent food stops, and historical perspectives combine to make this a great 64-mile day for fit riders. Alternatively, given the abundance of bed-and-breakfast inns on the route, this could be a two-day cruise for people who prefer to take more time on the hills. The 64-mile challenge through Wayne and Susquehanna counties can be shortened to cruises of 39 or 32 miles or even a ramble of 24 miles. *Note that two of the rides start in Lenox and the other two start in Susquehanna.*

The 64-mile challenge, contributed by Augie Mueller of Vestal, New York, covers an area in transition from industry to tourism. From a history of railways, coal, furniture making, quarries, logging, and subsistence farming, this ride will take you past a buffalo ranch (buffalo meat is featured in the Lenox Cafe), game lands for hunting, the Elk Mountain Ski Center, upscale shops, ski condos, B&Bs, and fine food. Outside the winter ski season, the roads are lightly traveled, reasonable in grade, and rich in pastoral scenes and scenic overviews—in short, ideal for cycling.

In Susquehanna, visit the Starrucca House, built in 1865 as a railroad hotel and restaurant and now a banquet hall. If it is open (it has limited hours, as it is often reserved for special functions), you will enjoy the food and atmosphere. Even if it is closed to the public, walk around the building and peer into the large windows for a glimpse of the glorious past. The nearby plaza houses several eateries and a grocery on the site that was once a huge round-house/repair shop for the Erie (later the Erie-Lackawanna) Railroad.

In Lanesboro, inspect the great Erie-Lackawanna Starrucca Creek Viaduct, built in 1847 to carry railroad tracks over the Starrucca Creek. Made of stone quarried in nearby Brandt, the unique bridge has eighteen arches fully 50 feet in diameter and 110 feet high spanning 1,200 feet over the sometimes rushing water of the creek. If you happen to be here in the late summer, at a time of limited flow, don't be fooled: Kayakers find this creek a great stream in early spring.

At mile 23.5, you'll ride over a bridge just 100 feet upstream from an excellent swimming hole (bring your swimsuit!). At mile 33.0 in Thompson, stop for ice cream before taking a detour to ride along a section of a rail trail more than 32 miles long. With a surface of hard-packed crushed cinder, the trail is most suitable for the wider tires of cross or off-road bicycles. (Actually, you can ride the rail trail about 8 miles from Thompson to Burnwood as an alternative to the paved roads between miles 33.1 and 41.1. If you wish an even longer rail trail ride, access it earlier at Stevens Point at mile 23.8 or Starrucca at mile 29.2.) At mile 42.0, as you start riding the ridge toward Elk Mountain, stop and enjoy the vista of at least 50 miles of hills and valleys.

The Basics

Start: For the 32-mile cruise or the 64-mile challenge: Lenox, Pennsylvania, 35 miles south of Binghamton, New York, or 20 miles north of Scranton, Pennsylvania. Take exit 64 off I–81. After leaving the exit ramp, park in the far back of the Bingham's Restaurant parking lot.

Alternate start for the 24-mile ramble or the 39-mile cruise: Susquehanna, Pennsylvania. From the south on I–81, take exit 64 as if going to Lenox, and then take PA 92 north to Susquehanna. From the north on I–81, take exit 68 (Great Bend/Halstead), and then take PA 171 east to Susquehanna. From the east on New York State Rte. 17 (the Southern Tier Expressway), exit at Windsor and take New York Rte. 79 south, which becomes PA 92 at the border and takes you to Susquehanna. Parking is readily available in the large shopping plaza at the junction of PA 171 and PA 92.

Length: 24, 32, 39, or 64 miles.

Terrain: Gently rolling. There is one steep climb on SR 2046 from Gelatt to SR 2077 on the 32-mile cruise; there is also a steep climb on SR 2046 from PA 171 to Burnwood on the 39-mile cruise and the 64-mile challenge.

Food: In Lenox, Bingham's Restaurant has excellent food and extended hours of operation. The owner is also bicycle-friendly, Mueller explains, as he had a BMX trophy-winning son, and for some time had a room filled with his bicycling mementos." Susquehanna, Thompson, and Clifford also have many food options. There are also convenience stores scattered on the route.

Miles & Directions

- 0.0 Turn right out of the Bingham's Restaurant parking lot to head north on PA 92.
- 8.7 At Gelatt, keep heading straight to stay on PA 92.

For the 32-mile cruise, do not go straight; turn right instead onto unmarked SR 2046—the first paved road heading right—and ride up the steep hill for about 3 miles. At mile 11.7, turn right again onto SR 2077, another paved road, and pick up the directions below at mile 43.2.

(Gelatt is also where the 39-mile cruise joins the 64-mile challenge.)

- 18.7 Turn right onto PA 171 (Main St.). You are now in Susquehanna, which is also the start for the 24-mile ramble and the 39-mile cruise. (If you turn left onto PA 171 instead, in 2 blocks you'll find the magnificent old Starrucca House, listed on the National Registry of Historic Buildings. Once a stopover for the railroad, now it is the site of an excellent restaurant and banquet facility.)
- 19.8 In Lanesboro, continue straight onto SR 1009 (South Main St.) as PA 171 turns right. *(This end of PA 171 is near the end of the 24-mile ramble.)*

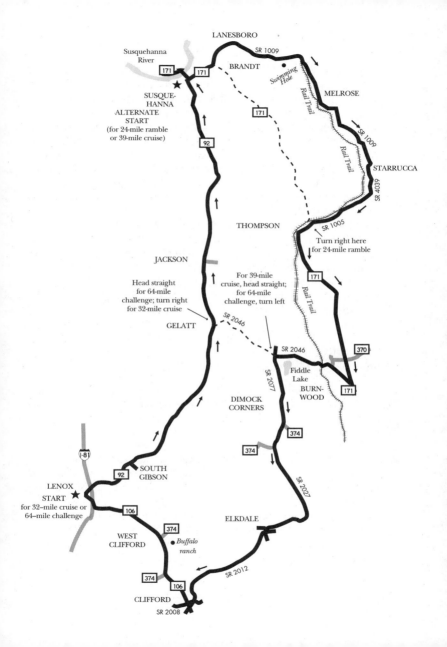

LANESBORO

SR 1009

BRANDT

Susquehanna
River

171 171

SUSQUE-
HANNA
ALTERNATE
START
(for 24-mile ramble
or 39-mile cruise)

92

171

Swimming
Hole

MELROSE

Rail Trail

SR 1009

Rail Trail

STARRUCCA

SR 4039

THOMPSON

SR 1005

Turn right here
for 24-mile ramble

171

JACKSON

Head straight
for 64-mile
challenge; turn right
for 32-mile cruise

For 39-mile
cruise, head straight;
for 64-mile
challenge, turn left

Rail Trail

GELATT

SR 2046

SR 2046

370

SR 2077

Fiddle
Lake

171

DIMOCK
CORNERS

BURN-
WOOD

I-81

JACKSON

92 SOUTH
GIBSON

LENOX
START
for 32–mile cruise or
64–mile challenge

106

374

374

374

SR 2027

374

WEST
CLIFFORD

374 Buffalo
ranch

ELKDALE

374 106

CLIFFORD

SR 2008

SR 2012

- 20.5 Turn right to stay on SR 1009, following the sign to Starrucca. At this intersection, you will ride under the dramatic Starrucca Viaduct. At mile 22.5, you will be passing through the nearly nonexistent town of Brandt, which was once an important center for logging, rail service, and furniture making, and the source of the stone for the Starrucca Viaduct. At mile 23.5, you'll cross a bridge over the meandering Starrucca Creek (*psst*—there is an excellent swimming hole just 100 feet downstream from this bridge). At about mile 25.0, bear right at the fork to stay on SR 1009 at Stevens Point. By the way, Stevens Point is one access to the rail trail.
- 29.2 In Starrucca, turn right onto SR 4039, following the sign to Thompson. (By the way, Starrucca is another access to the rail trail.) SR 4039 becomes SR 1005 when you leave Susquehanna County and enter Wayne County.
- 33.1 In Thompson, head straight onto PA 171. But if you're in the mood for a fun detour, turn right (north) instead onto PA 171 and ride 100 yards to the Jefferson Inn (food), Rooney's Ice Cream (in the old railroad depot), and another access to the rail trail path. Hobb's Market and Stone's Deli are additional possible food stops in Thompson. When ready, retrace your route and take PA 171 south, following the sign to Forest City.

For the 24-mile ramble, do not retrace your route; instead, continue on PA 171 north all the way back to Lanesboro—a net downhill. At the T intersection, turn left onto SR 4039 and ride another 1.1 miles back to Susquehanna.

- 40.0 Make a very sharp right onto SR 2046, the first clearly paved route off PA 171. It is about 2 miles after paved SR 370 enters from the left. At mile 41.1 in Burnwood, cross over the rail trail for the last time.
- 43.2 Turn left onto paved SR 2077, the first paved road after you pass Fiddle Lake on your left. *(This is where the 32-mile cruise joins the 64-mile challenge.)* Enjoy the view! You're now running along the top of the ridge.

For the 39-mile cruise, do not turn left onto SR 2077; instead, continue straight ahead on SR 2046 for another 3 miles downhill into Gelatt. At the T intersection, turn right onto PA 92 and follow the directions from mile 8.7.

- 46.0 Continue straight ahead as PA 374 comes in from the left and becomes your route. This intersection is Dimock Corners and marks the end of SR 2077.
- 47.1 Continue straight onto SR 2027 (Lyons St.), where PA 374 heads off to the right. A mile later, you'll pass the Stone Bridge Restaurant/Endless Mountain Resort, which has a nice view but few services (limited hours) in the non-ski season.
- 53.1 In Elkdale, turn right onto SR 2012, following the sign to Clifford. At mile 54.2, keep heading straight on SR 2012 toward Clifford.
- 56.7 In Clifford, turn right at the stop sign onto SR 2008.
- 56.8 Turn right at the stop sign onto PA 106 (Main St.). The Mountain View Motel and Restaurant (closed Mondays) is highly recommended. About mile 60, near West Clifford, just before the junction with PA 374, look for the buffalo herd on the right.
- 64.0 In Lenox, turn right at the bank onto PA 92, and then turn right into the parking lot of Bingham's Restaurant.

33

Ringing Rocks Ramble

*Kintnersville—Uhlerstown—
Ringing Rocks County Park—Kintnersville*

This ride between Kintnersville and Uhlerstown is among the most spectacular you'll find in Bucks County, with the Delaware River and Canal stretching out along the left side of the road and steep palisades rising above your right shoulder. Its beauty and its ease make it an ideal early-season ride, as well as a wonderful introduction to the charms of bicycle touring.

The canal, part of a system of state-built public works started in 1827 to connect Philadelphia, Pittsburgh, and Lake Erie, carried barges of freight for more than a century. The Delaware Canal section of the Pennsylvania Canal ran from the Lehigh River in Easton north of Kintnersville to Bristol in the south. Nine years after it was closed in 1931, it was turned into a state park. Now it is open to cyclists, picnickers, and others to enjoy.

At Uhlerstown pause to gaze at the historic collection of houses and canal buildings before passing through the Uhlerstown covered bridge. Built of oak in 1821 and spanning a remarkable 101 feet, this structure is the only covered bridge crossing the Delaware Canal, and it has windows on both sides, affording a view of the canal and locks. Shortly thereafter you'll ascend a steep wooded hill—the only steep climb of the trip, but it is mercifully short. If you must walk your bike, take advantage of your leisurely pace to enjoy the coolness of the forest.

At the top you'll pedal through rolling farmland, cycling past Ringing Rocks County Park. Stop for a few moments to hike out a few hundred feet on one of the trails to this small valley of boulders, deposited there during the Ice Age. The boulders rest on one another in such a way that sound is not damped, and if struck by a hammer or a thrown fist-size rock, they emit bell-like ringing tones. After leaving Ringing Rocks, you'll coast back down to Kintnersville.

This ride, one of the favorites of verifier Steven Getzow, member of the board of directors of the Bucks County Tourist Commission in Doylestown, should be taken only in the direction described in this cue sheet; the grades and crossings make it much less safe when taken in the opposite direction. Also, this ride can be taken only in the spring, summer, and fall, as the steep section of Uhlerstown Hill Road is closed from December 1 through April 1.

The segment between Kintnersville and Uhlerstown can be covered either on Route 32 or on the Delaware Canal towpath. Route 32 is smooth but without shoulders, and on lovely weekends it has fairly heavy traffic at 35 to 40 miles per hour; the towpath is somewhat bumpy so that speeds above about 6 miles per hour may not be comfortable, but it hugs the water's edge and is free of auto traffic. A cross (hybrid) or a mountain bike might handle best on the towpath's hard-packed dirt, although a thin-tire bike will also do fine. The towpath may be muddy, though, right after a heavy rain.

At the start, in Kintnersville, the Great American Grill at the intersection of Routes 611 and 32 makes huge deli sandwiches of all descriptions, some quite fancy. Take your goodies to go, as the canal towpath is dotted with picnic tables and an occasional pit-toilet rest room. There are also pit toilets at Ringing Rocks but no water, so take with you all you'll want to drink.

Four miles into the ride is the Chef Tell Manor House (610–847–0951) on your right. The pastry shop in the rear has great gourmet goodies, cold beverages, and outdoor seating with a view of the Delaware River. The owner, Chef Tell Erhardt, is not just bicycle-friendly; he is an accomplished racing cyclist. See if you can get him to tell you how he took third place in a grueling six-day race in Germany in 1959.

If you wish to stay overnight to allow yourself more time to explore the full length of the canal's towpath, two inns are worth noting. One is in Uhlerstown within a mile south of the turn at mile 8.1: EverMay-on-the-Delaware country inn (610–294–9100) for dining and lodging. The other is the Bridgeton House Bed and Breakfast, just 5.2 miles into the ride. (*Note:* For cyclists who would enjoy making a long-weekend minivacation of riding from one inn to another along the Delaware, the Bridgeton's owner, Beatrice Briggs, can arrange to transport luggage from one inn to the next. Both inns provide support for bicyclists and are within walking distance from good dining alternatives. For more information, call the Bridgeton House at 610–982–5856.)

The Basics

Start: Kintnersville, at the parking lot of the post office on Rte. 611, just 500 feet off Rte. 32. To get to the start from Easton, take Rte. 611S to Kintnersville.
Length: 17.5 miles.
Terrain: Generally flat to gently rolling, except for one steep climb. Traffic is very light on the second half of the route, although it can be moderately heavy on the first half; to avoid most cars for the first 8 miles, ride on the canal towpath.
Food: Kintnersville and a bit farther down the road; stock up on both snacks and drinks near the beginning.

Miles & Directions

- 0.0 Turn left out of the post office parking lot onto Rte. 611N (Easton Rd.).
- 0.1 Bear right at the Y intersection onto Rte. 32S (River Rd.). If you want to take the Delaware Canal towpath, 0.5 mile down Rte. 32S, use the footbridge on your left to cross the canal, and turn right onto the towpath to parallel Rte. 32S. The wide Delaware River will be on your left. On the right at mile 4.0 is Chef Tell Manor House, your last change for food. On the left at mile 5.2 is the Bridgeton House Bed and Breakfast.
- 8.1 Turn right onto Uhlerstown Hill Rd., just after the Uhlers-

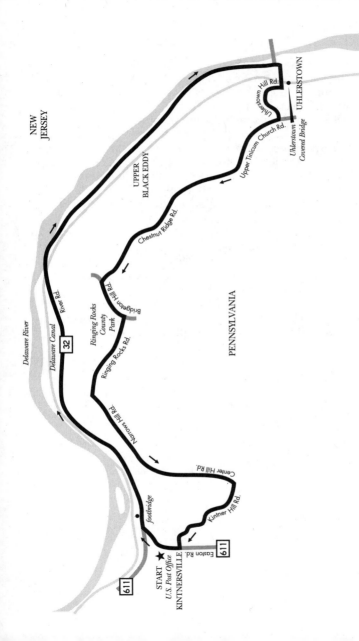

town-Frenchtown Bridge over the Delaware River. At mile 8.4 you'll pass through a covered bridge that was built in 1832. On the other side of the bridge, follow the road as it takes a sharp right. It rises very steeply and the pavement deteriorates. But at mile 8.8 it will level out again and then head downhill.

- 9.2 Turn right onto Upper Tinicum Church Rd.; this is the right turn immediately *before* the T intersection (with Perry Auger Rd.). At the Bridgeton Township line (mile 10.7), Upper Tinicum Church Road changes its name to Chestnut Ridge Rd.
- 12.3 Turn left at the T intersection onto Bridgeton Hill Rd.
- 12.8 Turn right onto Ringing Rocks Rd. At mile 13.0 is the entrance to Ringing Rocks County Park on your right.
- 13.9 Turn left at the T intersection onto Narrows Hill Rd., which climbs gently but steadily; it changes its name to Center Hill Rd. when you cross into Nockamixon Township.
- 16.1 Turn right onto Kintner Hill Rd., which is a fairly steep descent with winding switchbacks.
- 17.2 Turn right at the T intersection onto unmarked Rte. 611N (Easton Rd.). Watch for traffic as you enter Kintnersville.
- 17.5 Turn left into the post office parking lot.

Washington, D.C.

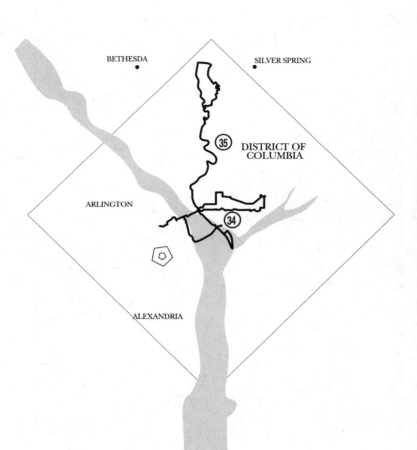

BETHESDA

SILVER SPRING

(35) DISTRICT OF COLUMBIA

ARLINGTON

(34)

ALEXANDRIA

Washington, D.C.

34

Washington Monuments Ramble

Washington, D.C.—Arlington, Va.—Washington, D.C.

In 1988 *Bicycling* magazine named the District of Columbia one of the top ten cycling cities in the United States. No wonder, as it has more than 670 miles of paved paths exclusively for bicycles and pedestrians and another 480 miles of bicycle routes marked on roads and streets shared with automobiles.

As you will see on this urban route, many of Washington's most famous monuments, memorials, and museums are accessible on two wheels, giving you the option of stopping where and when you wish without wondering where to park the car. You'll pedal right past the Lincoln Memorial, the Arlington Cemetery, the Washington Monument, nine Smithsonian museums (all of which are free), the Supreme Court, the U.S. Capitol, Union Station, the FBI Building, the White House, and the Vietnam Veterans Memorial.

Although this virtually flat 22-mile ramble can be ridden in only an hour or two, there is so much to see that you may well decide to take several days. This ride, which combines two routes in Michael Leccese's best-seller *Short Bike Rides in and around Washington, D.C.* (The Globe Pequot Press, third edition, 1996), is within the ability of even novice or out-of-shape cyclists. The route was verified by Shari Lawrence Pfleeger of Washington, D.C.

The most beautiful time of year for cycling in the District is the spring, especially in mid-April when thousands of blooming cherry and dogwood trees on both sides of the Potomac River are adorned in their lacy pink finery. Late autumn, with its crisper air and fiery leaves, is also a lovely time. Even on a mild winter's day this short outing can be done before early darkness falls. Avoid summer, however, when steaming humidity combines with automobile exhaust to make outdoor exercise in the city less than fun or healthful. And avoid mid-day during high tourist season if you don't enjoy riding in heavy traffic.

The Basics

Start: Washington, D.C., at the Harry T. Thompson Boat Center just off Virginia Ave. and the Rock Creek Potomac Pkwy. NW. (Bicycles can be rented at the boat center.) To get to the start from the north, take Rock Creek Potomac Pkwy. south to Thompson's parking lot and turn right. From the Mall, take Virginia Ave. west across Rock Creek Potomac Pkwy. to Thompson's parking lot.

Length: 22 miles. It may be combined as noted below with the "Rock Creek Park Cruise" (Ride 35) for a cruise of 38.8 miles.

Terrain: Flat except for Arlington Cemetery and Capitol Hill. Traffic ranges from nonexistent on the paved bicycle paths to very heavy on the main streets.

Food: Water and rest rooms at the start. Food is available at various spots on the Mall and at Arlington Cemetery.

Miles & Directions

- ■ 0.0 Turn right (southeast) out of the Harry T. Thompson Boat Center onto the bike path heading toward the Watergate apartments. The Potomac River will be on your right, and the Kennedy Center on your left. At mile 1.3 dismount and walk through two short bridge underpasses. Continue straight through the traffic circle at the John Ericsson Monument at Independence Ave. and Ohio Dr. SW.
- ■ 1.4 Proceed southeast on Ohio Dr., a one-way road with many potholes.
- ■ 2.3 After crossing over a graceful bridge with gargoyle foun-

tains, turn right at the circular flower bed to stay on Ohio Dr., following signs to East Potomac Park (Hains Point). Cross under four bridges for cars, Amtrak, and Metrorail.

- 2.9 Turn left at the stop sign onto Buckeye Dr. to follow a one-way loop around East Potomac Park. Follow the road as it makes a sharp right around Hains Point and passes Seward Johnson's 1980 statue *The Awakening.* Now you're headed back north, parallel to the Potomac River. At the end of the one-way loop, continue straight onto Ohio Dr. Pass again under the four bridges, following the signs to the Jefferson Memorial.
- 7.4 At the parking lot for the Jefferson Memorial, look for a curb cut leading to the wide, smooth bike path over the 14th St. Bridge. Cross the bridge.
- 8.0 At the base of the bridge on the Virginia side, bear right onto a bike path that parallels the George Washington Memorial Pkwy. You're now on the Mt. Vernon Trail, with the Potomac River on your right and the Boundary Channel on your left. Pass Lady Bird Johnson Park, with its 2,700 dogwoods and one million daffodils. Continue on the bike path toward the Arlington Memorial Bridge.
- 9.2 Bear left to avoid passing under the Arlington Memorial Bridge. Cross the George Washington Memorial Pkwy. at the crosswalks. Cross the traffic circle and turn left onto the sidewalk paralleling Memorial Drive.
- 10.2 Turn right onto Schley Dr. to enter Arlington National Cemetery.
- 10.3 Bear left onto Sherman Dr.
- 10.5 Bear right onto Meigs Rd., which leads to Arlington House (Custis-Lee Mansion).
- 10.9 Turn around at the gate to Ft. Myer. Retrace your route back to Arlington Memorial Bridge. Cross the bridge back to Washington, D.C., by riding on the sidewalk. Walk your bike across the traffic circle to the grounds of the Lincoln Memorial. Ride up a short road (where the sign reads TAXIS ONLY) to the Lincoln Memorial.
- 13.5 Facing east, head down a slight slope past a souvenir stand on your right and ride on the bike path parallel to the 0.5-mile-

long Reflecting Pool. Continue past the fountains and jog to the left on the sidewalk to the 17th St. pedestrian crossing (traffic light).

- 14.2 Take the bike path heading directly uphill to the Washington Monument. Ride on the bike/foot paths across 15th and 14th streets to Jefferson Dr.
- 15.0 Follow one-way Jefferson Dr. along the National Mall, past nine Smithsonian museums (including the Smithsonian Castle, the National Air and Space Museum, and the National Gallery of Art), an ice-skating rink, and a Dept. of Agriculture building.
- 15.9 Turn right onto 3rd St. and then immediately left onto Maryland Ave. On the right is the U.S. Botanical Gardens. Ride past the statue of James Garfield on the grounds of the U.S. Capitol.
- 16.1 Turn right onto footpaths that bear left around the south side of the U.S. Capitol to the east front, passing the Library of Congress and the Supreme Court. Pass through stone gates.
- 16.4 Turn right onto E. Capitol St.
- 16.5 Turn left onto 1st St. Ride about 0.75 mile to Columbus Circle in front of Union Station.
- 17.0 Turn right onto Columbus Circle and left into the service road in front of the train station. After exiting the station area on the service road, turn left. At mile 17.3, take the second right onto Louisiana Ave.
- 17.7 Bear right at the end of Louisiana Ave. onto Constitution Ave. Two blocks later bear right onto Pennsylvania Ave., riding along the same route the presidential inaugural parade has always taken since the inauguration of Thomas Jefferson. Pass the Canadian Embassy on your right, the National Archives on your left, the FBI Building on your right, and the Old (1897) Post Office on your left. *Note:* There are rest rooms at the post office.
- 18.8 Turn right onto 13th St. and immediately left onto Pennsylvania Ave. The park on your left, Freedom Plaza, often has entertainment at lunchtime. Pass the National Theatre and the Willard Hotel. Ahead of you at 15th St. NW, you will see barriers and a DO NOT ENTER sign. The sign is only for automobiles. You

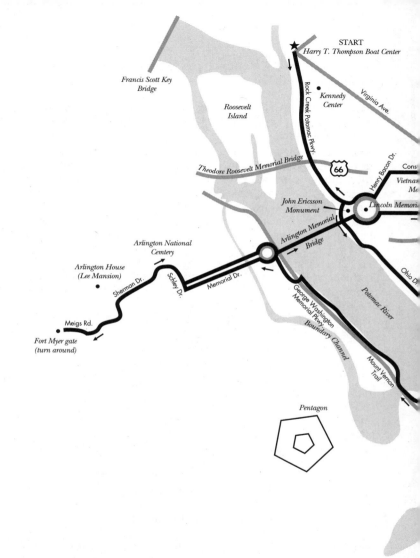

START
Harry T. Thompson Boat Center

*Francis Scott Key
Bridge*

*Kennedy
Center*

Virginia Ave.

Rock Creek Potomac Pkwy.

*Roosevelt
Island*

Theodore Roosevelt Memorial Bridge

66

Henry Bacon Dr.

Cons

*Vietnam
Me*

*John Ericsson
Monument*

Lincoln Memoria

*Arlington Memorial
Bridge*

*Arlington National
Cemetery*

Ohio D

*Arlington House
(Lee Mansion)*

Sherman Dr.

Schley Dr.

Memorial Dr.

Potomac River

Meigs Rd.

*George Washington
Memorial Pkwy.
Boundary Channel*

*Fort Myer gate
(turn around)*

*Mount Vernon
Trail*

Pentagon

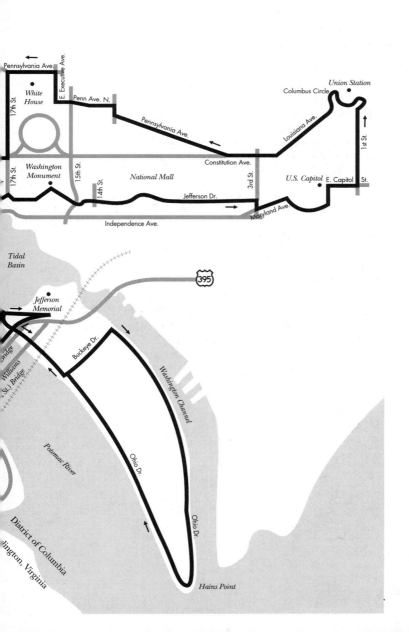

should cross 15th St. and continue along Alexander Hamilton Pl.
- 19.2 Turn right onto E. Executive Park. At the iron gates, turn right onto the sidewalk to arrive at Pennsylvania Ave. and view the White House. Turn left onto Pennsylvania Ave. NW—bicycles are allowed in the road, even though automobiles are not. Pass the White House on your left, then Blair House (the lodging for presidential guests) on your right. The Renwick Gallery, another Smithsonian museum, is on the righthand corner.
- 19.5 Turn left onto 17th St. and ride 3 long blocks (passing the Corcoran Gallery and the Organization of American States Building).
- 20.1 Cross Constitution Ave. and turn right onto a parallel bike path, passing Constitution Gardens and the Vietnam Veterans Memorial.
- 20.6 Turn left onto Henry Bacon Dr. to the Lincoln Memorial. Return to the Ericsson statue. Turn right onto the bike path to retrace the route back to the Thompson Boat Center.

To combine this route with the "Rock Creek Park Cruise" (Ride 35) for a total length of 38.8 miles, continue north past the boat center and pick up the directions at mile 0.0 of the Rock Creek Park ride.

35

Rock Creek Park Cruise

*Thompson Boat Center—Pierce Mill and Art Barn—
Rock Creek Park—Pierce Mill and Art Barn—
Thompson Boat Center*

The Rock Creek Park bicycle path is one of the best-known classic routes of Washington, D.C., cyclists. Right within the center of the nation's urban capital, the bike path is an escape to the country with deep wooded glades, cooling even in the hot summer's humidity. During the week the bike path is a regular commuter run for city cyclists riding to work from the north; on weekends it is a favorite of recreational strollers and hikers as well.

This ride, a combination of two routes in Michael Leccese's marvelously written best-seller *Short Bike Rides in and around Washington, D.C.* (The Globe Pequot Press, third edition, 1996), takes you north into the hilly reaches of Rock Creek Park—a superb aerobic workout for stronger riders. The ride can be turned into a longer cruise of 38.8 miles by joining it with the "Washington Monuments Ramble" (Ride 34). Ride carefully on nice-weather weekends, as the recreational traffic can be heavy and the path is both bumpy and narrow in spots—sometimes only 8 feet wide. But riding more slowly also gives you more time to take in its refreshing, rustic beauty. The route was verified by Shari Lawrence Pfleeger of Washington, D.C.

The most beautiful time of year for cycling in the District is the spring, especially in mid-April when the cherries and dogwoods are abloom. Autumn and even mild winter days are also good times to be cycling in D.C. Summer, however, is less than ideal, as steaming humidity combines with automobile exhaust to make outdoor exercise in the city physically stressful—and not much fun.

The Basics

Start: Washington, D.C., at the Harry T. Thompson Boat Center just off Virginia Ave. and the Rock Creek Potomac Pkwy. NW. (Bicycles can be rented at the boat center.) To get to the start from the north, take Rock Creek Potomac Pkwy. south to Thompson's parking lot and turn right. From the Mall take Virginia Ave. west across Rock Creek Potomac Pkwy. to Thompson's parking lot.

Length: 16.8 miles. It may be combined as noted above with the "Washington Monuments Ramble" (Ride 34) for a longer cruise of 38.8 miles.

Terrain: Rolling south of Pierce Mill and Art Barn; very hilly north of Pierce Mill and Art Barn. Automobile traffic ranges from nonexistent on the paved bicycle paths to heavy on the main streets; parts of Beach Dr. are closed to traffic on Saturdays and Sundays. Note that you're likely to share the bike path with many joggers and strollers on weekends.

Food: Water and rest rooms at the start and at Pierce Mill and Art Barn. None elsewhere on the route, so bring snacks or a picnic lunch.

Miles & Directions

■ 0.0 From the boat center cross the short one-lane bridge to the parking lot. At the curb cut, turn left (north) onto the Rock Creek Park bike path, keeping the Watergate apartment complex and the Kennedy Center on your right and the Potomac River on your left. For the next 3 miles, the path runs parallel to the Rock Creek Potomac Pkwy., crossing Rock Creek five times via bridges. (At mile 1.5 you may turn left onto the Massachusetts Ave. bike path and proceed 0.5 mile to reach the

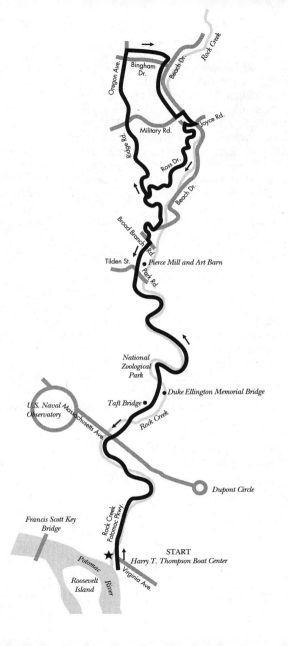

U.S. Naval Observatory.) After passing the exercise course that parallels the route, dismount and cross Rock Creek Potomac Pkwy. at the crosswalk and continue north.

- 2.2 Bear right at the fork in the path and ride under the arches of the Duke Ellington Memorial Bridge.
- 3.3 Just before the tunnel, turn left and ride through a gate onto a smooth path paralleling Rock Creek. (At the service road crossing, you can, if you wish, take a short detour to your left over a stone bridge into the National Zoological Park.) At mile 4.0 pass Pierce Mill and Art Barn and waterfalls, a nice spot for a snack.
- 4.3 Turn left onto the two-lane Broad Branch Rd. and make an immediate right onto Ridge Rd. Climb a steep hill for 0.5 mile.
- 4.0 Bear left at the sign for the Nature Center to stay on Ridge Rd.
- 5.6 At the Military Rd. traffic light, keep heading straight onto Oregon Ave. or take the bike path parallel to it.
- 6.3 Turn right onto Bingham Dr. or take the parallel bike path.
- 6.6 Turn right onto the Beach Dr. bike path.
- 7.5 At the four-way stop, turn right onto Joyce Rd. and make an immediate left onto Ross Dr.
- 8.3 Bear left onto Ridge Rd. near the Nature Center.
- 8.9 Turn left onto the two-lane Broad Branch Rd. and make an immediate right into the bike path, retracing your route south. At mile 13.1 pass the Pierce Mill and Art Barn parking area. At mile 16.8 arrive back at the Thompson Boat Center.

To combine this route with the "Washington Monuments Ramble" (Ride 34) for a total length of 38.8 miles, continue south past the boat center and pick up the directions at mile 0.0 of the monuments ride.

Virginia

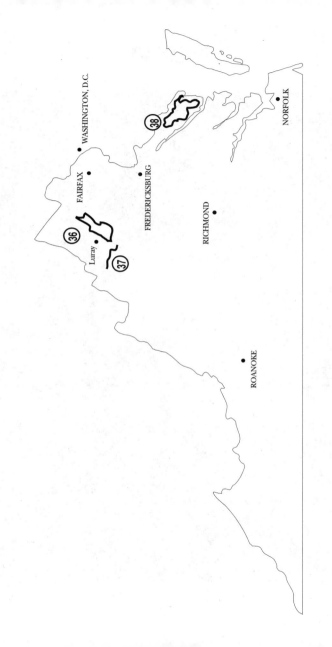

Virginia

36

Shenandoah Valley–Skyline Drive Classic

*Luray—Thornton Gap—Front Royal—Browntown
Bentonville—Luray*

This 72-mile classic will allow you to explore two of Northern Virginia's most famous areas: the lovely Shenandoah Valley and the northernmost third of the 105-mile-long Skyline Drive, which connects to the 469-mile-long Blue Ridge Parkway. You'll also have a chance to tour Luray Caverns (540–743–6551), arguably the most famous caverns in the eastern United States. Another attraction is historic Front Royal, where Stonewall Jackson fought a decisive Civil War battle during his brilliant valley campaign of 1862, and where today the south fork of the Shenandoah River is considered one of the finest canoeing streams in the East. This route, one of three devised and contributed by Mike Arnette of Powhatan, Virginia, is one of several offered by his commercial outfit Old Dominion Bicycle Tours (804–598–1808); a group tour with Old Dominion features arrangements made for overnight stays, meals, and mechanical support from a following sag wagon.

The most challenging part of this ride is the 2,000-foot climb up to Skyline Drive, which follows the ridge of the Blue Ridge Mountains. The second most challenging part of the ride is the 30-mile segment preceding the descent into Front Royal, because Skyline Drive gains and loses several thousand feet in altitude as it dances back and forth across both the Appalachian Trail and the border of Rappahannock County and Page and Warren counties. The compensation, of course, is the spectacular vistas alternately to your left and right over the 195,000-acre Shenandoah National Park, which encompasses the full 105 miles of Skyline Drive, along with the lovely dogwoods, redbuds, and rhododendrons that may be in bloom. The speed limit on the Drive is a mere 35 miles per hour—which, *caution!* bikes can exceed on the downhills—and the curvy, forested, two-lane road is well-marked and well-paved. Watch for deer, however, which can bound down out of the hills scarcely 30 feet in front of you! Also, keep your eyes alert for bear.

To take full advantage of the ride's attractions, you might consider breaking the tour into two portions. The first day would consist of a vigorous 42-mile challenge with plenty of climbing along Skyline Drive and an overnight in Front Royal (which would also give you a chance to visit Skyline Caverns, 703–635–4545). The second day would be a more relaxing 30-mile cruise back to Luray, leaving plenty of time to explore the caverns.

In Luray, possible places to spend the night include the Minslyn Inn (540–743–5105 or 800–296–5105) at mile 1.0, Yogi Bear's Jellystone Campground (540–743–4002 or 800–420–6679) at mile 5.3, and Brookside Restaurant and Cabins (540–743–5698) at mile 6.0; the single campground you'll pass on Skyline Drive—Mathews Arm at mile 20.3—is closed at least through 1998 for budgetary reasons. In Front Royal try the Pioneer Motel (540–635–4784) or the Skyline Resort Motel (540–635–5354). Those preferring being pampered at a bed-and-breakfast inn in Front Royal might try the Chester House (540–635–3937 or 800–621–0441), the Killahelin (540–636–7335 or 800–847–6132), or the Woodward House (540–635–7010 or 800–635–7011); seven miles south of Luray, consider Jordan Hollow Inn (540–778–2285) or The Ruby Rose Inn (540–778–4680) in Stanley. For more information, call the local Chamber of Commerce either in Luray (540–743–3915) or Front Royal (540–635–3185), the Foothills Travel Association (540–347–4414), or the Shenandoah Valley Travel Association (540–740–3132).

The Basics

Start: Luray, at the parking lot for Luray Caverns. To get there from I–81, turn east onto U.S. Rte. 211, which goes directly to the center of Luray. From I–66, take Rte. 340S through Front Royal all the way to the center of Luray. By either route, follow the prominent signs for the caverns.

Length: 72 miles.

Terrain: Ranges from rolling in the Shenandoah Valley to very hilly up to and along the Blue Ridge. There is one 4.7-mile-long climb from Luray (altitude 400 feet) up to Skyline Drive (altitude 2,300 feet); subsequent climbing on Skyline Drive reaches a peak altitude of nearly 3,400 feet. In the summer, traffic can be heavy on Rte. 211 from Luray to Skyline Drive; it is generally light along Skyline Drive and in the Shenandoah Valley, excepting for moderate traffic along Rte. 340 back toward Luray.

Food: Many options in Luray and Front Royal. Be forewarned: On Skyline Drive, the only places to get food are the Panorama Restaurant and Store (mile 10.6) just before Thornton Gap and at Elkwallow Wayside (mile 18.0), where there is a grill and camp store; thereafter, it's a 24-mile dry stretch until Front Royal. In the Shenandoah Valley there are scattered convenience stores.

Miles & Directions

- 0.0 Start at the entrance to Luray Caverns and ride toward the exit. At mile 0.1, turn right out of Luray Caverns parking lot onto the access road. At the stop sign at mile 0.2, keep heading straight to cross U.S. Rte. 211 Bypass, using extreme caution at this high-speed intersection.

- 0.3 Turn left onto U.S. Rte. 211 Business (West Main St.). At mile 0.9, you'll pass a convenience store and at mile 1.0 the Minslyn Inn on your right. At mile 1.4, cross Rte. 340, and then look for the Luray Visitor Center on your right.

- 2.0 Bear left to stay on Rte. 211 (Main St.). At mile 2.5, ride with caution as Rte. 211 Business becomes the four-lane divided Lee Highway. In 0.5 mile, you'll leave Luray.

- 4.2 Bear right to stay on U.S. Rte 211 (Lee Hwy.) toward Skyline Drive, where Rte. 211 Business joins Rte. 211 Bypass. At mile 6.2, begin the 4.7-mile climb up to Skyline Drive. At mile 10.6, pass the Panorama Restaurant and Store on your right, your penultimate chance to fuel up.
- 10.9 Turn left toward Skyline Drive. At mile 11.0, pass through Thornton Gap Entrance Center onto Skyline Drive; there even bicycles have to pay a few dollars to continue on the Drive. You can also obtain maps and other information here. Just after passing through the center, bear left on the drive to head toward Front Royal; you are now at an altitude of 2,300 feet. At mile 18.3, pass Elkwallow Wayside (2,445 foot altitude), which also has a camp store and food service—the last opportunity until Front Royal. At mile 21.5, pause at Hogback Overlook, which on clear days offers a spectacular view of the meandering Shenandoah River; at an altitude of 3,385 feet, this is the highest point on the route. At mile 42.0, coast down through the Front Royal (North) Entrance Station, leaving Skyline Drive.
- 42.6 Turn left (west) at the T intersection onto U.S. Rte. 340.

Note: If you are staying at the Pioneer Motel or Skyline Resort Motel, bear right (east) instead onto U.S. Rte. 340 and enter Front Royal; the motels are another mile ahead. The next day, to continue the ride, return on Rte. 340 to this spot and add 2 miles to your total mileage.

- 42.8 Turn left onto Rte. 649 (Browntown Rd.), passing the entrance to Skyline Caverns. Pass through the hamlets of Glen Echo and Boyds Mill, neither of which offers any services.
- 50.0 Turn right onto Rte 613 (Bentonville-Browntown Rd.) in Browntown (no services).
- 55.5 Turn left at the T intersection onto U.S. Rte. 340; watch for moderate traffic. In 0.5 mile, enter the town of Bentonville (no services).
- 61.8 Turn left onto Rte. 622 and then make an immediate right onto Rte. 611.
- 64.1 Turn right onto Rte. 661.

- 65.7 Turn left at the T intersection onto U.S. Rte. 340 in the hamlet of Big Spring (no services).
- 70.7 Turn right at the stop light to stay on Rte. 340, here called Broad Street.
- 71.8 Turn right onto the unnamed access road into the entrance of Luray Caverns park. At the stop sign at mile 71.9, take care in crossing the high-speed intersection with Rte. 211 Bypass.
- 72.0 Turn left into the parking lot for Luray Caverns.

37

Stanley to New Market Challenge

Stanley—New Market—Stanley

Even though this ride totals only 46 miles, it definitely does not rank as a cruise: Each direction, you will be crawling right over Massanutten Mountain for about 700 feet of climbing and descent in about 5 miles with some grades steeper than 7 percent. The good news is, this out-and-back ride through Page and Shenandoah counties divides neatly in half. Animal riders loving steep climbs can leave Stanley to lunch in New Market and still be back for dinner. More leisurely sightseers may elect to stay overnight at New Market to take in the many local attractions, such as nearby Shenandoah Caverns (540–477–3115) or Endless Caverns (540–740–3993). On the mountain, you'll be riding through the cooling pines of the George Washington National Forest (540–433–2491); elsewhere, you'll be cruising past cattle and poultry farms.

Known initially as Cross Roads because it was the intersection of two principal Indian trails, New Market was renamed in 1796 after New Market, England, as both were the sites of race tracks. New Market's place in history was secured in 1864 during a fierce Civil War battle in the rain and mud that resulted in a Confederate Army victory. History buffs may want to time their visit for Mother's Day weekend for New Market Heritage Days or for the Battle Reenactment by VMI cadets. But any time of the year, you can learn more about the Battle of New Market at the Museum of American Cavalry (540–740–3959), the Battlefield Military Museum (540–740–8065), and the Battlefield Historical Park and Hall of Valor Museum (540–740–3102), all in New Market. For a change of pace, also check out the Bedrooms of U.S. Museum (540–740–3512), where eleven different rooms show every major period in American history.

This ride is one of three devised and contributed by Mike Arnette of Powhatan, Virginia. If you prefer a group tour's prearrangements for overnight stays, meals, and mechanical support from a following sag wagon, you can take the same trip with Arnette's commercial outfit, Old Dominion Bicycle Tours (804–598–1808).

For those making a weekend of the ride—which is also easily joined to the Shenandoah Valley–Skyline Drive Classic (Ride 36) at Luray—there are two places in Stanley near the start: The Ruby Rose Inn (540–778–4680) or the Jordan Hollow Farm Inn (540–778–2285), which is an alternate starting place. Seven miles north on Route 340 Business in Luray, there are many other options (see Ride 36 for more information). In New Market, choose from the Days Inn (540–740–4100), the Battlefield Motel (800–296–6835), the Best Western (540–477–2911), and the Quality Inn (540–740–3141). For those preferring to camp in New Market, try the Endless Caverns Campground (540–740–3993) or the Rancho Campground (540–740–8313), both near Endless Caverns. New Market also has some bed-and-breakfasts, including the Cross Roads Inn (540–740–4157), A Touch of Country (540–740–8030), and the Red Shutter Farmhouse (540–740–4281). For more information, call the New Market Chamber of Commerce at (540) 740–3132.

The Basics

Start: The parking lot of The Ruby Rose Inn in Stanley, Virginia. To get there from I–81, take U.S. Rte. 211E all the way to Luray (you will actually pass through New Market and get a preview of Massanutten Mountain). Turn south onto U.S. Rte. 340 Business and drive 7 miles to Stanley; turn left onto Rte. 689 where Rte. 340 bends right, and 0.3 mile later turn left into the parking lot of The

Ruby Rose Inn. From I–66, take U.S. Rte. 340S through Front Royal and Luray to Stanley, and follow the directions above to The Ruby Rose Inn.

Length: 46 miles, with optional round-trips to Endless Caverns or Shenandoah Caverns of an additional 9 or 13 miles.

Terrain: Mostly rolling at either end with one 500-foot mountain in the middle; traffic is light on the back roads, but it can be heavy at time on Rtes. 211 and 340. There is a three-lane highway going up both sides of Massanutten Mountain.

Food: Many options in New Market. In Stanley, there is a diner on Rte. 340, a convenience store at the intersection of Rtes. 689 and 340, and a restaurant at the Jordan Hollow Inn. There are also a couple more convenience stores along the way.

Miles & Directions

- Turn right out of the parking lot of The Ruby Rose Inn onto Rte. 689.
- 0.3 Turn left at the T intersection onto U.S. Rte. 340.
- 0.4 Make the first left onto Judy Lane Rd. (unmarked Rte. 623).
- 1.0 Turn right at the T intersection onto Rte. 622.
- 1.5 Go straight over the railroad tracks on Rte. 622, and then immediately bear left onto Rte. 638. Follow Rte. 638 through several right-angle turns. At mile 2.2, pass a convenience store.
- 4.7 Bear right onto Rte. 650, entering the hamlet of Honeyville, which has no services.
- 5.5 Turn right onto U.S. Rte. 340.
- 5.8 Make the first left onto Rte. 616. At mile 8.7, you'll enter the village of Leaksville (no services).
- 8.8 Turn left onto Rte. 646.
- 10.8 Turn left onto U.S. Rte. 211.
- 11.6 Make the first left after crossing over the Shenandoah River onto Rte. 615, entering the hamlet of Salem (no services).
- 13.9 Turn left at the T intersection onto U.S. Rte. 211. At mile 14.5, keep heading straight to stay on U.S. Rte. 211. This is

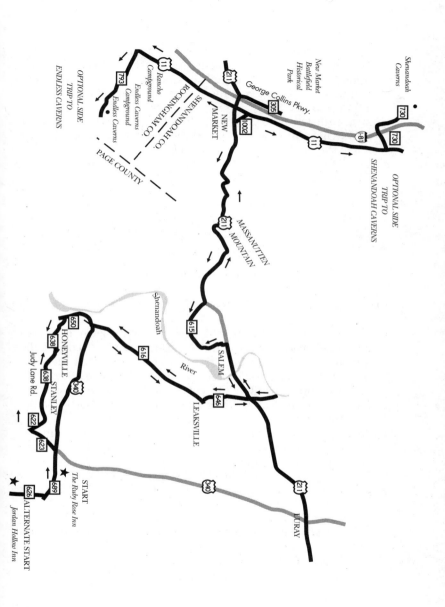

where the serious climbing begins through the forest. At mile 16.4, pass another convenience store. At mile 17.3 near the summit, you'll enter Shenandoah County, marked by the Massanutten Visitor Center of the George Washington National Forest on your left.

- 20.5 Turn left onto Rte. 1002. In about 500 feet, you'll enter New Market. At mile 20.7, keep heading straight onto Old Cross Rd. to stay on Rte. 1002.
- 21.5 At the traffic light, head straight onto U.S. Rte. 211 (West Old Cross Rd.), crossing Rte. 11 (Congress St.).

*Note: For an optional ride to Endless Caverns (540–896–CAVE or 800–544–CAVE) and the two campgrounds, turn **left** (south) instead onto Rte. 11; turn left onto Rte. 793 to Endless Caverns—an additional distance of 4.5 miles each way.*

*Note: For an optional ride to Shenandoah Caverns (540–477–3115), turn **right** (north) instead onto Rte. 11; turn left onto Rte. 730 to Shenandoah Caverns—an additional distance of 6.5 miles each way.*

- 21.9 Turn right onto Rte. 305 (George Collins Pkwy.), a dead-end access road paralleling the west side of I–81; you'll pass the Museum of American Cavalry on your left and then the Days Inn. At mile 22.3, you'll pass the New Market Battlefield Military Museum. At mile 23.0, you'll reach the terminus of the main ride at the Hall of Valor Museum and New Market Battlefield Historical Park.
- 23.0 To return to Stanley, retrace your entire route. From the Hall of Valor Museum and New Market Battlefield Historical Park, head south on Rte. 305 (George Collins Pkwy.).
- 24.1 Turn left onto U.S. Rte. 211 (West Old Cross Rd.).
- 24.5 Head straight at the traffic light onto Rte. 1002 (Old Cross Rd.).
- 25.5 Turn right at the T intersection onto U.S. Rte. 211. In a mile or two, begin climbing. At mile 28.7, you'll reach the summit.
- 32.1 Turn right onto Rte. 615.

- 34.4 Turn right onto U.S. Rte. 211.
- 35.2 Make the first right after crossing the Shenandoah River onto Rte. 646.
- 37.2 Turn right at the T intersection onto Rte. 616.
- 40.2 Turn right at the T intersection onto U.S. Rte. 340.
- 40.5 Make the first left onto Rte. 650.
- 41.3 Make the first left onto Rte. 638.
- 44.5 Turn right at the T intersection onto Rte. 622.
- 45.0 Make the first left onto Rte. 623 (unmarked Judy Lane Rd.).
- 45.6 Make the first right onto U.S. Rte. 340.
- 45.7 Turn right onto Rte. 689.
- 46.0 Turn left into the parking lot for The Ruby Rose Inn.

Northern Neck
Multiday Cruise

Montross—Warsaw—Lancaster—Gonyon
Reedville—Heathsville—Village—Montross

Tucked away in the upper Tidewater, on a peninsula created by the Potomac and Rappahannock rivers and the Chesapeake Bay, lies Virginia's Northern Neck. Although only an hour from Washington, D.C., it is geographically isolated. Thus, the Northern Neck has been largely bypassed by the inexorable march of twentieth-century progress, with its highways and subdivisions.

What a blessing for cyclists! On this ride through Lancaster, Northumberland, Richmond, and Westmoreland counties, you'll pedal past homes dating to the late eighteenth and nineteenth centuries, farmhouses in the middle of carefully tended fields, and watermen still using time-honored traditional methods of harvesting fish, crab, and oysters from the bay and rivers. The byways (not highways) follow old Indian trails and colonial roads, and on the entire peninsula there are only eight traffic lights.

Because of its unique geography, the Northern Neck's history has focused on transportation by sails or steam engines rather than by wheels. Traces of old wharves and turn-of-the-century houses still remain in several riverfront villages. Even today, the Northern Neck has 12,000 boats registered, so that just about every family has means of putting fresh seafood on the table. Don't miss out on the fresh crabs—especially soft-shell—served at the local restaurants.

The optional 26-mile round-trip from Gonyon to Reedville is

worth doing, not only for the Reedville Fishermen's Museum (804–453–6529), but also because Reedville is the seaside town where you can catch a day cruise to remote Tangier Island or Smith Island, where a version of Elizabethan English is still spoken. For cruise reservations, call either Smith Island & Chesapeake Bay Cruises at (804) 453–3251 or Tangier Island & Rappahannock River Cruises at (804) 453–BOAT (2628).

This Northern Neck route is based on two- and five-day rides offered by Mike Arnette of Powhatan, Virginia, as commercial tours through his company Old Dominion Bicycle Tours (804–598–1808), which specializes in Virginia bicycle tours. While the route can be ridden as a classic by a strong cyclist in a day, Arnette recommends making at least a long weekend of it to slow down to sniff the roses; one recommended four-day cruise of the full 143 miles for a moderately strong rider would be Montross to Lancaster (about 50 miles), Lancaster to Reedville (about 40 miles), a day cruise (a rest day), and Reedville to Montross (about 53 miles). Overnight stays are possible at the Washington and Lee Motel in Montross (804–493–8093), the Greenwood (804–333–4353) in Warsaw at mile 19.0, the Inn at Levelfields (804–435–6887 or 800–238–5578) in Lancaster around mile 50.0, the Fisherman's Inn (804–453–4309 or 804–453–5127) in Gonyon at mile 77.1, and the Bay Motel (804–453–5171) and numerous bed-and-breakfast inns in Reedville on the optional side trip, such as The Gables (804–453–5209) around mile 90.0. Those preferring to rough it—although it could scarcely be called that with hot showers and a pool!—might try camping at Warsaw's Heritage Park Resort (804–333–4038) or Reedville's Chesapeake Bay/Smith Island KOA (804–453–3430).

History buffs, take note: The start at Montross is only a few miles from the birthplaces of both George Washington, in Oak Grove (804–224–1732), and Robert E. Lee, at the Stratford Hall Plantation (804–493–8038); also in Montross, be sure to check out the historical exhibits at the Westmoreland County Museum and Visitor Center (804–493–8440). The Richmond County Museum (804–333–3607 or 804–394–4901) in Warsaw displays the agricultural history of the region. Lancaster boasts the Mary Ball Washing-

251

ton Museum (804–462–7280), which depicts life over the Northern Neck's 350-year history. In Heathsville, you can watch the restoration of the 110-foot-long Rice's Hotel/Hughlett's Tavern (804–529–6224).

The Basics

Start: Montross, Virginia, at the Washington & Lee Motel on Rte. 3. Take I–95 to Fredericksburg and then take Rte. 3E to Montross.
Length: 66, 117, or 143 miles.
Terrain: Flat to rolling; traffic is light on most roads, but moderate on Rtes. 3 and 360, and can be heavy on weekends around Reedville. For a multiday tour, plan to arrive at Reedville midweek.
Food: Food is available in the major towns and at scattered convenience stores. *Note:* The Fisherman's Inn does not serve any meals, but has a kitchen available for guests' use; the nearest stores are in Reedville.

Miles & Directions

- 0.0 Turn right out of the Washington & Lee Motel onto Rte. 3. You'll revisit Rte. 3 at several points along the Northern Neck.
- 2.0 Turn left onto Rte. 622 (Peach Grove Ln.). In 0.5 mile, you'll enter Richmond County.
- 3.2 Bear left onto Rte 638 (Oak Row Rd.).
- 5.9 Turn left at the stop sign onto Rte. 624 (Newland Rd.). At mile 7.0, you'll enter the village of Newland. At mile 13.9, cross over the wooden bridge.
- 14.5 Turn left onto Rte. 621 (Chestnut Hill Rd.).
- 16.2 Turn right at the T intersection onto Rte. 690 (Menokin Rd.).
- 19.1 Turn right onto Main St. (Rte. 3—the same one that passed through Montross) in Warsaw.
- 19.5 Turn left onto Rtes. 3/360 (Richmond Rd.). You'll pass

convenience stores at miles 19.7 and 20.2.

- 20.3 Turn right at the stop sign onto Rte. 3 (Historyland Hwy.). Cross over a bridge at mile 22.9 and pass a convenience store at mile 23.1.
- 25.7 Turn right onto Folly Neck Rd. (Rte. 614).
- 28.2 Turn left to stay on Rte. 614 (Folly Neck Rd. becomes Beaverdam Rd. on the curve). You'll have done it right if you cross over a bridge in 0.1 mile.
- 30.4 Turn left onto Rte. 642 (Suggetts Point Rd.) and then make an immediate right to stay on Rte. 642.
- 31.1 Head straight onto Rte. 608 (Farnham Creek Rd.) where Rte. 642 heads right.
- 32.2 Bear left and then, 0.1 mile later, bear right to stay on Rte. 608 (Farnham Creek Rd.). At mile 33.0, cross over a bridge. At mile 35.2, head straight to stay on Rte. 608 (Farnham Creek Rd.).
- 36.5 Turn right at the T intersection onto Rte. 3.
- 38.0 Make the first left at the convenience store onto Rte. 601 (Maon Rd.).
- 40.9 Bear right at the T intersection onto Rte. 600 (Ridge Rd.).

For the shorter cruise of 65.8 miles, turn left (instead of right) at this T intersection onto Rte. 600; in 2.5 miles, where Rte. 604 comes in from the right (the first road to your right), keep heading straight and pick up the directions from mile 94.5.

> At mile 44.1, where you enter Lancaster County, Ridge Rd. (Rte. 600) changes name to Lara Rd.

- 48.4 Turn left onto Rte. 201 (White Chapel Rd.).
- 48.9 Turn right at the T intersection onto Rte. 600 (Courthouse Rd.).
- 49.1 Bear right at the yield sign to stay on Rte. 600 (Courthouse Rd.).
- 50.6 Turn left at the T intersection onto Rte. 3 (Mary Ball Rd.). In 0.2 mile you'll pass the Mary Ball Washington Museum. At mile 51.0, pass a convenience store.
- 51.2 Make the first right at the Lancaster High School onto Rte.

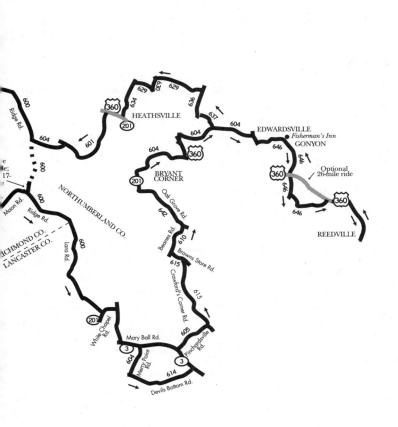

604 (Merry Point Rd.).

- 52.8 Make the first left onto Rte. 614 (Devils Bottom Rd.). In 1.5 miles, cross over a wooden bridge.
- 55.9 Turn left at the T intersection onto Rte. 3 (Mary Ball Rd.).
- 56.9 Turn right onto Rte. 605 (Pinckardsville Rd.).
- 58.7 Bear left onto Crawfords Corner Rd. (Rte. 615).
- 62.1 Turn left at the T intersection onto Rte. 615 (Browns Store Rd.).
- 62.8 Bear right onto Rte. 610 (Beanes Rd.).
- 64.2 Turn left at the T intersection onto Rte. 642 (Oak Grove Rd.). At mile 66.1, cross over a wooden bridge.
- 67.0 Head straight onto Rte. 201 at the stop sign and pass Howland School. In 0.6 mile, ride through the village of Bryant Corner (no services).
- 67.9 Turn right onto Rte. 604.
- 70.7 Turn left onto Rte. 360 (unmarked Horse Head Rd.).
- 71.4 Bear right onto Rte. 604, then take the immediate right to stay on 604.
- 75.4 Turn right at the T intersection onto Rte. 640; you are now in Edwardsville.
- 75.7 Turn left onto Rte. 646.
- 76.9 Head straight at the stop sign to stay on Rte. 646. You are now in Gonyon. In 0.2 mile, turn right into the Fisherman's Inn, which is on the corner. Continue straight on Rte. 646, however, for the main ride.

For the optional side trip of 25.8 miles to Reedville (making the total ride 142.7 miles), turn left out of Fisherman's Inn. At the stop sign at that corner, turn left onto Rte. 646. At mile 1.9, turn left at the T intersection onto Rte. 360. At mile 4.1 at the Lillia Elementary School, make the first right onto Rte. 646. At mile 8.9, turn left to stay on Rte. 646. At mile 11.0, turn right onto Rte. 360. At mile 11.1, bear left to stay on Rte. 360. In 0.5 mile, pass the Bay Motel. At mile 12.9, enter Reedville; there is a convenience store 0.2 mile after entering Reedville. Retrace your route to return to Gonyon and the Fisherman's Inn.

- 77.3 Head straight at the stop sign to stay on Rte. 646.

- 78.5 Turn right at the T intersection onto Rte. 640.
- 78.8 Turn left onto Rte. 604.
- 80.8 Turn right onto Rte. 637.
- 81.9 Turn right at the T intersection onto Rte. 636.
- 83.1 Make the first left onto Rte. 629.
- 85.4 Turn left at the T intersection onto Rte. 630.
- 85.9 Make the first right onto Rte. 629.
- 86.8 Make the first left onto Rte. 634. At mile 87.5, cross a bridge.
- 88.6 Turn right at the T intersection onto Rte. 360 in Heathsville.
- 89.3 Turn left at Northumberland High School onto Rte. 601.
- 91.8 Bear right onto Rte. 604.
- 93.0 Bear left to stay on Rte. 604.
- 94.5 Turn right at the T intersection onto Rte. 600 (Ridge Rd.). *Here the 65.8-mile route comes in from the left to join the two longer routes.*
- 99.2 Turn left at the T intersection onto Rte. 360 (Richmond Rd.). At mile 99.6, enter the town of Village (no services).
- 99.7 Turn right onto Rte. 600.
- 101.7 Bear left to stay on Rte. 600. At mile 102.5, enter Westmoreland County.
- 105.6 Head straight at the stop sign to stay on Rte. 600, crossing Rte. 203, and then follow Rte. 600 through all its right-angle turns.
- 108.4 Bear right to stay on Rte. 600 in the town of Kremlin.
- 108.8 Turn left to stay on Rte. 600, at the sign for Foxfield.
- 110.6 Turn right onto Rtes. 600/621.
- 111.5 Keep heading straight on Rte. 600 where Rte. 621 goes left.
- 113.5 Bear left to stay on Rte. 600.
- 114.8 Head straight at the stop sign to stay on Rte. 600.
- 114.9 Turn left onto Rte. 202Y.
- 115.0 Bear right onto Rte. 3. At mile 116.7, enter Montross.
- 116.9 Turn right into the Washington & Lee Motel.

West Virginia

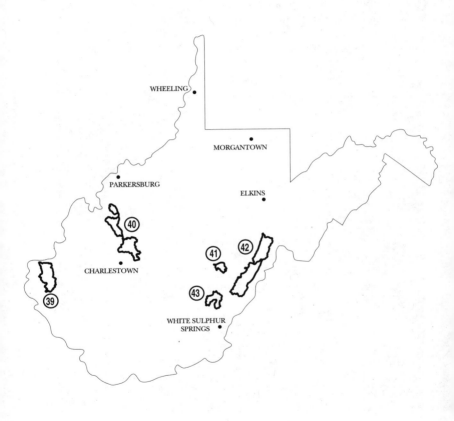

WHEELING •

MORGANTOWN •

PARKERSBURG •

ELKINS •

(40)

(41) (42)

CHARLESTOWN •

(43)

(39)

WHITE SULPHUR
SPRINGS •

West Virginia

Milton Getaway Challenge

Milton—Dudley Gap—Ona—Balls Gap—Milton

If you're hankering for some real hill climbing and the cure for too much civilization, this loop will exercise your granny gear and quest for solitude, along with providing lovely views of West Virginia's rows of forested ridges. The westernmost ride in this book, this route through Cabell County is a true challenge, despite its moderate length of 41 miles. A favorite of the Mountain State Wheelers Bicycle Club, it was contributed and verified by Jim Saulters of St. Albans, West Virginia.

At the start in Milton, you can take a public tour of Blenko Glass, famous for its hand-blown commemorative glassware. And 17.6 miles into the ride, you can make a 0.5-mile detour to Ona Speedway, a small country airport that offers rides in private planes. But outside of Milton and the town of Ona halfway through the ride, the route follows backroads in the Mountain State so isolated and so lightly traveled that you will not run across so much as a picnic ground. Accommodations are available in both towns, however. Milton features the Wine Cellar Bed and Breakfast (301–743–5665) while Ona offers the Foxfire Camp Grounds (304–743–5622), allowing you to turn this challenge into a two-day cruise. Despite the solitude, all the roads are paved.

The Basics

Start: Milton, at the Little League fields on County Fair Rd. To get to the ride's start, take the Milton exit (exit 28) off I–64; drive 0.3

mile south; turn right (west) at the traffic light onto Rte. 60; and drive 0.4 mile into downtown Milton. At the next traffic light, turn left (south) onto County Fair Rd. Drive 0.4 mile and park along the road near the Little League playing fields. Please do *not* park in the visitor lot for Blenko Glass.

Length: 41 miles.

Terrain: Hilly, no doubt about it. Traffic is normally light, except for around Milton and Ona.

Food: Convenience stores and fast-food restaurants in Milton and halfway through the ride at Ona; no other services along the route. Carry snacks, water, and tools.

Miles & Directions

Note: Follow directions carefully, as not every small street is shown on the map.

- 0.0 Head north (it could be either left or right, depending on the side of the road on which you parked) along County Fair Rd. back into Milton. At mile 0.4 you can stock up on snacks at the Chevron convenience store on your right. At the traffic light continue straight north.
- 0.6 Turn right at the stop sign onto Mason St.
- 0.65 Turn left onto Rte. 15 (Glenwood St.). At the stop sign at mile 0.9, continue straight under I–64.
- 4.4 Turn right onto Rte. 9 (Dudley Gap Rd.). In 0.75 mile, you'll begin a long climb up to Dudley Gap. "Hope you brought your granny!" notes Jim Saulters.
- 6.2 Turn left onto Rte. 11 (Barkers Ridge Rd.), which rolls and weaves in a wonderful rollercoaster ride, offering lovely views of the forested ridges. At mile 9.0, bear right at the unmarked Y intersection to stay on Rte. 11. At miles 11.0 and 11.7, you'll pass some television towers on your right.
- 12.5 Continue straight onto Rte. 1 (Union Ridge Rd.), which intersects from your right.
- 12.6 Bear left (south) to stay on Rte. 1; stay on the ridge, *not*

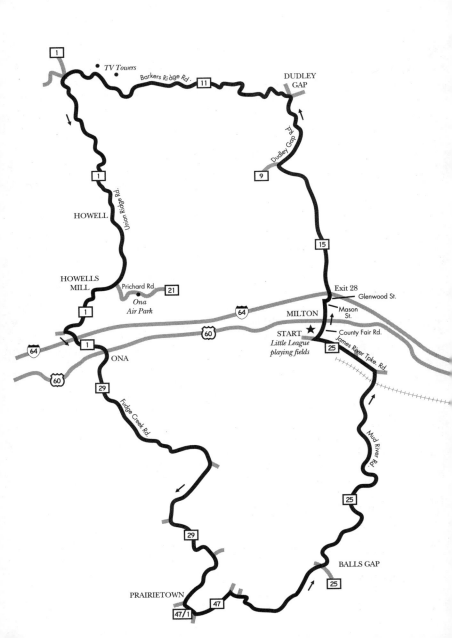

taking the obvious downhill to the right (which is Big Seven Rd.). In 0.25 mile you'll begin a long, pleasurable, winding downhill. At mile 15.0, bear right at the unmarked Y intersection to stay on Rte. 1.

- 18.0 Bear to the right to stay on Rte. 1, where Rte. 21 (Prichard Rd.) comes in from the left. If, however, you'd like a nice 0.5-mile detour and maybe take a ride in a private plane, turn left onto Rte. 21 to visit the Ona Speedway. Then return to this spot to continue the ride. At mile 18.6 cross the Mud River at Howells Mill. At mile 19.9, you'll pass underneath I–64.
- 20.8 Here you can refuel at the Exxon convenience store where Rte. 1 ends at Rte. 60. Then continue straight across the intersection onto Rte. 29. At 24.2, bear right to stay on Rte. 29. At mile 26.2, bear left at the Y intersection, following the sign to Salt Rock. At mile 26.5, you'll climb up to the top of a ridge; on the downhill use caution on the steep switchbacks.
- 29.0 Turn left at the T intersection onto unmarked Rte. 47/1 in the unmarked community of Prairietown. In 0.3 mile turn left onto Rte. 47, following the signs to Milton and Balls Gap. In 1.2 miles you'll grind up a *steep* hill, followed by a slightly less steep descent.
- 33.0 Turn left onto Rte. 25 (Mud River Rd.) and ride over the top of Balls Gap, marked by a church on your right. Watch your speed on the left-hand sweeper on the other side!
- 35.8 Before crossing the Mud River, turn left at Zoar Baptist Church onto Rte. 25/12 (W. Mud River Rd.).
- 40.3 After passing under a railroad trestle, turn left onto Rte. 25 (James River Tpke. Rd.). At mile 41.0 pass the warehouse for Supervalu Food Distributors.
- 41.2 Bear right at Blenko Glass onto County Fair Rd.
- 41.4 Arrive back at your car.

40

Sternwheel Regatta Century Classic

*Elkview—Sissonville—Liberty—Given—
Fairplain—Sissonville—Elkview*

This 100-mile ride north of Charleston takes you on a challenging tour through Kanawha, Putnam, and Jackson counties in western central West Virginia. You will climb forested ridges to behold panoramic vistas, soar down slopes into a river valley, and cycle through cultivated farmland. You may choose to picnic at the top of Allen Fork Road where it intersects with Route 34 about 35 miles into the ride and then take a tour of Fisher Ridge Winery a few miles later.

The ride's unusual name originated from the Sternwheel Regatta, a festival that started in Charleston on Labor Day in 1970 and whose highlight is a boat race among sternwheel riverboats. Over the years the Sternwheel Regatta has grown to a celebration ten days long that attracts more than 100,000 spectators for the events and concerts, all of which are free. In 1979 the Mountain State Wheelers Bicycle Club was asked to organize a bike ride for the festival; now the challenging ride attracts some 400 cyclists each year. "You can mention that if riders do the Regatta bike ride the last weekend in August during the festival, they will enjoy full support, which includes sag wagons, food, water, security and emergency services, and a dinner the night before the ride," notes Dennis A. Strawn of Elkview, West Virginia, who contributed and verified the map and cue sheet.

Although the Sternwheel Regatta classic was originally conceived as a one-day century ride, you can modify it in several ways. Because the 103-mile ride is three successive loops, it can be shortened to a 42-mile challenge or an 83-mile classic by returning after only the first or second loop. Alternatively, the ride can be turned into a two-day weekend by staying overnight at the Wildwood Campground (304–372–2436) at Staats Mill, 6 miles from Fairplain, about 70 miles into the ride.

Like most locales isolated enough to be ideal for road riding in West Virginia, here, too, places to get food are few and far between. There are a few convenience stores, but load up on snacks, water, and tools—unless, of course, you join the riders with sag support at the actual Sternwheel Regatta!

The Basics

Start: Elkview, at Crossings Mall, just off the Elkview exit from I–79.
Length: 42, 83, or 103 miles.
Terrain: Very hilly. Traffic is light on weekend mornings, but during the week it can get heavy with commuter traffic in the mornings and evenings.
Food: Occasional restaurants and convenience stores, but places can be up to 15 miles apart; carry snacks, water, and tools.

Miles & Directions

- 0.0 Turn right out of the parking lot at Crossings Mall onto Rte. 45 (Little Sandy Creek Rd.).
- 6.3 Turn right onto Rte. 119.
- 8.3 Turn right onto Rte. 114. Here there are a Hardee's and Smith's Grocery Store.
- 9.0 Turn right onto Rte. 41 (Coopers Creek Rd.) and stay on the obvious main road as it changes number from Rte. 41 to Rte. 28 (at mile 12.6, where the road is marked Five Mile Rd.) to Rte. 26 to Rte. 26/1. At mile 13.8 start climbing. At mile 14.2

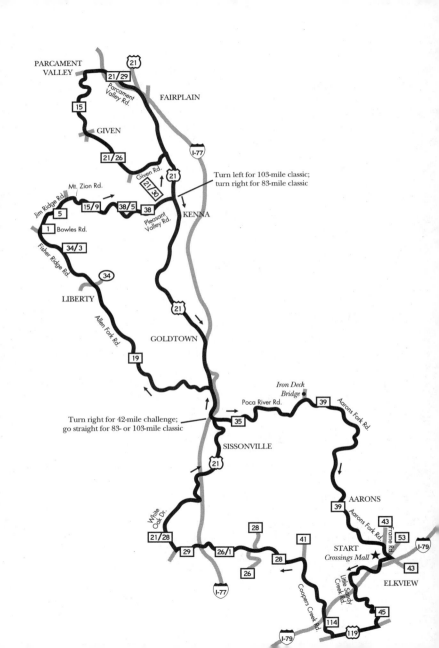

PARCAMENT VALLEY

21

21/29

Parcament Valley Rd.

FAIRPLAIN

15

GIVEN

21/26

I-77

Mt. Zion Rd.

Given Rd.

21

21/30

Jim Ridge Rd.

15/9

38/5

38

5

Bowles Rd.

Turn left for 103-mile classic; turn right for 83-mile classic

KENNA

1

Pleasant Valley Rd.

Fisher Ridge Rd.

34/3

34

LIBERTY

Allen Fork Rd.

21

19

GOLDTOWN

Iron Deck Bridge

Poca River Rd.

39

Aarons Fork Rd.

35

Turn right for 42-mile challenge; go straight for 83- or 103-mile classic

SISSONVILLE

21

AARONS

39

Aarons Fork Rd.

43

Frame Rd.

53

I-79

White Oak Dr.

21/28

29

26/1

28

41

START
Crossings Mall ★

43

I-77

28

26

ELKVIEW

Coopers Creek Rd.

Little Sandy Creek Rd.

114

119

45

I-79

you'll reach the crest and start a steep downhill. At mile 15.7 start another climb, followed 0.2 mile later by a very steep downhill. Control your speed on the sharp turns.

- 16.8 Bear right at the sharp turn to stay on Rte. 26/1. Watch your speed—the safe maximum is 15 mph.
- 17.5 Turn right onto Rte. 29 (Tuppers Creek Rd.), just before I–77.
- 18.4 Turn left onto Rte. 21/28 (White Oak Dr.); this stretch of the ride is exceptionally scenic. Watch for the sharp S turns on the downhill after mile 19.8.
- 20.1 Turn right onto Rte. 21N. (For a grocery store and restaurant, turn left instead and go 0.7 mile.) At mile 23.8 you'll enter the limits of Sissonville. At mile 25.4 continue straight on Rte. 21 at the intersection of Poca River Rd. (Dolly's convenience store is here.)

For the 42-mile challenge: At mile 25.4 turn right onto Poca River Rd. (instead of continuing straight) and pick up the directions below at mile 87.5.

- 27.0 Turn left onto Rte. 19 (Allen Fork Rd.), which passes under I–77. At mile 33.5 start a steep but short climb.
- 34.4 Turn left onto Rte. 34S.
- 34.6 Make the first right onto Rte. 34/3 (Fisher Ridge Rd.), passing the Fisher Ridge Winery at mile 37.3. At mile 41.3, be careful! This is the start of a very steep downgrade, which has a stop sign at the bottom.
- 41.7 Turn right onto unmarked Rte. 1 (Bowles Rd.). At mile 41.9 begin climbing.
- 44.4 Bear right at the Y intersection onto Rte. 5 (Jim Ridge Rd.). In 500 feet you can refuel at the Jim Ridge convenience store on your right, where the owner is friendly toward visiting cyclists. *Note*: Between miles 44.7 and 47.0, there are a few gravel sections anywhere from 20 to 100 feet long. Ride with caution!
- 46.2 Turn left at the T intersection onto Mt. Zion Rd. At mile 50.1 continue straight at the intersection of Rock Castle Rd. (Rte. 15/9). After Rock Castle the road you are on will change

route numbers several times (from Rte. 15/9 to Rte. 38/5 to Rte. 38 to Rte. 21/30), but continue to follow the evident main road.

- 55.4 Turn left at the T intersection onto Rte. 21N.

For the 83-mile classic: Turn right onto Rte. 21S instead, and pick up the directions at mile 74.2.

- 57.8 Turn left onto Rte. 21/29 (Given Rd.), which changes to Rte. 38. At mile 62.3 you'll pass through the community of Given, which has no services. Continue north of Given onto Rte. 15.
- 65.6 Bear right at the Y intersection onto Parcament Valley Rd. to Fairplain.
- 66.4 After crossing over I–77, bear right to stay on Parcament Valley Rd. (Rte. 21/26).
- 68.8 Turn right at the T intersection onto Rte. 21S (where there is a convenience store with a small restaurant) and proceed under the interstate. You'll stay on Rte. 21S for the next 18 miles. At mile 71.9 pass the intersection of Given Rd. At mile 74.2 pass the intersection of Pleasant Valley Rd. *This is where the 83-mile classic joins the 103-mile route.* At mile 75.3, just after passing a country store, continue straight as Rte. 34 joins from the left. At mile 76.1 begin climbing Divide Hill. At mile 76.6, at the crest of the hill, continue straight on Rte. 21S where Rte. 34 turns right. Coast down Divide Hill. At mile 82.2 pass under I–77 at Goldtown (a small community with no services). At mile 85.2 pass the intersection of Allen Fork Rd. (Rte. 19) and a convenience store 0.3 mile later.
- 87.5 Turn left onto Rte. 35 (Poca River Rd.). *This is where the 42-mile challenge joins the 103-mile route.* Once again you can refuel at Dolly's convenience store. After crossing Iron Deck Bridge over Hicumbottom Creek, bear right onto Rte. 39 (Aarons Fork Rd.). Use caution on the one-lane bridge at mile 102.2.
- 102.3 Continue straight onto Rte. 43 (Frame Rd.).
- 103.0 Turn right onto Little Sandy Creek Rd., and then make an immediate right into Crossings Mall.
  Congratulations!

41

Williams River Trail Cruise

Little Laurel Overlook—Woodrow—
Tea Creek Campground—Little Laurel Overlook

West Virginia is famed for its mountain biking, not its road riding, so it's only right to include an easy introduction to that very distinct sport. This ride along a well-marked former railroad grade paralleling the Williams River in Pocahontas County is accessible even to novices. But if you're one of those road riders who love to coordinate the color of their water bottle cages with their Descente jackets and their Pearl Izumi shorts, be forewarned: Mountain biking is a filthy sport. On the Williams River Trail, several springs run off the mountain and can make the trail wet and slippery; you must also ford Little Laurel Creek about halfway through the ride. Mud can be liberally splashed all over your clothes and equipment, finding its way into your bottom bracket and even into your pockets and onto your glasses. Save the fashion statement for a dry day on the highway.

For safety's sake do this ride only on the 2-inch knobbies of a true mountain bike; otherwise you risk injury slipping on the moist trail or down the first gravel descent. If you've brought only a road bike, never fear: You can readily rent a true West Virginia mountain steed from the Elk River Touring Center in Slatyfork (304–572–3771), just 12 miles from the ride's start. In fact, the touring center includes ten rooms and two cabins at a bed-and-breakfast lodge, a hot tub where overnight guests can soak the aches out of their quadriceps, and a very nice restaurant (The Restaurant at Elk River, also 572–3771)—one of the few in the state that caters to the high-carbo, low-fat nutritional needs of active cyclists. Other overnight options can be found in Marlinton, about 10 miles south (see Ride 42).

This ride, based on one in the book *Mountain Bike Rides in Pocahontas County, West Virginia* (Roadrunner Press, 1992), written by the owners of the Elk River Touring Center, veteran mountain-bike tour guides Gil and Mary Willis, gives you several options. Although the ride is written to start from the Little Laurel Overlook on the Highland Scenic Highway 150, you could also start from the Tea Creek Campground or from the Handley Public Hunting and Fishing Area.

The cue sheet below, which was verified by Dennis A. Strawn of Elkview, West Virginia, directs you only on the paved and gravel roads and not on the trail. Taking the actual Williams River Trail would cut off either U.S. Forest Service (USFS) Road 115 or USFS 86. The least hilly option (only about 300 feet of altitude gained) for riding the trail would be to start at either campsite and take USFS 86; the option taking full advantage of the views from the scenic highway—but requiring much more climbing—would be to take USFS 115 after starting at Little Laurel Overlook on the scenic highway.

The Highland Scenic Highway 150, a fantastic two-lane road running for 23 miles along the tops of ridges, would itself make a wonderful road trip (although there are no services along its length outside of the primitive campgrounds). Reminiscent of the gorgeous Blue Ridge Parkway in Virginia, the scenic highway commands spectacular views of line after line of the forested ridges that are so beautifully characteristic of West Virginia. Moreover, its pavement is so superb and the automobile traffic so light that "we Rollerblade all over it," remarks Gil Willis, and in the winter locals cross-country ski on it because it remains unplowed.

There is *nowhere* to buy food or drink on this ride, so you must stock up at Slatyfork. The Little Laurel Overlook has a sheltered picnic table and a chemical toilet (as well as a great view). At both Handley and Tea Creek there are primitive campsites with pit toilets and drinking water (at Tea Creek you heave the long handle of an old-fashioned hand pump to draw up the frosty well water). Bring any tools you anticipate needing.

Oh, yes, one other note: Hunting season in West Virginia starts the last week in November. Mountain biking during hunting season is *not* recommended.

The Basics

Start: Little Laurel Overlook on Highland Scenic Hwy. 150. From the Elk River Touring Center in Slatyfork, drive (or pedal) 8 miles south on U.S. Rte. 219/State Rte. 55; turn right onto Hwy. 150; in 3.9 miles turn left into the overlook's parking lot.

Length: 18 miles if only the paved and gravel roads are taken (as the ride is written); 14 or 15 miles if the Williams Creek Trail is taken.

Terrain: One long descent at the beginning; one stiff climb at the end. Traffic is light.

Food: *None*—stock up in Slatyfork; water is available at the Tea Creek and Handley campgrounds.

Miles & Directions

- 0.0 Turn right out of Little Laurel Overlook onto Highland Scenic Hwy. 150N toward Rte. 219/Rte. 55.
- 1.8 Turn right onto the gravel Friel Run Rd. and make an immediate left onto the gravel unmarked USFS 115. Descend slowly on the gravel, taking care when passing over the cattle grates at miles 4.1 and 4.6.
- 5.3 Turn right at the T intersection (stop sign) onto paved Rte. 17/3, passing some of the trailer homes and farm buildings of the community of Woodrow. As the road passes right through cow pastures, watch out for cow pies in your path. At mile 5.7 use caution when riding over the cattle grate.
- 6.7 Bear right at the church, and immediately turn right at the next T intersection (stop sign) onto the nicely paved two-lane

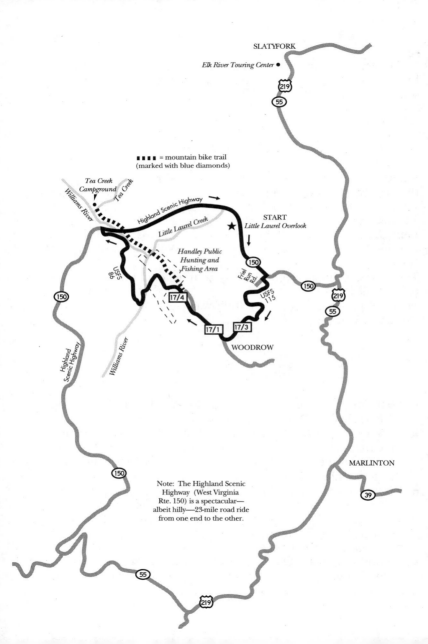

SLATYFORK

Elk River Touring Center ●

219

55

■■■■ = mountain bike trail
(marked with blue diamonds)

*Tea Creek
Campground*

Williams River

Tea Creek

Highland Scenic Highway

Little Laurel Creek

START
Little Laurel Overlook

★

150

USFS
86

*Handley Public
Hunting and
Fishing Area*

Friel Run Rd.

150

USFS
115

150

219

55

17/4

17/1

17/3

WOODROW

Williams River

*Highland
Scenic Highway*

150

MARLINTON

39

Note: The Highland Scenic
Highway (West Virginia
Rte. 150) is a spectacular—
albeit hilly—23-mile road ride
from one end to the other.

55

219

unmarked Rte. 17/1, following the sign WILLIAMS RIVER 5 MI. Soon you're riding through a farm valley.

■ 8.4 Bear left onto the blacktop of unmarked Rte. 17/4.

To ride the Williams River Trail, keep heading straight here (instead of bearing left) to enter the Handley Public Hunting and Fishing Area (the sign reads handley wildlife management area). In 1.0 mile bear left at the Y intersection, following the sign to manager's residence (the right-hand fork goes to the campground); 0.1 mile later pass through a gate marked with a blue diamond onto an old two-track dirt road. This is one end of the Williams River Trail, which is marked with blue diamonds all along its 3.75-mile length to the Tea Creek Campground. At Tea Creek Campground you'll emerge at a circular parking area, in the center of which is the hand water pump. Exit the campground by heading left onto the bridge over the Williams River. Turn left at the T intersection and ride another mile on gravel USFS 86. Immediately after passing under the overpass for Scenic Hwy. 150, turn right onto the paved on-ramp and follow the directions from mile 12.3 below.

■ 10.8 Cross the bridge over the Williams River.
■ 11.3 Bear right at the Y intersection onto the unmarked gravel USFS 86, following the sign TO SCENIC HIGHWAY 150, and begin climbing. You'll reach the crest at mile 12.4. At about mile 14.0 you'll approach the concrete bridge over the Williams River that is part of Scenic Hwy. 150.
■ 14.3 Turn left onto the paved on-ramp leading up to the overpass of Scenic Hwy. 150.
■ 14.4 Turn right at the T intersection onto Scenic Hwy. 150. Begin a 3.5-mile-long, arduous, steady climb.
■ 17.9 Turn right into Little Laurel Overlook.

42

Observatory and Railroad Classic

Marlinton—Green Bank—Bartow—Cass—Marlinton

This entire classic is within the Monongahela National Forest, which spreads 848,000 acres over nine counties. The first half of the ride is a 35-mile-long, relatively gentle uphill all the way from Marlinton to Bartow. You'll pass through the Seneca State Forest (304–799–6213), where there is picnicking and primitive camping. The entire ride is within Pocahontas County.

If you don't feel like pedaling the whole 81-mile classic, you can still hit the two main attractions in a shorter challenge of 58 miles, whose cue sheet I devised based on the suggestions of Rachel Alpert, program director of the Greenbrier River Leadership Center in Bartow (which, among other activities, offers a variety of mountain-bike tours—call 304–456–5191), and Karen G. Carper, owner of the Bikeworks bicycle shop in Elkins. The entire route was verified by Dennis A. Strawn of Elkview, West Virginia.

The first attraction, some 27 miles into the ride, is the National Radio Astronomy Observatory (NRAO) in Green Bank (304–456–2011). The observatory is open to the public at no charge. You may walk around and gaze at the giant dish-shaped telescopes, which stand in the open air and are used to listen to radio emissions from the heavens twenty-four hours a day. Free tours are given in the summer.

If it is late afternoon when you leave NRAO, you can easily turn the 81-mile classic into a two-day ride by spending the night in Bartow 9 miles north (36 miles into the 81). The nicest place in

Bartow is The Hermitage (304–456–4808), a motel and restaurant on the bank of the east fork of the Greenbrier River. The rear door of every room opens onto a long porch, which overlooks a large green and the river—perfect for enjoying a sunset drink and listening to the peepers as the stars come out.

Five miles after leaving Bartow, the second half of the ride becomes almost like mountain biking on pavement: winding, rolling, with rollercoaster-sharp turns and steep climbs, on the appropriately named Back Mountain Road. Fifty-seven miles into the classic, stop for the second main attraction: a ride on a turn-of-the-century, ninety-ton steam-powered Shay logging locomotive at the Cass Scenic Railroad State Park (304–456–4300). On selected Saturday evenings throughout the summer, you can make reservations on a "dinner train," which includes a barbecue and live bluegrass entertainment. Cass also has The Shay Inn (a bed-and-breakfast) and fully equipped six- or eight-person cottages, complete with linens and kitchen utensils. For reservations, call either (304) 456–4652 or 572–3771.

The last half of the classic, from Bartow through Cass and back to Marlinton, has almost no services. Stock up well at the ride's start in Marlinton, at Green Bank, or at Bartow if you're taking the 58-mile challenge. Route 66 passes The Amish Bakery—an unmarked white farmhouse open Wednesday through Saturday from noon to 5:00 P.M. Don't rely on Cass except during the summer: Even in late May right before Memorial Day, daytime services—including the country store, snack bar, and rest rooms—are closed except for an outdoor soft-drink machine. As there are no bike shops anywhere, be sure to take all the tools you may need.

Marlinton has several places to stay overnight, among them the Marlinton Motor Inn (304–799–4711) and the Jerico B&B (304–799–6241). A night at Marlinton would allow you also to explore the Greenbrier River Hike, Bike, and Ski Trail. The restored railroad depot that is now the Marlinton Visitors Center is an access to the Greenbrier River Trail, the level former bed of the Greenbrier Division of the C&O Railway built at the turn of the century to serve the booming timber industry of the time. Now the public trail passes through numerous small towns and traverses thirty-five bridges and two tunnels, much of the route adjacent to the beautiful Greenbrier River. You can ride along the hard-packed gravel bed as far north as Cass (24 miles) or as far south as North Caldwell (53 miles). For a detailed map and guide to the trail, write to the Greenbrier River Trail Association, Inc., Slatyfork, WV 26291.

The Basics

Start: Marlinton, at the parking lot of the Marlinton Visitor Center (an old converted railroad station) on Rte. 39 0.2 mile east of Rte. 219/15.

Length: 58 or 81 miles.

Terrain: Rolling to hilly. Traffic ranges from moderate to light on the main roads outbound and is practically nonexistent on the return.

Food: Convenience stores and restaurants in Marlinton, Green Bank, and Bartow; food available at Cass between Memorial Day and Labor Day; that is *it!* Moreover, on the 81-mile ride other than in the summer, there could be a stretch of *37 miles without food or water* (from Durbin to Marlinton). Take all necessary tools.

Miles & Directions

- 0.0 Turn left out of the Marlinton Visitor Center parking lot onto Rte. 39E (Main St.). Ride through the quaint, brick downtown district of Marlinton. Load up here on snacks and water; your next opportunity is in 21 miles. After leaving the outskirts of town, you'll begin climbing.
- 5.2 Turn left onto Rte. 28N, continuing your gradual climb through farm land. At mile 15.5 you'll pass the entrance to the Seneca State Forest.
- 21.0 Turn left at the stop sign to stay on Rte. 28N, where Rte. 92N joins your route. At this intersection are an Exxon gas station and a small convenience store—the first in 21 miles.
- 24.4 At this intersection with Rte. 66W, continue straight to stay on Rte. 28N/92N.

- 27.6 Turn left to enter the grounds of the National Radio Astronomy Observatory. To continue the 81-mile route, leave the observatory grounds by turning left to continue north on Rtes. 28N/92N.

For the 58-mile challenge, leave the observatory grounds by turning right instead and retracing 3.2 miles south along Rte. 28S/92S. Then turn right onto Rte. 66W, coast 4.6 miles down to Cass, and pick up the directions at mile 67.3.

By the way, only 0.6 mile down Rte. 66 from Rtes. 28N/92N is The Amish Bakery; a small sign will direct you to turn right and continue for 0.5 mile. The bakery is actually a white farmhouse with no sign but with a small gravel area for cars to park; walk in the front door and you'll know you've arrived.

- 36.2 Bear left to stay on Rte. 92N/250 as Rte. 28N heads right. You are entering Bartow. Not 500 feet later, just after crossing over the east fork of the Greenbrier River, The Hermitage motel is on your left. At mile 38.9 you'll pass a grocery market in the town of Durbin. At mile 40.0 you'll pass a gas station on your left, which has a small convenience store. This is your *last chance* before Cass—or possibly Marlinton—to stock up on food and drink.
- 41.4 Turn left onto Rte. 1 (Back Mountain Rd.).
- 43.0 Make a *sharp* right to stay on Rte. 1 (Back Mountain Rd.), where Rte. 251/11 (Grant Vandevender Rd.) goes straight. This is real backwoods West Virginia, where tumbledown farms with rusting trucks and buses in the muddy yards overlook boulder-strewn fields and forested hills of stunning beauty. Just keep going for nearly 15 miles.
- 57.6 Turn left at the T intersection onto unmarked Rte. 66E. This is Cass. In a few hundred feet, just across the railroad track, you'll be at the Cass Country Store and Soda Fountain and Restaurant, the terminus for the scenic railroad in the Cass Scenic Railroad State Park. Across the parking lot there are picnic tables with barbecue grills on the bank of the Greenbrier River.

- 57.7 To resume the ride turn right out of the Cass Scenic Railroad State Park parking lot onto unmarked Rte. 66W. You'll pedal through the restored village of Cass, past the rental cabins and gift shops, rejoining Rte. 1. Cass is also the northernmost access to the Greenbrier River Trail, which is an alternate return to Marlinton (24.6 miles to the south by the trail).

- 59.4 Turn left onto the continuation of Rte. 1 (Back Mountain Rd.), heading south. At mile 62.5 you'll descend into Stony Bottom, where amid all this wildness you'll suddenly encounter Moore's Lodge Motel (304–456–4721) on your right next to the river; there are no other services. Then you'll begin a very steep climb. At mile 65.4 Rte. 9 (Linwood Rd.) joins Rte. 1 (Back Mountain Rd.) from the right. A mile later you'll enter the small community of Clover Lick—another access to the Greenbrier River Trail for an alternate return to Marlinton (15 miles south by the trail through its most wild and remote section).

- 66.6 Turn right at the T intersection to stay on unmarked Rte. 1/9, following the sign reading MARLINTON 14 MI. At mile 72.3, stop and enjoy the view for miles around.

- 73.4 Bear right at the Y intersection to stay on Rte. 1 (Back Mountain Rd.) where Rte. 1/6 (Fairview Rd.) heads left.

- 74.1 Turn left at the triangle onto Rte. 15 (Airport Rd.), a two-lane road of excellent pavement that now seems like a veritable freeway. This is a lovely downhill glide past farms.

- 79.5 Turn left at the T intersection onto the unmarked and very busy Rte. 55/219. Watch for cars! If you're hungry, you now have a choice between Kentucky Fried Chicken and Dairy Queen.

- 80.5 Turn left onto Rte. 39E into Marlinton.

- 80.8 Turn left into the parking lot of the Marlinton Visitor Center.

43

Hillsboro Farmland Cruise

Hillsboro—Lobelia—Droop Mountain—Hillsboro

For a true appreciation of West Virginia farmland and countryside, this 25-mile tour in Pocahontas County can't be beat. You'll start in the town of Hillsboro, birthplace of Pearl S. Buck (1892–1973)—the only American woman to be awarded both the Pulitzer Prize in literature (in 1932 for *The Good Earth*) and the Nobel Prize in literature (1938). In fact, just 0.75 mile north of this ride's start on Route 219, the white clapboard home where she was born is now a museum, open to the public Monday through Saturday (for hours call 304–653–4430).

The ride, suggested in part by Cara H. Rose, director of the Pocahontas County Tourism Commission, and verified by her colleague Todd Gay, first meanders through farms where you may see sheep and cattle grazing. But this is no tame and pastoral farmland like the somnolent rolling fields of Pennsylvania. No, this is red-knuckled farmland clinging to the steep sides of hollows, surly in its strong beauty lying naked among the tree-covered rocky hills.

And those rocky hills you will climb. The roads become very twisty, very narrow, and very steep—up to 9 percent grade as you approach and leave Droop Mountain, site of the most extensive Civil War battle in West Virginia. The site is now a state park with a small museum, picnic areas, and a stacked-log lookout tower commanding a spectacular view.

But there's a great payoff for all that climbing: the gorgeous land and its sheer isolation. There is nothing to disturb your contemplation of nature other than the rhythmic sound of your own deep breathing in grinding up switchbacks; in the whole route it is doubtful you'll encounter as many as half a dozen cars (except for the brief stretch on Route 219).

The first half of the ride (up Droop Mountain) is a net climb, with the second half being a net descent, from a high of 3,060 feet above sea level to a low of 2,200 feet. But as in Nepal, there are considerable ups and downs in between; the probable total of a couple of thousand feet gained and lost is the reason this short ride is definitely not a ramble. But it is one of the simplest routes in this book, taking only four roads: Lobelia Road its full length, left onto Route 219 for 2.6 miles, right onto Locust Creek Road for 3 miles, and left onto Denmar Road until its end back in Hillsboro.

These roads are so little traveled that there are *no* services outside of Hillsboro. Stock up there on food and water before you leave, and be sure to take your tools. There are, however, a couple of inns in the area to stay a night: the Yew Mountain Lodge (304–653–4821) and The Current Bed & Breakfast (304–653–4722) halfway through the ride. (The Current, by the way, is adjacent to the Greenbrier River Trail, a generally level former railroad bed now devoted to hiking and biking along the river.) Bicycle campers can pitch a tent and enjoy a hot shower at the 10,000-acre Watoga State Park a few miles northeast of Hillsboro (304–799–4087).

The Basics

Start: Hillsboro, on Rte. 219 at the corner of Rte. 29 (Lobelia Rd.). Park along Rte. 219 across from the Four Winds Cafe.
Length: 25 miles.
Terrain: Very hilly. Virtually no traffic on the side roads, although traffic may be moderately heavy on the unavoidable 2.6-mile stretch on Rte. 219. *Watch for gravel.*
Food: No services outside of Hillsboro. Take more snacks, water, and tools than you think you might need.

Miles & Directions

■   0.0 From Rte. 219 through the center of Hillsboro, head west (the only direction you can go) onto Rte. 29 (Lobelia Rd.). First

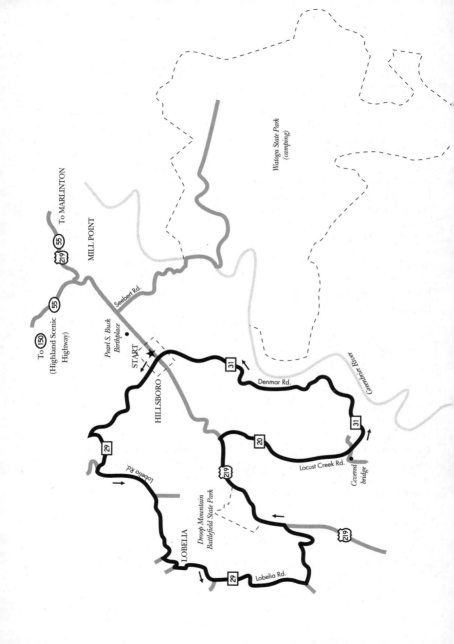

you'll ride through open farmland with cows and sheep, and soon you'll be climbing through forest. At mile 4.9 you'll pass Rte. 22 (Russell Scott Rd.) on your left; at mile 6.6 you'll pass Rte. 29/21 (Bruffy's Creek Rd.) on your right. At mile 7.2 follow Rte. 29 (Lobelia Rd.) as it makes a ninety-degree left turn through the town of Lobelia (a few sagging buildings with no services), following the sign TO 219. At mile 8.4 keep heading straight through the intersection of two gravel and dirt roads (George Hill Rd. and Briery Knob Rd.), following the sign TO 219.

- 10.9 Bear left at the unsigned Y intersection to stay on Rte. 29 (Lobelia Rd.). A mile later begin a *steep* climb up the back of Droop Mountain, taking time to enjoy the expansive vista at your left over the valley to forested West Virginia ridges.

- 13.1 Turn left at the T intersection onto Rte. 219. Watch for cars! At this point you are nearly at the summit of the mountain, which has an altitude of 3,060 feet. At mile 13.7 you'll pass one entrance to Droop Mountain State Park on your left. At mile 14.1, after passing a second park entrance, you'll begin a *steep* descent of a 9 percent grade down tight switchbacks for the next 0.75 mile. *Caution! Watch for gravel and cars!*

- 15.7 Turn right onto Rte. 20 (Locust Creek Rd.).

- 18.8 Turn left at the T intersection onto unmarked Rte. 31 (Denmar Rd.). But before you make the turn, you might want to detour 100 feet to your right to walk through the century-old covered bridge, no longer in service for automobile traffic but preserved for posterity as a landmark.

- 20.1 Bear left at the small white church to stay on Rte. 31 (Denmar Rd.). At mile 20.7 you'll have descended to the lowest point on the ride, 2,200 feet. The rest is a relatively gentle ascent.

- 21.4 Turn right at the T intersection to stay on unmarked Rte. 31 (Denmar Rd.). Now you're pedaling through farmland.

- 25.1 Arrive back at Rte. 219 at your starting point, across the highway from Rte. 29 (Lobelia Rd.). (To visit the Pearl S. Buck Birthplace, turn right onto Rte. 219 and ride another 0.75 mile.)

Appendix

Below are some selected references pertinent to bicycle touring in the Mid-Atlantic states. The list is not exhaustive. If any organization, set of maps, or other reference that should have been included has been omitted or if an address has changed, please send the necessary information to the author for inclusion in the next edition of this book: Trudy E. Bell, c/o The Globe Pequot Press, P.O. Box 833, Old Saybrook CT 06475 (e-mail: tebell@mcimail.com).

National Cycling Organizations

Adventure Cycling Association
P.O. Box 8308
Missoula, MT 59807
(406) 721–1776

The Adventure Cycling Association is a national, nonprofit organization for recreational cyclists, founded in 1974 as Bikecentennial; since then it has established the 19,000-mile National Bicycle Route Network, for which it publishes maps and marks cross-state and cross-country roads as bicycle routes. It publishes the magazine *BikeReport* nine times a year for members, including the annual reference *Cyclists' Yellow Pages;* sells panniers, tents, guidebooks, and other touring merchandise; and conducts guided bicycle tours, including ones up to three months long across the country.

League of American Bicyclists
190 W. Ostend Dr., Suite 120
Baltimore, MD 21230-3755
(410) 539–3399

The League (a century-old organization until 1994 called the League of American Wheelmen) is a national, nonprofit bicycle-advocacy organization, serving the interests of touring, utilitarian, and club cyclists. It has a full-time government relations advocate, who represents the League's concerns with legislation and other activities to gain for cyclists greater legal rights and safer access to roads. It publishes the magazine *Bicycle USA* eight times a year for members, including the annual *TourFinder* and *Almanac* reference issues.

State Cycling Organizations

Some telephone numbers are not included, following club policy.

Delaware

Delaware Bicycle Council
c/o Tom Hartley
980 Lochmeath Way
Dover, DE 19903
(302) 697–0430

White Clay Bicycle Club
c/o Donovan Carbaugh
49 Marsh Woods Ln.
Wilmington, DE 19810

Maryland

Baltimore Bicycling Club
P.O. Box 5906
Baltimore, MD 21208
(410) 792–8308

Cumberland Valley Cycling
Club
P.O. Box 711
Hagerstown, MD 21740

Frederick Pedalers Bike Club
P.O. Box 1293
Frederick, MD 21702-0293
(301) 845–8307

Oxon Hill Bicycle & Trail Club
P.O. Box 81
Oxon Hill, MD 20750-0081

Salisbury Bicycle Club
c/o Edward K. Payne
708 Walnut St.
Pocomoke City, MD 21851
(410) 957–3089

New Jersey

Bicycle Touring Club of North
Jersey
446 Ellis Pl.
Wyckoff, NJ 07481

Central Jersey Bicycle Club
P.O. Box 2202
Edison, NJ 08818-2202
(908) 225–HUBS

East Coast Bicycle Club of
Orange County
P.O. Box 260
Bayville, NJ 08721
(609)693–0983

Jersey Shore Touring Society
P.O. Box 8581
Red Bank, NJ 07701-8581
(908) 747–8206

Morris Area Freewheelers
P.O. Box 252
Convent Station, NJ 07961-0252
(201) 691–9275

North Jersey Bicycle Club
c/o John P. Quinn
100 Ridgewald Ave.
Waldwick, NJ 07463-2109
(201) 445–6140

Princeton Freewheelers
P.O. Box 1204
Princeton, NJ 08542-1204
(609) 921–6685

Shore Cycle Club
P.O. Box 492
Northfield, NJ 08225-0492
(609) 652–0880

South Jersey Wheelmen
c/o Arthur Schalick
P.O. Box 2705
Vineland, NJ 08360-1076
(609) 848–6123

The Wayfarers
P.O. Box 211

Fair Lawn, NJ 07410
(201) 796–9344

Western Jersey Wheelmen
41 Philhower Rd.
Lebanon, NJ 08833-4515
(908) 832–7361

New York
Big Wheels Bicycle Club
4456 Beachridge Rd.
Lockport, NY 14094
(716) 625–8308

Buffalo Area Recreational
   Cyclists, Inc.
P.O. Box 922
Niagara Falls, NY 14302

Canton Bicycle Club
P.O. Box 364
Canton, NY 13617-0364

Cruise Brothers Bike Club Inc.
P.O. Box 456
Copiague, NY 11726-0456
(516) 541–1707

Fast & Fabulous Cyclists
P.O. Box 87
Ansonia Sta., NY 10023

Finger Lakes Cycling Club
1431 Mecklenburg Rd.
Ithaca, NY 14850-9301

Five Borough Bicycle Club
American Youth Hostels
891 Amsterdam Ave.
New York, NY 10025
(212) 932–2300

Long Island Bicycle Club
c/o Bill Selsky
100 S. Ocean Ave.
Freeport, NY 11520-3539
(516) 562–5844

Massapequa Park Bicycle Club
c/o Kay Page
P.O. Box 231
Massapequa, NY 11758-0231
(516) 221–3948

Mid-Hudson Bicycle Club
P.O. Box 1727
Poughkeepsie, NY 12601
(914) 679–8188

Mohawk-Hudson Cycling Club
P.O. Box 12575
Albany, NY 12212-2575
(518) 437–9579

New York Cycle Club
P.O. Box 199, Cooper Station
New York, NY 10276
(212) 886–4545

Niagara Frontier Bicycle Club
P.O. Box 211
Buffalo, NY 14226-0211

(716) 632–2820
Onondaga Cycling Club, Inc.
P.O. Box 6307
Syracuse, NY 13217-6307

Orange County Bicycle Club
c/o Deborah White
68 South St.
Warwick, NY 10990-1621
(914) 986–2659

Paumonok Bicycle Clubs
P.O. Box 7159
Hicksville, NY 11802
(516) 842–4699

Rochester Bicycle Club
P.O. Box 10100
Rochester, NY 14610
(716) 473–7494

Southern Tier Bicycle Club
c/o Augie P. Mueller
4009 Drexel Dr.
Vestal, NY 13850-4016
(607) 722–6005

Staten Island Bicycling Club
P.O. Box 141016
Staten Island, NY 10314-0004

Suffolk Bike Riders Association
P.O. Box 404
Saint James, NY 11780-0404
(516) 842–4699

Pennsylvania

Berks County Bicycle Club
c/o Tom Moyer
4624 Pheasant Run N.
Reading, PA 19606-3542
(215) 370–1239

Bicycle Club of Philadelphia
P.O. Box 30235
Philadelphia, PA 19103-8235
(215) 440–9983

Brandywine Bicycle Club
P.O. Box 3162
West Chester, PA 19381-3162

Central Bucks Bicycle Club
P.O. Box 295
Buckingham, PA 18912-0295
(215) 346–8483

Hanover Cyclers
129 Baltimore St.
Hanover, PA 17331-3111
(717) 259–7387

Harrisburg Bicycle Club
1011 Bridge St.
New Cumberland, PA 17070-
     1631
(717) 975–9879

Lackawanna Bicycle Club
P.O. Box 149
Dunmore, PA 18512-0149
(717) 347–7620

Lancaster Bicycle Club
P.O. Box 535
Lancaster, PA 17603-0535
(717) 396–9299

Lehigh Wheelmen Association,
     Inc.
P.O. Box 356
Bethlehem, PA 18016-0356
(610) 967–2653

Suburban Cyclists Unlimited
P.O. Box 401
Horsham, PA 19044-0401
(215) 628–8636

The Anthracite Bicycle Club
83 N. Church St.
Hazleton, PA 18201

The Wayfarers
P.O. Box 142
Danville, PA 17821-0142
(717) 275–1707

Two-Tired Bicycle Club
3447 Wilmington Rd, Suite C
New Castle, PA 16105

Valley Forge Bicycle Club
2003 Bridle Ln.
Oreland, PA 19075
(215) 233–4183

Western Pennsylvania
     Wheelmen Bicycle Club
P.O. Box 6952

Pittsburgh, PA 15212-0952
(412) 782–1341

Willaimsport Bicycle Club
P.O. Box 5119
Williamsport, PA 17701-0919
(717) 322–2553

Wyoming Valley Bicycle Club
P.O. Box 253
Dallas, PA 18612-0253
(717) 675–4866

Virginia
A. P. Hill/Rappahannock Bicycle
Club
c/o James S. Day, Jr.
P.O. Box 682
Bowling Green, VA 22427-0682
(804) 633–6500

Eastern Tandem Rally, Inc.
c/o Bob Friedman
5514 Callander Dr.
Springfield, VA 22151-0402
(703) 978–7937

Fredericksburg Cyclists
P.O. Box 7844
Fredericksburg, VA 22404-7844
(540) 371–0398

Potomac Pedalers Touring Club
6729 Curran St.
McLean, VA 23612-2115
(804) 875–1594

Reston Bicycle Club
P.O. Box 3389
Reston, VA 22090
(703) 904–0900

Richmond Area Bicycling Association
409-H N. Hamilton St.
Richmond, VA 23221-2014
(804) 270–9506

Shenandoah Valley Bicycle
Club
P.O. Box 1014
Harrisonburg, VA 22801-1014

Winchester Wheelmen
P.O. Box 1695
Winchester, VA 22604
(703) 662–1510

Washington, D.C.
Washington Area Bicyclist
Association (WABA)
818 Connecticut Ave. NW, #300
Washington, DC 20006
(202) 872–9830
waba@capaccess.org

West Virginia
Blennerhassett Bicycle Club
P.O. Box 2262
Parkersburg, WV 26102-2262
(304) 422–7808

Harrison County Bicycle Club
c/o David Young
35 Park Dr.
Fairmont, WV 26554-2401
(304) 366–5613

Mountain State Wheelers Bicycle Club
P.O. Box 8161
South Charleston, WV 25303-0161
(304) 345–5886

Tri-State Wheelers
Alan Winkler
208 Beacon Dr.
Weirton, WV 26062-4904
(304) 723–5036

State Bicycling Maps and Guides

The DeLorme Mapping Company has published an *Atlas & Gazetteer* for Delaware and Maryland (together), New York, Pennsylvania, and Virginia. The large-format book of topographic maps also shows dirt and paved roads and suggested bicycle routes, and it lists wildlife areas and other local attractions. These maps are accurate and are superb in rural areas; their scale is too small, however, to be helpful in towns and cities. For a list and prices, contact DeLorme Mapping Co., P.O. Box 298, Freeport, ME 04032; (800) 227–1656.

The tabloid-size newspaper *Spokes,* published ten times a year, covers bicycle touring, racing, off-road, recreation, triathalon, and commuting news in the southern Mid-Atlantic states. It is available for free at many area bicycle stores, fitness centers, and sporting establishments in Maryland, Virginia, Washington, D.C., and parts of Delaware, Pennsylvania, and West Virginia. For more information contact the editor and publisher, Neil W. Sandler, at *Spokes,* 5334 Sovereign Pl., Frederick, MD 21710; (301) 846–0326.

Another regional tabloid published ten times a year, *Cycling Times*, covers similar subjects for the New York metro area, including New York, New Jersey, Pennsylvania, Connecticut, and Delaware. For more information, contact the editor, J. P. Partland, at *Cycling Times*, 12-32 River Rd., Fairlawn, NJ 07410; (201) 796–8634; CycleTimes@aol.com.

DELAWARE
Delaware State and County Road Maps and Maps for Bicycle Users
Contract Administration,
    Delaware Department of
    Transportation
P.O. Box 778
Dover, DE 19903
(302) 739–4318
Send for free map index.

Delaware Valley Commuters Bicycle Map
Greater Philadelphia Bicycle
    Coalition
P.O. Box 8194
Philadelphia, PA 19101
(215) 387–9242
$5.75 ppd. Map (1982) of preferred commuting roads in Delaware, New Jersey, and Pennsylvania counties surrounding Philadelphia.

MARYLAND
Maryland State and County Road Maps
Map Distribution Section
State Highway Administration
2323 W. Joppa Rd.
Brooklandville, MD 21022
(410) 321–3518

The Maryland Department of Transportation has a toll-free number for information about bicycle-compatible transportation facilities and other bicycling information. Call 800–252–8776 Monday–Friday between 8:30 A.M. and 4:30 P.M.

Baltimore Area Bike Map

Baltimore Regional Council of
    Governments
2225 N. Charles St.
Baltimore, MD 21218
(301) 554–5614
$2.50. Waterproof and tear-
proof. Routes for commuting
and touring in Baltimore and
surrounding counties (1984).

Bicycling in Maryland

Bicycle Affairs Coordinator
Maryland State Highway
    Administration
707 N. Calvert St.
P.O. Box 717
Baltimore, MD 21203
(800) 252–8776
Free. Cross-Maryland routes,
plus information on Maryland's
bicycle laws, pertinent
addresses, and sources of local
and statewide information.

Bicycle Tours of Frederick County, Maryland

Tourism Council of Frederick
    County, Inc.
19 E. Church St.
Frederick, MD 21701
(301) 663–8687; (800) 999–3613
$4.00 plus tax at the visitor cen-
ter; $5.25 ppd. Packet of cue
sheets and maps (1989) for nine
bicycle tours in Frederick
County.

Carroll County Classic Country Bicycle Tours

Carroll County Visitor Center
210 E. Main St.
Westminster, MD 21157
(800) 272–1933
Free. Packet of cue sheets and
maps for ten bicycle tours in
Carroll County.

Chesapeake & Ohio Canal Maps

C&O Canal National Historic
    Park
P.O. Box 4
Sharpsburg, MD 21782
(301) 739–4200
Free. Map of 184.5-mile-long bicycling and hiking trail on the
canal towpath from Cumberland to Georgetown.

NEW JERSEY

New Jersey county maps can be
obtained at many local stationery stores and newsstands;
the major local publishers are
Geographia, Hagstrom, and Patton.

New Jersey Bicycling Information Packet

Pedestrian/Bicycle Advocate
New Jersey Department of
    Transportation
1035 Parkway Ave., CN600
Trenton, NJ 08625
(609) 530–8051, 530–4578
Free packet, including a detailed information booklet listing clubs, tour organizations, map sources, Hudson River crossing information, touring and commuting tips, state cycling laws, etc.

Bicycling Suitability Map of Western Jersey

Dan Rappaport
Holly House, #5M
Princeton, NJ 08540
$7.50.

NEW YORK

Maps of New York counties near New York City can be obtained at many local stationery stores and newsstands; the major local publishers are Geographia, Hagstrom, and Patton.

New York State and County Road Maps

Map Information Unit
New York State Department of
    Transportation
State Campus, Building 4,
    Room 105
Albany, NY 12232
(518) 457–3555
Send SASE for complete list and prices.

PENNSYLVANIA

Pennsylvania State and County Road Maps

Pennsylvania Department of
    Transportation (PennDOT)
    Sales Store
P.O. Box 2028
Harrisburg, PA 17105-2028
(717) 787–6746
County maps, $2.50 each folded, $133.00 per set, one map per county.

Pennsylvania County Maps

County Maps
821 Puetz Place
Lyndon Station, WI 53844
(608) 666–3331
$11.90 ppd. Book of county maps with information on history and natural and recreational areas.

Bicycling Directory of Pennsylvania

Pennsylvania Department of
    Transportation (PennDOT)
    Sales Store
Distribution Services Unit

Room G-123
Transportation and Safety
    Building
Harrisburg, PA 17120
PennDOT Publication 316, is a
twenty-eight page bookliet on
bike clubs, annual rides, bike
shops, campsites, rail trails,
transit company bike policies,
and more. Free.

WASHINGTON, D.C.
Washington, D.C., Street Map
Maps
D.C. Committee to Promote
    Washington
415 12th St. NW, Suite 312
Washington, DC 20004
(202) 724-4091

ADC's Washington Area Bike Map
ADC, "The Map People"
6440 General Green Way
Alexandria, VA 22312
(703) 750-0510
$6.95. 3rd edition (1993) map,
compiled by the Metropolitan
Washington Council of Governments, marks roads suitable
for bicycling, along with 64
miles of paved bicycle paths.

Greater Washington Area Bicycle Atlas
Washington Area Bicyclists
    Association
818 Connecticut Ave. NW,
    Suite 300
Washington, D.C. 20006-2702
(202) 872-9830
Maps seventy-one rides in
Delaware, Washington, D.C.,
Maryland, Pennsylvania, Vir-
ginia, and West Virginia; 4th
ed., 1992, $13.45 ppd.

VIRGINIA
Virginia County Maps
Virginia Department of
Transportation
Office of Public Relations
1221 E. Broad St.
Richmond, VA 23219
(804) 786-2838
$2.00 each for maps with a
scale of 1 inch to 1 mile; $.25
each for maps with a scale of 1
inch to 2 miles. Traffic vol-
ume book with information
on interstate, arterial, and primary road systems, $1.50.
Make checks out to Treasurer
of Virginia; include 4% sales
tea.

Trail Guide, Washington & Old Dominion Railroad Regional Park

Northern Virginia Regional
Park Authority
5400 Ox Rd.
Fairfax, VA 22039
(703) 729–0596;
(703) 352–5900
This fifty-six page, four-color
guide (1991) has twenty-five
strip maps for the 45-mile-
long rail trail in Northern
Virginia that runs. between
Shirlington in Arlington
County and Purvellville in
Loudoun County. From the
same source, you can also ob-
tain a free map and guide
"Playing It Safe on the W&OD
Trail" (1993).

Winchester Wheelmen Ride Booklet

Winchester Wheelmen
    Bicycle Club
P.O. Box 1695
Winchester, VA 22601
This 1987 booklet with
twenty-five rides through the
northern part of the Shenandoah Valley is $6.95.

Bicycling the Blue Ridge
Elizabeth and Charlie Skinner
Menasha Ridge Press
P.O. Box 59257

Birmingham, AL 35259-9257
This 1990 book ($10.95) to
the entire Skyline Drive and
the Blue Ridge Parkway features maps and elevation pro-
files, the best routes on and
off the highway, and information about campgrounds,
lodging, and bicycle shops.

WEST VIRGINIA
West Virginia County Road Maps

West Virginia Department of
    Highways
Transportation
Map Sales
1900 Kanawha Blvd. E.,
Rm. A-848
Charleston, WV 25305
(304) 558–2868
Call for information and price
list. These official county maps
are as accurate as U.S. Geologi-
cal Survey topographic maps,
minus the contour lines; the
mileages of all segments of
numbered roads are given to
the nearest 0.1 mile. Names of
roads are omitted, however, as
are all named but unnumbered
city streets.

West Virginia County Maps and Recreational Guide

County Maps
821 Puetz Pl.
Lyndon Station, WI 53944
(608) 666–3331
$14.85 ppd. Fifty-five county maps, with table of state parks and natural and wild areas.

Greenbrier River Trail Guide

Elk River Touring Center
Highway 219, Star Route
Slatyfork, WV 26291
(304) 572–3711
$2.00 ppd. Map (1989) of 75-mile-long unpaved railroad right of way along the Greenbrier River, along with information about access points and places to stay overnight.

West Virginia Adventure Guide to Rail Trails

by Frank Proud and Lynn Hartman
West Virginia Rails-to-Trails Council
P.O. Box 8889
South Charleston, WV 25303
(304) 722–6558
Maps (1995), descriptions, and a land trail-rating system for seventeen of West Virginia's rail trails. $7.95 plus $2.00 shipping.

West Virginia Cycling Maps

Bill Foster
515 S. Linden
Clarksburg, WV 26301
Write for list of maps and prices.

Bicycle Touring Companies

This is only a partial list of locally based commercial touring companies that concentrate their efforts in the Mid-Atlantic states. Many reputable touring companies headquartered outside the area also offer lovely Mid-Atlantic tours. For more information consult the Adventure Cycling Association's *The Cyclists' Yellow Pages* or the League of American Bicyclists' *Bicycle USA TourFinder*.

In addition, charities such as the American Cancer Society, the American Diabetes Association, the American Lung Association, the March of Dimes, the National Multiple Sclerosis Society, and the United Way sponsor one-day and weekend fund-raising tours, whereby participants take pledges per mile traveled. Contact your local office of the charity for information about fund-raising rides in your area.

American Youth Hostels
P.O. Box 37613
Washington, DC 20013-7613
(202) 783–6161

Appalachian Valley Bicycle Touring
31 East Fort Ave.
Baltimore, MD 21230
(410) 837–8068

Brooks Country Cycling and Hiking Tours
140 W. 83rd St.
New York, NY 10024
(212) 874–5151 or (800) 284–8954 (outside New York, New Jersey, and Connecticut)

Elk River Touring Center
Hwy. 219, Star Route
Slatyfork, WV 26291
(304) 572–3771
Mountain-bike tours. Also offers the book *Mountain Bike Rides in Pocahontas County, West Virginia* by Gil and Mary Willis (1992).

Finger Lakes Cycling Adventures
P.O. Box 457
Fairport, NY 14450
(716) 377–9817

Lancaster Bicycle Touring, Inc.
3 Colt Ridge Ln.
Strasburg, PA 17579
(717) 396–0456

Old Dominion Bicycle Tours
3620 Huguenot Trail

Powhatan, VA 23139
(804) 598–7815
Specializes in Virginia; offers
family tours.

True Wheel Tours
P.O. Box 366
Long Lake, NY 12847-0366
(518) 624–2056
Specializes in the Adirondacks,
Finger Lakes, and Catskills re-
gions in New York.

Wayfarers
P.O. Box 211
Fair Lawn, NJ 07410
Specializes in Maryland, New
Jersey, and Pennsylvania.

Acknowledgments

This book would not have been possible without the generous help of scores of people.

First, my deepest thanks go to the contributors of the individual routes, each of whom is credited in the ride's description. In some cases the contributor is also the person who painstakingly created the ride you may now enjoy. Many of these people spent hours traveling over the route specifically to answer questions I raised while writing this book; they also sent me helpful brochures and maps.

Equally, I would like to thank the volunteer army of experienced cyclists who verified each and every route for this second edition; their names are also credited in the individual ride descriptions. In some cases, the verifier was the original contributor. In many cases, however, the verifier was simply a cheerful respondent to a classified ad printed in *Bicycle USA* or a rider of the bike lane of the Internet superhighway who answered a post on a biking bulletin board. These people rode the routes, painstakingly checking each mileage, direction, spelling of street and road names, and phone number of cited attractions—and charting alternate routes when the original had become unsuitable. To Gil Gilmore of Norwalk, Connecticut, Bill Ingalls of Arlington, Virginia, Larry Sturm of Shoreham, New York, and Jim Yannaccone of Watsontown, Pennsylvania—who all heroically came to my rescue at the eleventh hour—I owe a particular debt of gratitude. Special thanks also go to Neil Grotenstein of Silver Spring, Maryland, who set up and monitored the post on the computer bulletin board, thus finding these rescuers.

My deep gratitude goes as well to the contributors of the photographs that appear at the beginning of the state sections: for Delaware, Barbara Lloyd of the New Devon Inn in Lewes; for Maryland, the Carroll County Tourism Office; for Pennsylvania, Mark Scholefield of Birdsboro; for Virginia, Nancy Taylor of Maryland; for Washington, D.C., the Washington, D.C., Convention & Visitors Association; and for West Virginia, Pamela "Sam" Withrow of Camera One in White Sulphur Springs.

Next, I wish to thank those people who donated rides that, for myriad reasons, unfortunately could not be published in this second edition. I also wish to thank the many people who did not submit rides but were most helpful in steering me to people who did or who sent me useful maps and other supplemental material. These wonderful people include Greg Cook and Stephanie R. Hughart of the West Virginia Division of Tourism and Parks in Charleston; William N. Hoffman of Lancaster, Pennsylvania; Peter C. Lemonides of Syracuse, New York and Reno, Nevada; Gene Martin of Narberth, Pennsylvania; Robert Moore of Baltimore, Maryland; Bert Nixdorf of Mount Holly, New Jersey; Shari Lawrence Pfleeger of Washington, D.C.; Dennis Strawn of Elkview, West Virginia; Bruce Williams of Hawk Mountain Sports in Cherry Valley, New York; Gill Willis of Elk River Touring Center in Slatyfork, West Virginia; Larry Wonderlin of Rehoboth Beach, Delaware; and David W. Young of Clarksburg, West Virginia. I also wish to thank all the bed-and-breakfast innkeepers who contacted me and sent me descriptive brochures of their inns.

Behind the scenes was my husband, Craig B. Waff, who cared for our daughter, Roxana, on the Saturdays I was furiously coordinating volunteer cyclists verifying all the routes and correcting the cue sheets and maps. Thank you for your steady and daily support and love.

This book is dedicated to my mother, Arabella J. Bell, and to my late father, R. Kenneth Bell, for all their love, guidance, encouragement, and support throughout my life.

About the Author

Trudy E. Bell is an avid touring cyclist and a certified bicycle mechanic (East Coast Bicycle Academy, Harrisonburg, Virginia, 1989). She has taught an introductory course in bicycle touring at the South Orange–Maplewood Adult School in New Jersey and at the Learning Annex in New York City.

Either with groups or solo, she and her 1984 Univega SportTour have cycled all over the Mid-Atlantic states and in Colorado, Utah, and California, including down the length of Baja California. In addition, she commuted by bicycle on the streets of New York City for five years (worth about 6,000 miles).

A former editor of *Scientific American*, *Omni*, and *IEEE Spectrum* magazines in New York City, she is now a communications specialist for McKinsey & Co., Inc. in Cleveland, Ohio. She has a master's degree in the history of science (American astronomy) from New York University. Her articles on bicycling have been published in *Adventure Cyclist*, *Collier's Encyclopedia*, *The Encyclopedia of New York City*, *The New York Times*, *Bicycle USA*, *Essence*, *Science Probe*, and *The Bicyclist's Sourcebook* (edited by Michael Leccese and Arlene Plevin, Woodbine House, 1991). She is the author of *Bicycling Around New York City: A Gentle Touring Guide* (Menasha Ridge Press, 1994) and is working on books on bicycle commuting and bicycling with children.

She lives with her husband, historian of science Dr. Craig B. Waff, and daughter, Roxana, in Cleveland, Ohio (previously in Maplewood, New Jersey).